Augustus Caesar in "Augustan" England

AUGUSTUS CAESAR
in
"Augustan" England

THE DECLINE OF A CLASSICAL NORM

by Howard D. Weinbrot

PRINCETON UNIVERSITY PRESS

Princeton, New Jersey

Library of Congress Cataloging in Publication Data will
be found on the last printed page of this book

Publication of this book has been aided by a grant from
the National Endowment for the Humanities

This book has been composed in Linotype Baskerville

Printed in the United States of America
by Princeton University Press,
Princeton, New Jersey

To the memory of my sister Ellen,
who knew it was hers

Contents

CONTENTS

Preface

Contemporary literary scholarship has made impressive gains in reclaiming the classical background of eighteenth-century literature. We no longer think of Pope's *Dunciad* as a plotless ramble, or of his imitations of Horace as unfortunately derivative. Instead, they are recognized as carefully wrought poems that include and evaluate the classical past as transmitted by Continental and British commentators. Modern writers who hold this view regard the classics as normative, as one of the eighteenth century's main sources of inspiration, emulation, and imitation, particularly in the case of the ultimate royal patron, Augustus Caesar, and Horace and Virgil, the poets he apparently nurtured with such handsome results. This approach has yielded much fruit, only some of which is nourishing. We too often look at classical aspects of Restoration and eighteenth-century Britain and forget that two of its most representative dates are the "modern" landmarks 1688 and 1776, that however much Samuel Johnson admired some parts of some classics, he was, in the words of a recent commentator, at war with them and their values.[1] This book was, in fact, originally conceived as a study in the rejection of classical standards in the so-called neoclassical age, with special emphasis on the inadequacies of Roman religion, philosophy, science, politics, and humanitarian ethics in general. It gradually became clear that so ample a task would go on for longer than writer, reader, or publisher would care to contemplate. It also became clear that many of the blind spots and optical illusions regarding the classics were located in the figure of Augustus and his satellites, and that "Augustanism" had become more fashionable, more prescriptive and thus more negatively formidable than "neoclassicism" had ever been.

[1] See Richard Peterson, "Johnson at War with the Classics," *ECS*, 9 (1975): 69-86.

This phenomenon is the more puzzling when one realizes that Augustanism is an incongruous enclave in what has come to be called, with deserved suspicion, the Whig interpretation of history and literary history.[2] To speculate why this happened is interesting, but useless; it is, however, useful to take as our motto Johnson's remark in the Preface to his edition of Shakespeare (1765): "Let the fact be first stated, and then examined."[3] Once we do that, we will, I hope, have a better way of evaluating the role of Roman classical, and specifically Augustan, history and literature in eighteenth-century Britain. My frankly revisionist interpretation of Pope's *Epistle to Augustus* should serve as a test case for the practical value of the historical reclamation in earlier chapters.

Wherever possible I have used seventeenth- or eighteenth-century English translations of Latin and French texts. When the former are not translated I have tried (often with others' help) to do so myself, sometimes paraphrasing and occasionally taking liberties, especially with complex Renaissance Latin. The relevant original Latin is supplied in the notes. I have assumed that such help is not necessary for untranslated French sources; the context should be an adequate guide to meaning when difficulties occur.

In many cases I have combined related sources into one omnibus footnote, so that there might be less disruption of

[2] Herbert Butterfield's *The Whig Interpretation of History* (1931) long ago discussed such historiography. More recently Henry Knight Miller extended the concept in "The 'Whig Interpretation' of Literary History," *ECS*, 6 (1972): 60-84. Miller rightly observes that R. S. Crane's reviews and essays "were of inestimable value in exposing the illogicalities of the 'Whig Interpretation' of literary history, and in contributing to a revised estimate of its dogmas" (p. 79, n. 33). Donald Greene's review of the facsimile of William Minto's *Literature of the Georgian Era* (1894) is also relevant. See *The Scriblerian*, 3 (1971):45-46.

[3] The Yale Edition of the Works of Samuel Johnson, vol. 7, *Johnson on Shakespeare*, ed. Arthur Sherbo, intro. Bertrand H. Bronson (New Haven: Yale Univ. Press, 1968), p. 66.

the reading process. Those who do not wish this work long-er will, doubtless, be comforted to hear that the materials offered within represent but the tip of the note cards and scarcely begin to exhaust the available evidence.

I have been fortunate in having generous bibliographic, financial, and intellectual support. Most of the research was carried out at the British Library, at the libraries of the University of Wisconsin, the University of Chicago, and Yale University, and at the Newberry Library. It is a pleas-ure to thank the staffs and collections of those institutions. The Graduate School of the University of Wisconsin sup-plied research assistance (most usefully that of Dorothy Driver), travel funds, and a semester's leave. A National Endowment for the Humanities Fellowship for Independ-ent Study and Research allowed me to finish the project, and several efficient, friendly, and patient secretaries in Wisconsin's English Department typed and retyped the manuscript.

Many friends and colleagues have provided their time, information, and wisdom. Thanks are due to Bertrand Goldgar, Peter Verdurmen, Manuel Schonhorn, Paul Al-kon, Robert H. Drew, Alex Chambers, William Kuper-smith, Martin Battestin, and Robert Hume for helpful comments and evaluations, as well as information. I owe special debts to Phillip Harth and Donald Greene for their help with what I thought a final draft, and most of all to Eric Rothstein for his frequent "Augustan" discoveries, in-valuable reading of an earlier draft, and useful suggestions and corrections thereafter. I am indebted to my native wit for whatever lamentable stylistic infelicities and errors of omission or commission still remain.

Augustus Caesar in "Augustan" England

CHAPTER 1

The Classical Legacy of Augustus Caesar in "Augustan" England

THE PEACE OF THE AUGUSTANS DIED SOME YEARS AGO. UN-
fortunately, the "Augustans" themselves are not only
alive, but also the subject of squabbles concerning who they
are and how they wrote—whether they lived between 1660
and 1700 or 1700 and 1745; whether they belong to another
specified period, or are all the "conservative" and "orthodox"
humanists between 1660 and 1800; whether they are essentially pessimistic or optimistic, realistic or unrealistic,
gloomy moralists or comic writers. Such vague terminology
has obvious pitfalls; but it would be harmless if it were, as
one of its recent advocates claims, merely a neutral form of
shorthand for some authors in Britain during some of the
years between 1660 and 1800.[1] Within the last two decades
or so, however, "Augustan" has become prescriptive rather
than descriptive; readings of particular texts or authors,

[1] For some of these discussions, see William K. Wimsatt, Jr., "The
Augustan Mode in English Poetry," in *Hateful Contraries: Studies in
Literature and Criticism* (Lexington: Univ. of Kentucky Press, 1965),
pp. 149-64, especially pp. 158-59; Paul Fussell, *The Rhetorical World
of Augustan Humanism: Ethics and Imagery from Swift to Burke*
(Oxford: Clarendon Press, 1965), pp. vii-viii, 20-21, 210; Carey Mc-
Intosh, "The Scheduled Quest," in *Proceedings of the Modern Language Association Neoclassicism Conferences 1967-1968*, ed. Paul J.
Korshin (New York: AMS Press, 1970), p. 27; V. de Sola Pinto, "Augustan or Augustinian? More Demythologizing Needed?" *ECS*, 2 (1969):
291; Irvin Ehrenpreis, *Literary Meaning and Augustan Values* (Char-
lottesville: Univ. Press of Virginia, 1974), p. 3. For the "neutral" shorthand, see Pat Rogers, *The Augustan Vision* (New York: Barnes and
Noble, 1974), pp. 1-2. There are, of course, many other books with
"Augustan" in the title, including my own *The Formal Strain: Studies
in Augustan Imitation and Satire* (Chicago: Univ. of Chicago Press,
1969).

the "age," genres, taste, and literary practice in general often regard the Augustan as good and the non-Augustan as less good, less interesting, and suspiciously aberrant.

In an influential work, for example, Reuben Brower states that the unnamed Augustans, also called the "true Augustans," saw in "Horace's poetry a concentrated image of a life and civilization to which they more or less consciously aspired."[2] Students of Pope commonly argue that the *Epistle to Augustus* contrasts ironic with real praise of an Augustan monarch.[3] V. de Sola Pinto believes that Augustan is an appropriate label for the Restoration and eighteenth century, since it was "actually used during the period" and, he implies, used positively: "It is difficult for us to realize the enormous prestige enjoyed by the Roman Augustan age all over Europe in the seventeenth and eighteenth centuries."[4] In light of these and comparable remarks, it is no wonder that, as David L. Evans observes, " 'Augustanism' is gradually replacing 'neo-classicism' as a term for what we admire in the literature of the eighteenth century."[5]

[2] *Alexander Pope: The Poetry of Allusion* (Oxford: Clarendon Press, 1959), p. 176. See also pp. 183, 305, 307.

[3] See Wimsatt, "Rhetoric and Poems: The Example of Pope," in *English Institute Essays 1948* (New York: Columbia Univ. Press, 1949), p. 183; Brower, *Alexander Pope*, pp. 305-7; Maynard Mack, " 'Wit and Poetry and Pope': Some Observations on His Imagery," in *Eighteenth-Century English Literature: Modern Essays in Criticism*, ed. James L. Clifford (New York: Oxford Univ. Press Galaxy Book, 1959), p. 34; Thomas E. Maresca, *Pope's Horatian Poems* (Columbus: Ohio State Univ. Press, 1966), pp. 21, 58-59, 91; William Frost, ed., *John Dryden: Selected Works* (San Francisco: Rinehart, 1971), p. xi. For exceptions to this view, see Jay Arnold Levine, "Pope's *Epistle to Augustus*, Lines 1-30," *SEL*, 7 (1967): 427-51; Howard D. Weinbrot, "Augustan Imitation: The Role of the Original," in *Proceedings* (n. 1, above), pp. 57-61; idem, "History, Horace, and Augustus Caesar: Some Implications for Eighteenth-Century Satire," *ECS*, 7 (1974): 407-410, and chap. 6, below.

[4] "Augustan or Augustinian?" p. 292 (n. 1, above). See also Donald Greene's reply to Pinto, *ECS*, 2 (1969): 293-300.

[5] "*Humphry Clinker*: Smollett's Tempered Augustanism," *Criticism*, 9 (1967): 257. For some of the other uses of a normative "Augustan,"

The use of Augustan by the twentieth century thus assumes favorable use by the eighteenth century. Then as now, Augustan implied a variety of excellences, but may be reduced to the omnibus belief that during the reign of Augustus Caesar the throne was a center of value. The exalted character of the monarch induced stable government, the arts of peace, protection by heaven, refinement of literary style, and patronage of great authors. These characteristics combined to create civilizing forces of permanent achievement for all mankind and standards against which further achievements should be measured. This pretty notion now dominates the view of the relationship between the Augustan eighteenth century and its presumed Roman parent and is, accordingly, being disseminated in lecture halls as well as scholarly publications. Hence a college anthology, entitled *English Augustan Poetry*, tells us about Augustus' establishment of "peace, consolidation, and expansion" after turmoil and civil war, and of his protection of literature and frequent thanks from the populace during his reign from 27 B.C. to A.D. 14. We also hear of the many parallels between Augustus and Rome and post-Restoration English monarchs and civilization, as in the restored Charles II and the London—"Augusta"—he ruled. Under George II the Augustan backdrop was used ironically, and so in *To Augustus* Pope adapts a satire "where Horace flatters Augustus on his bravery and taste—as if George II represented no falling off." English Augustan poetry has certain identifiable traits that stem, it would seem, from its Roman forebears. "As distinguished from mid-seventeenth-century poetry, the poetry we recognize as Augustan is written within a consciousness of taking place in a safe environment, or at least an environment, like that in Gay's *Trivia*, where the threats are interesting and amusing rather than really terrifying. English poetry *which deserves to be*

see Sanford Budick, "The Demythological Mode in Augustan Verse," *ELH*, 37 (1970): 390-91, and W. B. Carnochan, "Satire, Sublimity, and Sentiment: Theory and Practice in Post-Augustan Satire," *PMLA*, 85 (1970): 260, 264, 266, et passim.

called Augustan assumes a world so well lighted and stable that menaces to its felicity can be kept at bay largely by satire or clarity or honesty or belittlement."[6]

J. W. Johnson, Jay Arnold Levine, and Ian Watt have challenged the concept of benevolent English Augustanism and made clear that by the early eighteenth century Augustus was often regarded as a tyrant, murderer, and threat to the order of the state.[7] These beliefs were so firmly a part of the Tory opposition to George II and Walpole that once the *Craftsman* finished its work, it was no longer possible, in Johnson's words, to regard Augustan "as a political accolade."[8] As the proliferation of modern pro-Augustan remarks suggests, however, these revisionists have had little influence and much resistance; in some cases they themselves are uncertain of the scope of the eighteenth-century rejection of Augustus.[9] Howard Erskine-Hill reviews the

[6] Paul Fussell (Garden City, N. Y.: Doubleday Anchor Books, 1972), pp. 3-4, italics added. A glance at the contents of this volume suggests the inadequacy of the assumption. Rochester's *Satire against Mankind*, Johnson's *London*, and Pope's fourth book of the *Dunciad* hardly portray a world in which felicity has been preserved and menaces have been "kept at bay."

[7] Johnson, *The Formation of English Neo-Classical Thought* (Princeton: Princeton Univ. Press, 1967), pp. 16-30 (originally, "The Meaning of 'Augustan,'" *JHI*, 19 [1958]: 507-22); Levine, "Pope's *Epistle to Augustus*" (n. 3); Watt, "Two Historical Aspects of the Augustan Tradition," in *Studies in the Eighteenth Century: Papers Presented at the David Nichol Smith Memorial Seminar, Canberra, 1966*, ed. R. F. Brissenden (Toronto: Univ. of Toronto Press, 1968), pp. 67-79.

[8] Johnson, p. 26.

[9] Ian Watt, for example, reprints part of his essay in the Introduction to his collection called *The Augustan Age: Approaches to Its Literature, Life and Thought* (Greenwich, Conn.: Fawcett, 1968). There one sees that Pope and Swift were more "intransigent" than most of their contemporaries in judging the classical Augustus, and that "it is hardly too much to say that the Augustan model became the main cultural pattern for the English educated classes throughout the period between the Civil War and the French Revolution; it was a pattern not only for literature and the arts but for a very wide range of psychological, moral, social, and national attitudes" (p. 18).

6

evidence, as he sees it, and concludes that though it was "journalistically convenient to the Tories to attack George II by stressing the bad side of Octavius Augustus," there is little basis for Professor Johnson's "astonishing generalisation"; that "is refuted by Pope's *Imitations of Horace,* especially by *To Augustus,* and by the fact that Hume, Warton and Goldsmith could use the term [as positively] as they did in the 1750s."[10]

I suggest that Professors Johnson, Levine, and Watt have been cautious, not astonishing. As I hope to show, disapproval of Augustus Caesar was a bipartisan venture common to Whig court "favorites" like Thomas Gordon and Conyers Middleton, "Tories" like Bolingbroke and Pope (who were only part of the opposition), ordinary citizens who did not meddle with political office or ambition, and students of art, poetry, history, and biography, among others. The firm tradition of Augustus as usurping tyrant actually has roots in the classical historians themselves.

We need, then, to study Augustus' reputation in Britain between about 1660 and 1800 and to determine whether his values and achievements are consistent with dominant native values and achievements of those years. By so doing, we should be able to determine the validity of modern and prescriptive uses of the term *Augustan.* In the process I hope that we will do more than turn a thriving cottage industry into a depressed area. The current Augustanism not only allows us to read history through purple-tinted glasses, but also induces sloppy scholarship by encouraging us to ignore massive contrary evidence; it distorts our perception of the realities that Augustus represented for the eighteenth century; it offers an erroneous "vision" of the past that makes it seem distant, unapproachably "mythic"

As the rest of my own study will suggest, Augustus was more likely to offer a negative than positive "pattern" for the eighteenth century.

10 "Augustans on Augustanism: England, 1655-1759," *Renaissance and Modern Studies,* 11 (1967): 82-83.

in outlook, and far less immediate and valuable than it is; and it inhibits our seeing the major implications that the eighteenth century's rejection of Augustus had for literature, history, and politics.

If we reexamined the notion of positive Augustanism, surely new and more appropriate hypotheses would suggest themselves, and surely some would cast new light on Restoration and eighteenth-century Britain. For example, Augustus' miserable reputation as transmitted by several classical historians helped to place him at the heart of fervid discussion of an important constitutional issue—the proper balance between the people, aristocrats and monarch. It also influenced the way in which modern historians would look at Roman history and portray it as a positive or negative model for Britain; it would influence some aspects of the historical and literary tactics used both by the opposition to Walpole and by his defenders; it would have the highest significance for judgments regarding the value and morality of the classical authors Virgil, Horace, and Juvenal, and the relative merits of the different kinds of satire the latter two wrote; and it would have comparable significance for the interpretation of a specific literary text, Pope's imitation of Horace's epistle to Augustus (*Epistles*, bk. ii, epistle 1).

These developments were not likely to have been limited to Britain, since Voltaire read the same Tacitus and Suetonius as Gibbon. The French were chronologically about a generation behind the British in judging Augustus harshly; but they also had to clear away the rubbish of absolutism before they could begin to build their new republic (Napoleon, of course, had other things to say). As Jean Dusaulx pointed out in 1770, once the philosophes finished with Augustus, his reputation was very tarnished indeed.[11] Du-

---

[11] *Satires de Juvénal traduites par M. Dusaulx* (Paris, 1770), p. xxix. "Le caractère de cet usurpateur est enfin dévoilé, depuis que des Philosophes ont écrit sur l'Histoire." Dusaulx's observation is verified by several French statements in the text and notes, below.

saulx himself contributed to this movement through his characterization of the servile Horace, the antityrannical Juvenal and the value of each as a satirist. The philosophes were plainly anglophiliac in their admiration for Britain's freedom and balanced constitution; they learned to make some of the same literary and historical as well as political judgments. Moreover, anti-Augustanism, or more broadly anti-Caesarism, was a force in framing the American Revolution and constitution, or at least some of the thought behind it, for its insistence on checks and balances is as much anti-Roman imperial as anti-Georgian-Britannic.[12] The rejection of Augustus thus tells us a great deal about the eighteenth century's literary, political, and historical concerns, far more than the amorphous and fossilized talk of an Augustan age's "enormous prestige," or the ungenerous acceptance of Augustanism as "what we admire" in eighteenth-century literature. Considering the subject's complexity, it would be best to start with the attitudes toward Augustus of the classical historians and, in some cases, the makers of Roman history. Such an examination should help to determine the classical legacy of Augustus Caesar in Augustan Britain.

I: SOME POSITIVE VIEWS AND NEGATIVE REACTIONS

There were, to be sure, numerous positive remarks made about Augustus, a remarkable man who turned himself from the sickly boy with few hopes of survival into the master of the world's most extensive empire and most effective propaganda machine. Messala, Zosimus, Eutropius, Cicero, commentators on Livy, Tacitus, Velleius Paterculus, Suetonius, Florus, Appian, Dio Cassius, and Sextus Aurelius Victor, all offer varying forms of approval. A conflation of their praise would include the following: Young Octa-

[12] See chap. 7, note 14, below for brief discussion of colonial anti-Caesarism.

vian was quickly recognized as the brilliant and proper
heir of his uncle Julius. Under Cicero's wise sponsorship,
the senate elevated him to praetor and defender of the state
and senate against the malicious Antony. In concert with
Hirtius and Pansa, both of whom died during the battle
at Mutina, he defeated Antony and drove him out of Italy.
Owing to the exigencies of the situation and the need for
a unified front, he later joined Antony and defeated the
assassins Brutus and Cassius. Shortly thereafter he formed
the triumvirate with Lepidus and Antony and was forced
to kill Cicero and many others, though he himself preferred
clemency. As governor of Rome he made a naval war in
Sicily against Sextus Pompeius, and though often defeated
by the more experienced sailor, showed his strength in ad-
versity and his wisdom in selecting his lieutenant Agrippa,
who finally helped him to defeat Pompey and return free
navigation to the seas and food to Rome. Thereafter, Octavian bravely stripped the wicked and ineffectual Lepidus
of his army, made the city of Rome a safe and pleasant
place to live, restored discipline and loyalty to the legions,
and made the Roman people love him as the father of the
country. When Antony proved himself an enemy to Rome
and friend to the Egyptian whore Cleopatra, Octavian
reluctantly went to war again and conquered Antony at
Actium, for the gods had ordained that he was to be the
sole ruler. Upon returning to Rome, he was idolized by the
people, established peace and plenty, encouraged the arts
and sciences, made kings bow to him and nations bow to
Rome, defeated the barbarians, reformed the senate and the
law, earned the title of Augustus, which the grateful people
and senate bestowed upon him, ruled with great moderation as prince of the senate rather than king, and left a
solid empire that not even many evil successors could
shake.

This view was supported by various subsequent translators and scholars. For example, commentators often noted
that Livy's apparent republicanism, perhaps clear in the

books now lost, earned the label of "Pompeianus" from Augustus. "Yet," Edmund Bohun reports in 1686, "that Generous Prince did not for all that refuse him his Friendship." In 1744 an anonymous translator repeats Bohun's belief that Livy wrote "at a time which afforded not only the noblest patterns, but the strongest encouragements to cultivate his natural endowments." A later adapter of this edition seconds René Rapin's eulogy upon the historian and his emperor, and mentions the "sublime delight" that the imagination obtains in contemplating those noble times.[13]

Other Renaissance and later commentators and historians also add affirmative observations. Justus Lipsius praises Augustus' restraint in reducing the number of praetors from 67 to 12; Giacomo Filippo Tomasini insists on Augustus' perception in offering Livy his patronage; Joannes Rosinus urges the excellent military achievements and victories of Octavian, who deserved to be called imperator; and Joannes Braun praises Augustus' restoration of civil and moral order, financial solvency, moral achievements, and his introduction of major new architecture.[14]

But the classical historians and history-makers themselves are the most important, and so I shall report representative remarks by Cicero, Velleius Paterculus, and Dio Cassius.

Cicero hopes that Octavian will counterbalance Antony and help restore the republic. He offers important praise of Octavian in his fifth Philippic, against Antony, in which he urges the senate to confer the office of praetor upon the

13 Bohun, *The Roman History, Written in Latine by Titus Livius* (London), sig. A1r; anon., *The Roman History By Titus Livius*, 6 vols. (London), 1:xiv; *Titus Livius's Roman History*, 8 vols. (London, 1761), 1:x.

14 Lipsius, *Tractatus ad historiam romanum* (Cambridge, 1607), cap. 10, sig. B8r; Tomasini, *T. Livii . . . Historiarum* (Amsterdam, 1764), p. 6; Rosinus, *Antiquitatum romanorum* (Amsterdam, 1743), p. 502; Braun, *Historia augusta, seu vitae romanorum caesarum* (Augsburg and Dillingen, 1698), pp. 9-11. Many other commentators, however—especially Casaubon on Suetonius—were hostile to Augustus.

valuable defender of Roman liberty. One need not fear the ambition or passions of Octavian, since that young man is "the very opposite" of Julius, has already recovered Rome's safety, and supports her hopes of liberty. Cicero is confident that the youth wishes "only to strengthen, not overturn" the state, and that "nothing is dearer to him" than the republic, "nothing more important than" the authority of the senate. Cicero promises, pledges, undertakes, and solemnly engages that Octavian will always subject himself to the command and authority of the senate.[15]

Velleius Paterculus was the warmest in praise of Augustus. At nineteen, after having already attempted and performed difficult and honorable deeds, Octavian "discovered a greater Concern for the State, than the whole Senate," and, with the aid of Hirtius and Pansa, defeated Antony at Mutina and forced him to flee Italy.[16] Upon the later victory over Pompey, Lepidus attempted to expel Octavian from Sicily and evoked an act beyond anything that "the Scipio's, or the Bravest of the *Roman* Heroes have attempted or executed." Wrapped only in his cloak, and armed only with his name, he entered the camp of Lepidus, escaped the arrows and lances thrown at him and bravely "seized the Eagle of the Legion. Now . . . the armed follow the Unarmed, and . . . *Lepidus* . . . sculking among the last of those who stood gazing at *Caesar* . . . threw himself along at his feet" (p. 176: bk. ii, par. 80).

After Augustus' comparably brilliant generalship at Actium, all civil and foreign wars were over and the happiness in Rome made clear that "Mankind could desire nothing more from the Gods" and the gods grant nothing more to men. "The Force of the Laws, the Authority of the Judge,

15 *Cicero: Philippics*, trans. Walter C. A. Ker. The Loeb Classical Library (New York: G. P. Putnam, 1926), pp. 303-9; Philippic v. 17. 47–v. 19. 52.

16 *The Roman History of C. Velleius Paterculus*, trans. Thomas Newcomb (London, 1721), pp. 143-44: bk. ii, chap. 61. Subsequent references are cited in the text.

and the Majesty of the Senate was restored." The old form of government was revived, as were the lands, religious rites, stability of estates, elections, and the authority of government itself. Indeed, Augustus "constantly rejected the Dictatorship, which the People obstinately forced upon him" (pp. 189-90: ii. 89).

Like almost everyone else in the third-century empire, Dio Cassius was reconciled to the inevitability of the principate, and therefore was viewed as a monarchist in Restoration and eighteenth-century Britain. His translator Francis Manning believes that Rome's alteration from republican to absolute government confirmed and heightened her glory. "The Empire," he says, "was more flourishing from *Augustus*'s time to that of *Trajan* than the Commonwealth had ever been."[17] Manning takes his cue from his own temperament and Dio's history—or at least Xiphilinus' epitome—where we see that Brutus and Cassius were defeated because "Heaven had decreed to give a better form of government, by making a Monarchy of a Popular State" (vol. 1, p. 84: xlvii. 39-40). After Actium and the metamorphosis of Octavian into Augustus, the emperor "redoubled his cares for the well-governing of the Empire, . . . publish'd abundance of Laws" in which the people, the senators, and other patricians were able "to change what they thought fit" (1:143) and thus gained "the esteem of all the world" (1:144-45: liii.20-22). The princeps' many excellences as a ruler compensated for his excesses as a triumvir, and the "most virtuous" loved him and regarded him as an indulgent father. Finally, Augustus was beloved by the Romans because "he had blended Monarchy and the Popular State together, . . . every body was happy . . . under a Royalty, which leaving an honest freedom, took not away the form of a Common-Wealth, but only banish'd all the Disorders of it" (1:203-4: lvi.44).

This file of favorable attitudes towards Augustus seems

[17] *The History of Dion Cassius Abridg'd by Xiphilin*, 2 vols. (London, 1704), 1:sig. A3v-4v. Subsequent references are cited in the text.

impressive in both quality and quantity, especially when one recalls that Suetonius—who is represented in the earlier omnibus section of positive remarks—was famous for writing lives of the emperors with as much freedom as they lived them. But this solid appearance of Augustan virtue collapses when we see that during the eighteenth century several of these historians were criticized or rejected altogether for their stands, that the historians who offer some praise also offer at least as much blame, and that others— like Tacitus—must be badly misrepresented, by eighteenth-century standards, before they can be called partisans of Augustus. As the political reaction to Messala will suggest, even a more-obscure pro-Augustan might be subject to proscription in Augustan Britain.

This history-maker and historian, whose works are lost, had been Brutus' worthy lieutenant at Philippi, was sentenced to death but reconciled to Octavian, and fought with him at Actium when, according to Plutarch, he regarded Octavian's as "the best and justest side." Though Gibbon praised Messala, Lyttelton used his association with Augustus to cast him into moral darkness. In the ninth of Lyttelton's *Dialogues of the Dead* (1760) Cato Uticensis labels Augustus as the murderer of the commonwealth, of Cicero and the noblest Romans, scoffs at the apparent flowering of letters, and claims: "Your Augustus and you, after the ruin of our liberty, made Rome a Greek city, an academy of fine wits, another Athens under the government of [the absolute] Demetrius Phalareus. I would much rather have seen her under Fabricius and Curius, and her other honest consuls, who could not read." For Lyttelton's Cato, Augustus has perverted Roman letters, and Messala slinks off, finally concluding: "I see you consider me as a deserter from the republick, and an apologist for a tyrant."[18]

---

[18] "Marcus Brutus," in *Plutarch's Lives*, adapted from the "Dryden" trans., 8 vols. (London, 1771), 7:371; Gibbon, *The Decline and Fall of the Roman Empire*, ed. J. B. Bury, 7 vols. (London, 1900), 2:168, chap.

The major pro-Augustans fared no better. Hostility to
Cicero begins almost as soon as the Renaissance publication
of his private correspondence with Brutus and Brutus'
letters about him. In spite of the orator's other defenses of
the republic, Brutus tells Atticus, he feels "no gratitude to
one who, to avoid being the slave of a bad-tempered master [Antony], does not deprecate slavery itself," but in fact
encourages Octavian to be as great a despot as Julius.
Cicero "has no aversion to servitude, if it be but tempered
by a show of respect." Thus, "Long live Cicero—as he may
well do—to cringe and serve!"[19] The fault for any subsequent Caesarian tyranny, Brutus insists to Cicero himself,
falls upon that orator "if its occurrence might have been
prevented by foresight."[20] The same readers may already
have known Plutarch's life of Cicero, which affirms these
points and the common blame of Cicero's actions, and proclaims that "he himself perceived that he was ruined" and
had betrayed Rome's liberty.[21]

These reasoned outbursts against the scourge of Catiline
permanently influenced Cicero's reputation in England and
blended well with dislike for his perceived timidity and
self-serving. The anonymous tragedy of *Marcus Tullius*

17, II. A point similar to Gibbon's was quoted by John Langhorne in
the *Monthly Review*, 47 (1772): 566-67, while reviewing the *Histoire
de l'académie royale des inscriptions et belles-lettres, 1764-1766*. The
attribution to Langhorne is in Benjamin Christie Nangle, *The Monthly Review First Series 1749-1789: Indexes of Contributors and Articles*
(Oxford: Clarendon Press, 1934), p. 106. For Lyttelton, see *The Works
of George Lord Lyttelton*, ed. George Edward Ayscough, 3 vols., 3rd
ed. (London, 1776), 2:157-58. At least one (unknown) commentator,
however, believed that Lyttelton's Dialogue gave Messala the better of
the argument. See *Candid and Critical Remarks on the Dialogues of
the Dead* (London, 1760), pp. 38-39.
19 Brutus to Atticus, Brutus, i. 17, in *The Letters of Cicero*, trans.
Evelyn S. Schuckburgh, 4 vols. (London: George Bell, 1899-1909), 4:
250-51.
20 Brutus to Cicero, i. 4, ibid., p. 254.
21 Dryden's *Plutarch* (see n. 18, above), 7:248.

Cicero (1651), portrays him as vain, foolish, the instrument
of his own and the republic's subversion, and criminally
blind to the true character of the ruthless boy. Quintus complains that his brother Marcus has "put the reins of Tyranny" into Octavian's hand and will "indiscreetly kindle /
The fire already glowing in his breast." Octavian thus will
increase his ambition

> When he perceives the authors of our liberty
> Commended to his care, and that by you
> Who have been hitherto the chiefest prop
> And pillar of it.[22]

Cicero confesses that he encouraged the dangerous youth,
soon sees that the republic is "past recovery, lost for ever,"
and laments that he himself has been made "the mark of
accusation" for that fatal act (sigs. D1^r, D2^v).

Such accusations, and their consequences for Octavian's
reputation, appear throughout the Restoration and eighteenth century. In 1663 Cowley reluctantly quotes Brutus' attack upon Cicero. John Rowe later tells the readers of his
Sallust (1709) that the historian should not be blamed for
giving so skimpy a portrait of Cicero's role in Catiline's defeat. Exclusion "might not be such a Disadvantage to him
as some People may be apt to Imagine," because we would
otherwise see that "he was of a Spirit too Low and Timerous to Bear up against the Power of Tyrants: That, in fine,
on the Loss of the *Roman* Liberty He was little better
than a Temporizer." John Sheffield's Cassius scarcely laments the death of Cicero—"that talking Friend of CAESAR"

22 (London), sig. C4^r. Subsequent references are cited in the text.
Quintus paraphrases Brutus' letter (n. 19) when he argues that his
brother is guilty of Octavian's crime "if you might have prevented
it, / Which moderation would have done." Cicero himself is aware
of his guilt and pleads, "Cease Good Quintus, / You wrack me too
severely" (sig. C4^r). Addison Ward has studied the decline in Cicero's
reputation, but thinks it a mid-eighteenth-century, rather than Renaissance, innovation. See his useful essay, "The Tory View of Roman
History," *SEL*, 4 (1964): 413-56. Ward is also a helpful complement
to the discussion of the British historians of Rome in chap. 3, below.

—and believes that "Octavius has well paid him for his pains." Conyers Middleton's partisan *Life of Cicero* (1741) admits that its subject "speaks always of Octavius, in terms highly advantageous, even where he was likely to give disgust by it."[23] In *Observations on the Life of Cicero* (1741), Lyttelton uses Brutus' and Cicero's own letters to show that Cicero "sacrificed the Welfare or his Country to his private Interests and Passions." He also laments the "Baseness and Indiscretion in so meanly courting the Enemy of the Commonwealth, and . . . having planted and supported a Tyranny" of such deep and strong roots. Indeed, he himself was killed because of "that Tyranny his Mismanagement had established." Several years thereafter William Melmoth repeats the already traditional reservations regarding Cicero's character and concludes that "Cicero was by no means at this juncture acting the part of a patriot."[24]

[23] "Of Liberty," in "Several Discourses by way of Essays, in Verse and Prose," *The Works of Mr. Abraham Cowley*, 5th ed. (London, 1678), p. 82 of new pagination after *Davideidos*; Rowe, *Caius Crispus Sallustius The Historian Made English* (London), p. xv; Sheffield, *The Works of John Sheffield, . . . Duke of Buckingham* [ed. Alexander Pope], 2nd ed., 2 vols. (London, 1729), 1:376 ("A Dialogue Between Augustus Caesar, and Cardinal Richelieu," 2:153-65, is also interesting for its anti-Augustanism. See chap. 2, sec. iv, at n. 52 in text, below); Middleton, 2 vols. (London), 2:460. For a more modern discussion of the relationship between Cicero and Octavian, see David Stockton, *Cicero: A Political Biography* (Oxford: Oxford Univ. Press, 1971), pp. 280-332.

[24] Lyttelton (London), pp. 9, 54, respectively (see also pp. 49-53); Melmoth, trans. of Cicero's *Letters to Several of his Friends*, 3 vols. (London, 1753), 3:381-82, n. 10. Cicero's timidity and insufficient patriotism were criticized throughout the century. See William Guthrie's version of *Cicero's Epistles to Atticus* (1752), 3 vols. (London, 1806), 3:268, where Guthrie rejects Middleton's defense of Cicero: "he could not . . . be ignorant of the views of Octavius . . . who had the address to . . . make use of him in all his most pernicious designs upon the public liberty"; Robert Jephson, *Roman Portraits* (London, 1794), pp. 89, 105, n. 5, 173-74; and Alexander Adam, *Classical Biography* (Edinburgh, 1800), p. 129. According to Jephson, "to form a correct judgment of Cicero" one should temper "the severity of Melmoth with the panegyrick of Middleton" (p. 255).

Cicero was not alone in being so criticized. Middleton berates Dio Cassius for his apparently monarchic pro-Augustan stand; Thomas Blackwell finds both Dio and Appian
Caesarean fawners; Joseph Warton calls Dio a "fulsome
court historian"; and Velleius Paterculus is reduced to the
role of lovely stylist and unlovely historian. Even René
Rapin, who was not hostile to strong kings, thinks that
Paterculus "strews every thing with flowers." Readers of
Dryden's *Tacitus* (1698) would see Paterculus identified as
one who wrote "an Epitome of the Roman History, in very
elegant Latin, but full of gross Flattery."[25] In 1722 James
Patterson admits that his author is "generally censured, for
his excessive and gross Flattery of *Augustus* and *Tiberius*."
Thomas Gordon, among others, was unpersuaded by Patterson's attempted defense and deplored the content of the
well-written history: "he destroyed his moral Character, by
his boundless Flattery to *Tiberius*, and his Minister *Sejanus*,
and has been ever since discredited."[26] It seems reasonable to
say that during the eighteenth century, those historians or
history-makers clearly sympathetic to Octavian or Augustus
were widely rejected. Such rejection was a broadly based ele-
ment of political and historical thought, one common to

[25] Middleton, *Life of Cicero*, 1:xxv-xxvi; Blackwell, *Memoirs of the
Court of Augustus*, 3 vols. (Edinburgh and London, 1753-1763), 1:315;
Rapin, trans. [R. Midgely], as *The Modest Critick* (London, 1689), p.
67; Dryden, *The Annals and History of Cornelius Tacitus*, 3 vols. (London), 1:341 n. *

[26] Patterson, *The Roman History of C. Velleius Paterculus* (Edinburgh), p. 11; Gordon, *The Works of Sallust . . . With Political Discourses on that Author* (London, 1744), p. xvi. See also *Caii Velleii
Paterculi . . . ex historiae romanae* (Glasgow, 1752), p. iii: "tenuis
alioqui verbis, neque satis accuratus. adulationis, supra quam credi
potest, vitio laboravit. praesertim cum Augustu et Tiberii Caesaris
gesta narravit"; Blackwell, *Memoirs of the Court of Augustus*, 1:317.
Perhaps the bluntest of such comments comes in the *Biographia
Classica*, 2 vols. (London, 1740), which translates Aldus Manutius'
objections: "In short, he is nothing but a Court Prostitute" (2:188).
Thomas Gordon, *The Works of Tacitus*, 2 vols. (London, 1728-1731),
1:49, is a respectable second.

court and opposition, Whig and Tory, and to thoughtful citizens who may not have been active followers of either side.

Moreover, most historians who praised Augustus also offered him comparable or greater blame. In Livy's case that negative material was supplied by the reader's imagination. George Baker's comment in 1797 borrows from Bolingbroke's *Letters on the Study and Use of History* in 1752 and is typical of one contemporary view of Livy. Assuming that Livy is a republican, Baker and Bolingbroke lament the loss of his several books regarding the later commonwealth and ask: "What delight would it not afford us, to see the whole progress of a free Government from liberty to servitude? the whole series of causes and effects . . . at the time; . . . I own, says a noble author, I should be glad to exchange what we have of this History, for what we have not."[27]

If Livy's non-extant books could so easily be 'listed in the cause, it is logical to assume that the real words of other historians and their commentators would be as well. Their complaints fell into four related and overlapping classes, and were recorded in whole or in part by most of the major classical historians. They objected to the methods by which Octavian acquired power, his lack of courage and martial ability, his unusual sexual preferences in his private life, and his influence upon the empire after he became its head.

Even Octavian's partisans often deplored his ugly rise to power. Florus was largely pro-Augustan and rivaled Paterculus in praise of the *"Wisdom and Dexterity"* that re-ordered the broken state; but his commentators sometimes added remarks that emphasized the ruler's bloody approach

---

[27] *The History of Rome, By Titus Livius*, 6 vols. (London), 1:vii-viii. Baker is quoting from Bolingbroke's Letter iv. 2. See his *Letters on the Study . . . of History*, 2 vols. (London), 2:164. Affection for Livy as a republican who "retained the fire of freedom" during an age of servitude was commonplace from Machiavelli to Baker and beyond. For the words just quoted, see [Charles Hereford], *The History of Rome*, 3 vols. (London, 1792), 3:126.

to the throne. Blankardus' edition comments upon the triumvirate of Antony, Lepidus, and Octavian, and analyzes
Octavian's motives. He insists that the young man hoped to
eliminate his colleagues as soon as he had the power and,
during the proscription, consciously destroyed all those
who were "eminent in virtue, wealth, or dignity," including his friends, and especially Cicero, "to whom he owed
all things, . . . lest he stand out as an overseer of great liberty in behalf of the republic."[28]

Plutarch and Appian were no less incensed regarding the
death of Cicero and the horrors of the proscription. "Nothing was ever heard of so barbarous," Plutarch insists in the
life of Antony.[29] Octavian is scarcely less ugly in "Brutus"
(7:343-44), and in the comparison of Demetrius with Antony
he seems merely a superior analogue to the unjust Antony
who tyrannically enslaved the Romans. He performed his
"most illustrious" work in hunting Brutus and Cassius in
order "to destroy the freedom of his fellow citizens and
country" (7:152). Plutarch's audience knew that young
Octavian, however ineffectual, was Antony's colleague in
those battles.

Dio Cassius is comparably severe, though some of his
eighteenth-century readers found him too friendly by far
toward "the Caesarean Success."[30] Dio is anything but blind

[28] *Lucius Annaeus Florus. Epitome rerum romanorum*, trans. John
Clarke, 6th ed. (London, 1763), p. 174: bk. iv, chap. 3; *L. A. Florus ex
recensione N. Blankardi. Accedit eiusdem ex omnium observationibus
editis, ac ineditis Salmasii commentarius* (Leiden, 1648), p. 375n:
"ceteros qui virtute, opibus, aut dignitate eminebant, proscriptione
tolli maluit, ut invidiam cum aliis potius communicaret, quam ea
oneraret se solus. Hinc etiam amicos prodidit, inter quos cui omnia
debebat, Ciceronem, ne aut pro Rep. gravis libertatis exactor. . ´. ."
Florus himself says that the Roman people were in "a State of *Slavery*"
under Augustus, whose role in the triumvirate was shameful. See pp.
174, 177 of Clarke's translation, and Florus iv. 3, and iv. 6.

[29] Dryden's *Plutarch* (n. 18), 7:365. Subsequent citations are given
in the text.

[30] For Middleton's and Blackwell's remarks regarding Dio (Blackwell is quoted), see n. 25, above, and for Joseph Warton, *An Essay on
the Genius and Writings of Pope*, 5th ed., 2 vols. (London, 1806), 2:33.

to the manifold faults of Augustus, and his transcription of Agrippa's speech urging restoration of the republic often was cited as a model of virtue.[31] Degory Wheare, following Colerus, seems to prefer Maecenas' countering tirade supporting the principate, but he also praises *"the splendid Oration of Agrippa."*[32] In 1658 one A. R. abstracted those splendors for separate publication and lamented that a heathen would not "betray the cause of his Country and Truth," whereas "professing Christians in this Generation" will in fact commit "Treachery, Perjury, and Corruption" against their God and nation.[33]

These three traits are also part of Dio's portrait of Octavian; we see his suppression of liberty with Antony and their joint "tearing of the Commonwealth in pieces," his debasing of the senate and its values (1:99: xlviii. 31-34; liii. 2-12), his violation of his own laws regarding adultery (1:156-57), his cruelty and love of blood (1:66, 184-85: e.g., xlvii. 3-5; lv. 21), and his cowardice and incompetence in battle (1:95, 104, 109-111: e.g., xlviii. 18; xlix. 4-10). While stating the relative virtues of Octavian metamorphosed into Augustus, Dio nevertheless includes a variety of additional unpleasant incidents and facts, perhaps the worst of which is his belief that Tiberius "was nam'd to succeed *Augustus* only for this reason, that the Vices of Ti-

[31] But Appian also was admired by monarchists like Henry Binniman. See his translation of Appian, *An Auncient Historie and exquisite Chronicle of the Romanes Warres, both Civile and Foren* (London, 1578), sig. Aij[r]: "How God plagueth them that conspire against theyr Prince this Historie declareth at the full. . . . this Author hathe a pleasure to . . . affray all men from disloyaltie toward their Soueraigne."

[32] *The Method and Order of Reading . . . Histories,* 2nd ed. (London, 1694), p. 109 (originally *De Ratione et methodo legendi historias,* 1623). Wheare's book was a historical text at Cambridge until the early eighteenth century (*DNB*).

[33] *An Oration of Agrippa to Octavius Caesar Augustus, Against Monarchy Taken out of the LII Book of Dion the Philosopher, Caelius, S. C. being the Interpreter* (London, 1658), sig. A1[v]. The title page includes a Biblical comment relevant to contemporary England and Augustan Rome: "Wo to him that buildeth a Town with blood, and establish a City by Iniquity" (Habakkuk, 2:12).

21

berius, might give a greater lustre to the Vertues of the other!" (1:205: lvi. 45).

This suspicion reappears and is weakly rejected in Suetonius, a historian, Jabez Hughes reports, who "is distinguish'd by his Integrity" and impartiality. He "praises and censures, and reports the good and bad Actions of the Emperors without Passion òr Flattery." Degory Wheare, Thomas Blackwell, Edward Gibbon, and others shared a faith in Suetonius' accuracy and impartiality.[34]

The candid Suetonius demonstrates that Octavian was made consul before the legal age only because his soldiers demanded it "for him in the Name of the Army." When the senate demurred, the officer in charge "threw back his Robe, and shewing the Hilt of his Sword, had the Face to declare in open Court, *This shall give it him if you refuse it.*" Confronted with such logic the senate reconsidered, and so the young man "invaded the Consulship" (1:78: Augustus 26). Octavian rarely was in battle, was heartlessly cruel thereafter, probably killed his generals Hirtius and Pansa

[34] Hughes, *The Lives of the XII. Caesars, Or the First Twelve Roman Emperors*, 2 vols. (London, 1717), 1:sig. A6ᵛ (subsequent citations are given in the text); Wheare, *Method and Order*, p. 105; Blackwell, *Memoirs of . . . Augustus*, 2:317; Gibbon, *Decline and Fall*, 2:86. See also Gibbon's remark in his *Vindication of Some passages in the XVth and XVIth Chapters of the Decline and Fall of the Roman Empire* (1779): "if Laertius had concealed the defects of Plato, if Suetonius had disguised the vices of Augustus, we should have been deprived of the knowledge of some curious, and perhaps instructive, facts, and our idea of those celebrated men might have been more favourable than they deserved" (*Miscellaneous Works*, ed. John Lord Sheffield, 5 vols. [London, 1814], 4:632). The compiler of Suetonius' *Lives of the Twelve Caesars* (London, 1688) reports the praise of their author by Pliny, St. Jerome, and Erasmus (sig. A4ᵛ). The *Biographia Classica* (n. 26, above) also gives a generous, largely favorable sample of responses to Suetonius: 2:234-39. The translation of Suetonius (1672) sometimes attributed to Andrew Marvell may have encouraged—or been a sign of—its author's antiroyalism, but the translator offers neither preface nor critical apparatus to feed our suspicions. The *DNB* thinks the attribution to Marvell is based on insufficient evidence (a contemporary hand's note in the Bodleian copy).

(at Mutina), and certainly punished innocent tribes and towns. After Philippi "he observ'd no Moderation," decapitated Brutus, "treated every illustrious Prisoner with Taunt and Passion," denied burial rites, and received "the blackest Reproaches" from the defeated prisoners being led to death (1:66: Augustus 12). This barbarity extended into his reign as a triumvir. Though he resisted the proscription, "when it was once begun, he executed it more severely than either of" his colleagues. Among other indecencies, he murdered the praetor O. Gallius for carrying a book under his toga while Gallius was waiting to see him. Octavian thought "he had conceal'd a Dagger there; and not venturing to make any Inquiry, lest it should prove otherwise," he had him removed from the court and tortured. "When he confess'd nothing, he commanded him to be kill'd, having first crush'd out his Eyes with his own Hands" (1:79-80: Augustus 27).

The reader who suspects that sexual perversion accompanies such sadism will not be disappointed by Suetonius' minute inquiries. Here is the private life of so hopeful a youth, who, it seems, teaches us that only Caesar's wife, and not his grand-nephew, need be above suspicion.

> In his Youth he labour'd under an infamous Character for several Actions of Lewdness. *Pompey* charg'd him with being effeminate, and M. Anthony told him he had purchas'd his Adoption by his Uncle by becoming his Prostitute. And *Lucius*, the Brother of *Marcus*, affirms that he was deflower'd by *Caesar*, and that he let himself out to *Hirtius* in *Spain* for Three hundred thousand Sesterces, and us'd to singe his Thighs, with Nut-Shells, to make the Hairs come up the softer. And the whole Body of the People one Day at the Games, with vast Acclamations, apply'd in his Disgrace a Verse spoken on the Stage concerning a Priest of *Cybele* beating his Tabor. . . .

> See how the Pathick, with his Finger, still
> Commands th' obsequious Orb and tempers at his Will?
> (1:116-17: Augustus 68)

Lest the uninitiated reader not understand the allusion and the joke, Jabez Hughes explains that "The Priests of *Cybele* were castrated, and prostituted themselves." The verse suggests "that the Priest, who was a Catamite, play'd on the Tabor (*Orbis*) with his Finger, or that *Augustus* was a Pathick, and commanded the World at his Pleasure. The first is the direct Meaning, and the People apply'd it in the latter" (1:117, n. †). [35]

With versatility worthy of an emperor, the married Augustus also enjoyed heterosexual misadventures, even though he himself passed laws against such adultery. As Augustus' friends pointed out, he was not unfaithful merely "to gratify his Lust, but out of Reasons of State, that he might discover the counsels of his Enemies by their Wives" (1:117: Augustus 69). Later in his life " 'tis said, he was most addicted to Deflowering of Virgins, who were provided for him from all Parts, even by his own Wife" (1: 120: Augustus 66). Suetonius does not say whether Livia also supplied Augustus' daughter Julia, but he long labored under the charge of banishing Ovid because the poet discovered that incestuous affair. No less a person than the depraved Emperor Caligula asserted that "his Mother was begotten by Augustus on his Daughter *Julia*" (2:267: Caligula 23).[36] Such a man is not quite the paragon or even neutral symbol we have been led to expect.

[35] Hughes was not alone in bringing this Suetonian swipe to the attention of his readers. Voltaire's *Questions sur l'encyclopédie*, 9 vols. (Geneva [?] 1770-1772) did so as well (2:347), and Gilbert Stuart's approving review for the *Monthly*, 44 (1771): 527 (attribution, Nangle, p. 105) translates Voltaire but leaves the scandalous Latin in its native idiom. Voltaire's entire essay on "Auguste Octave" is filled with outrage against Augustus, Virgil, and Horace.

[36] See also Hughes' note: " 'tis certain *Julia*'s character was abandon'd enough to admit [this possibility], and *Augustus* himself was too dissolute to make such a Suppositon impossible. It has been thought, that *Ovid* ow'd his Banishment to his surprising the Emperor . . . unaware in these infamous Embraces . . ." (2:267, n. ††). This hypothesis for Ovid's banishment was common from the later Middle Ages on, and it is discussed, together with the other hypotheses, in John C. Thibault,

The writers in Augustus' stable, however, did their best to support the appropriate myths, including his military accomplishments; but those who were not house-historians had a different view. Appian, for example, tells us that shortly before the battle against Brutus at Philippi, word was brought that Antony advanced alone, "having left *Caesar* sick at *Epidamnum*."[37] When Brutus' men later took Octavian's camp, "*Caesar* was not there because of a Dream, by which he was advertised to absent himself" (2:206: iv. 14. 110). At the end of the day Antony encamped opposite Brutus, awaiting the decisive battle. "*Caesar* having watched till Midnight, being sick, withdrew" (2:214: iv. 17. 130). He remained sick during crucial encounters, and so all the honor of the victory goes to Antony and all the contempt to Octavian (2:225: v. 2. 14). Whatever the soldiers' action, Appian is aware that immense suffering had been caused in a war that was undertaken "to satisfy the ambition of the Chiefs" who were "Usurpers of the Government" (2:224: v. 2. 12).

Nor, Appian continues, is the young triumvir any better as a commander at sea. During the Sicilian war, that bungling and frightened captain was consistently defeated and forced to flee from young Pompey. Only Agrippa's leadership, courage, and invention of a new weapon that caused terrible damage (2:262: v. 12. 118) allow Octavian's ultimate victory.

Dio Cassius offers similar stories and confirms that Octavian was so inept in naval combat and strategy that he

---

The Mystery of Ovid's Exile (Berkeley and Los Angeles: Univ. of California Press, 1964).

[37] *The History of Appian of Alexandria*, 2 vols., trans. J[ohn] D[avies] (London, 1679), 2:204: iv. 13. 106. Subsequent quotations are cited in the text. The importance of such historians in clarifying Augustus' true achievements was urged by S.N.H. Linguet, in *Histoire des révolutions de l'empire romain*, 2 vols. (Paris, 1766), 1:36. They offer necessary correctives to the misrepresentations of Horace and Virgil: see chap. 2, n. 56, below. A set of these volumes was in the library of George III.

planned to attack Pompey in ox-hide-covered osier barks. "But finding that his Project was ridicul'd" as obviously dangerous, "he provided a more solid Fleet, with which nevertheless he was defeated," leaving Pompey with control of the sea and the food bound for Rome (1:95: xlviii. 18). The people hold Octavian and Antony responsible for the subsequent famine, insist that they make peace, and attempt to kill them when peace remains distant and stomachs empty. Both Dio and his eighteenth-century readers must have noticed the difference in behavior. "*Caesar* seeing some of his People hurt, tore his cloaths, and presented himself to them in that equipage, and after having ask'd them pardon, begg'd them to spare his Life. As for *Antony*, he call'd his friends to his Assistance, and repuls'd their Violence" (1:98: xlviii. 31).

These readers would also have been aware of the difference between Dio's and Paterculus' description of the capture of Lepidus. For one, Octavian's achievement transcended the highest republican martial virtue; for the other, the deception and superior forces of a bully awed a "naturally timerous" man (1:113-14: xlix. 2). Finally, not to be outdone in proclaiming imperial weaknesses, Suetonius lets us know that it was always with the swords of others that Octavian prospered, and that "he manag'd but two Foreign Wars in Person," those in Dalmatia and Cantabri. "The rest of his Wars he wag'd by Lieutenants" (1:73: Augustus 20). Suetonius does not see this as the wisdom of an emperor with better things to do than be slain by a mindless barbarian, and so his translator draws the appropriate conclusion: "*Augustus* . . . was at Bottom a Coward" (1:30, n.*). This opinion was shared by Antony, who knew of his rival's "profound sleep" during the final battle against Pompey and thus claimed "*That he was not able to turn his Eyes directly upon the Line of Battle . . . and wou'd not get up and shew himself to his Men, before* Marcus Agrippa had put the Enemies Ships to Flight" (1:68: Augustus 16).

The outlook for future rule by such a man could not have been promising. Even Florus admits that though Rome was secure, it was so in a *"State of Slavery"* under Octavian (p. 174: iv. 3). The gods themselves gave warning of that state, as Appian shows in his tale of a soothsayer's prediction of tyranny after the triumvirate. During the battles against Brutus and Cassius there were so many prodigies that "the Senate sent for Divines out of *Tuscany*: the eldest of which told them, that the Royalty should be reestablished, and they all Slaves but only He: and therewith stopping his Mouth, held his Breath so long, till he fell down dead in the place" (2:164: iv. 2).[38] Similarly, as Dio reports, the astrologer Nigidius Figulus knew the fates of the infant Octavian, and the aging republic and a possible reaction to the budding emperor. "One Day seeing Octavius [the father] come to the Senate a little later than the rest, by reason of the Birth of his Son, he said to him, you have begot a *Master* for us. *Octavius* troubled at what he said, would have killed his Son, but he prevented him by telling him, that 'twas not his Fate to dye after that manner" (1:60: xlv. 1). According to Appian and Dio, reactions to the birth of the future princeps include suicide and contemplated filicide.

Later British reactions were necessarily less destructive in deed but not in spirit. For John Clarke, Suetonius' translator in 1732, this excellent and impartial historian shows that after "the Civil Wars betwixt *Pompey* and *Caesar*" the story of Rome becomes one of butchery, misery, barbarity, and "the most brutish Folly." Clarke, who admires the Whig Gordon's anti-Augustan "admirable Discourses" to Tacitus, believes that Suetonius should be taught in the schools, so that students will see "the dismal Effects of arbitrary Power lodged in the Hands of a single Person." The teacher should help Suetonius by making "proper Remarks and Reflections."[39] Clarke himself was a schoolmaster of

[38] The tale from Nigidius Figulus was remembered. See Adam, *Classical Biography* (n. 24, above), p. 278.

[39] Clarke, *C. Suetonii Tranquilli XII Caesares. . . . Or, The Lives of the Twelve Caesars* (London). p. v. This work reached a third edition in 1761. The latter remark is by Paul Fussell, *English Augustan Poetry* (n. 6, above), pp. 3-4.

distinction and influence; he and his students probably would have been puzzled by the view that English *Augustan* poetry was "written with a consciousness of taking place in a safe environment, or at least an environment . . . where the threats are interesting and amusing rather than really terrifying."

Many of these crimes, however, are the property of Octavian rather than Augustus, and it is the latter who has become the golden center of the golden age acclaimed as the model for the British Augustans. After all, as several commentators on Rome said, the change in Octavian Caesar from before to after Actium was enormous, and the chief objection to his life is that he should never have been born or never died. Others, however, thought that "Augustus" was merely mutton dressed as lamb. They saw the boy as father to the monster, refused to distinguish between the old and the new Augustus, or to allow that one could be a good emperor with a background of sadism, murder, treachery and, above all, the eradication of representative government and the constitutional balance that made the republic great. Tacitus, Gibbon said, was "the first of historians who applied the science of philosophy to the study of facts" (*Decline and Fall*, 1:213); and Tacitus, defined as an antityrannic republican by fifteenth-century Florentines, told much of Western Europe about the frightening implications of the reign of Augustus Caesar. Examination of the relevant parts of the *Histories*, and especially the *Annals* and their libertarian influence, supports the conclusion towards which our other classical evidence leads: regardless of casual remarks, conventional panegyric, wishful thinking, or simple appeals for patronage, Augustus Caesar was an unlikely norm for eighteenth-century Britain.

II: TACITUS AND TACITEAN HISTORY

From the outset of the *Annals* Tacitus makes clear that Augustus was the successor of Julius Caesar, even though he "assum'd the Government, under the *Modest* Title of Prince of the Senate."[40] He also makes clear that Augustus inherited a large body of "Famous Wits" to transfer his actions "to *future Ages*," but that "they were hinder'd by the Growth of Flattery," which started, Dryden's note tells us, under Augustus (1:6).[41] Once he established his authority and soothed the fears of the people and the senate, he began to encroach upon them and to acquire their powers and the power of the law, "none daring to oppose him, the most violent of his Enemies being either slain in Battle, or cut off by Proscriptions." The remaining nobles were rewarded in the degree that they were ready "to enter into Servitude," and were "more willing to embrace the Present Slavery, with an assur'd prospect of Ease and Quiet, than to run the Hazard of new Dangers for the recovery of their Ancient Freedom" (1:7-8). By means of successful completion of wars, reasonable government, and moderation, Augustus solidified his rule while allowing the magistrates to retain their earlier names rather than functions. Moreover, he was aided by the inevitable course of nature, since most of the older citizens who "had seen the times of Lib-

40 *The Annals and History of Cornelius Tacitus: His Account of the Antient Germany, and the Life of Agricola. Made English by several Hands*, 3 vols. (London, 1698), 1:5. Book One of the *Annals* was translated by Dryden. Subsequent references are given in the text.

41 The title page tells us that the volumes include "the Political Reflections and Historical Notes of Monsieur Amelot De La Houssay, and the Learned Sir Henry Savile." The note above—like the others and the division of the page into text, political reflections, and historical notes—comes from Amelot. For this remark, see his *Tacite avec des notes politiques et historiques*, 2 vols. (The Hague, 1692), 1:8, n. 2. This edition is especially valuable for its prefatory abstracts of several modern translators and commentators on Tacitus. Ignorance of Dryden's source —Amelot rather than Tacitus—has led to some curious generalizations regarding the development of English prose style. See George Williamson's *The Senecan Amble: A Study in Prose Form from Bacon to Collier* (1951; rpt. Chicago: Univ. of Chicago Press, 1966), p. 322, n. 1. Williamson is followed by Irvin Ehrenpreis, *Literary Meaning and Augustan Values*, p. 4.

erty" were dead, and those born after Actium knew only
his administration: "Nothing of the Form or Force of the
Ancient Government was left. Equality and Freedom were
at once distinguish'd; the Common Interest was to obey
and serve the Prince" (1:13). He presided over the permanent dissolution of the republic by establishing "a large
Provision of Heirs" (1:26). Upon his death a debate
emerged regarding his virtues and vices. It is worth dis-
cussing at length, since it is almost a paradigm of the arguments on either side of the case.

Some argued that "his filial Piety to *Caesar*," the necessity
of the times and laws, had forced him into a civil war, which
could not be managed with strict justice. Antony and Lepidus were responsible for most of the violence and were
tolerated merely to help avenge Julius' death. The ef-
feminacy of Lepidus and the debauchery of Antony required
their elimination and Augustus' sole governance. Even so,
he ruled only as Prince of the Senate, secured the empire's
boundaries, the military's strength, the citizens' rights, and
Rome's glory, while rarely using force and then "always for
the preservation of the Publick Safety" (1:27-29).

So much for the positive side. "On the other side," Tacitus
declares, all his "boasted Piety . . . and the Necessities of a
Common-Wealth" were merely his pretext; owing to his
"insatiable desire of reigning," he bribed the veteran troops
and turned them to his own use. Others argued that after
he "extorted" the office of praetor from the senate, he seized
the troops of the suspiciously slain Hirtius and Pansa, forced
his own elevation to consul, and then turned the arms of the
republic against her noblest citizens.

> The Proscription . . . was charg'd on him; and the di-
> vision of the Lands disapprov'd even by those to whom
> they fell. The Death of *Cassius* and the two *Bruti*, must
> indeed be own'd for a just Vengeance on the Murderers
> of his Father; though still it had been more glorious for

him, to have sacrific'd his private hatred, to the Publick Interest: But the younger *Pompey* had been unworthily betray'd under the shadow of a pretended Peace; and *Lepidus* by a dissembled Friendship: *Anthony* sooth'd and lull'd asleep, . . . had paid with his Life the forfeit of that fraudulent Alliance. After this a Peace was of necessity to ensue, but it was a bloody Peace; and infamous for the punishment of the *Varro's*, the *Egnatii*, and the *Julii* of *Rome*; to which succeeded the Defeats of *Lollius* and *Varus* in Germany. (1:30-31)

Augustus' contemporaries, like Englishmen some 1700 years later, were offended by his life as a private citizen. Hence "they reproach'd him for having forcibly taken from her Husband a Woman [Livia] then with Child; and for having made a Scoff of Religion, by demanding of the Priests if it were lawful for him to espouse her before she was deliver'd." He permitted the luxury of his family, allowed himself to be governed by Livia, "a heavy Burden to the Common-Wealth, and a worse Step-mother to the Family of the *Caesars*," and caused his own virtual deification. Tacitus offers his harshest attack on Augustus' motivation in selecting Tiberius "to succeed him, not out of any Affection which he bore him, nor out of any Consideration for the Publick Good, but only to add a Lustre to his own Glory, by the Foyl of that Comparison; as having a perfect Insight into his Nature, and knowing him at the bottom to be Proud and Cruel" (1:31-33: i. 4). For Dryden's Tacitus, the superficially attractive Augustan settlement corrupts the people, the senate, the arts, and the ruler himself. In addition, Tacitus' weighing of Augustus' strengths and weaknesses speaks volumes, since the latter abound and the former are diminished by the defensive tone of their presentation and their admission of several faults. Readers of Tacitus in the eighteenth century probably would have sympathized with Sir Ronald Syme's modern judgment of the debate regarding Augustus: "bold and subversive, Tacitus arraigns the whole moral and social programme of the Princeps, a failure when it was not deleterious."[42]

Perhaps most important of all, however, Tacitus' remarks are prologue to the story of the decline and fall of the Roman Empire. Like his later student Gibbon, Tacitus quietly urges that the origin of imperial degradation may be traced to the creator of the empire, that the moment of splendor and equilibrium was purchased with the death both of thousands of human beings and of the foundations of liberty. The crimes of the young Octavian are enormous; the crimes of the mature Augustus are catastrophic. The establishment of his power and the death of Rome are synonymous acts.

Tacitus' views often were shared by the numerous readers of Dryden's (1698), Gordon's (1728), and Murphy's (1796) versions of the *Annals*. These translators would have agreed with the "Politick Reflection" of Amelot de la Houssaye (1690) that Dryden borrows: "*Augustus* effaced all the Footsteps of his Triumvirate, by quitting the Title of Triumvir; and it may be said, that his Clemency did the Roman Common-Wealth more mischief than his Triumvirate, seeing it made the People tame for Servitude, by

---

[42] *Tacitus*, 2 vols. (Oxford: Clarendon Press, 1958), 1:432. For some eighteenth-century reaction to this passage in the *Annals*, see Dryden's *Tacitus*, 1:32-33, n. 10 and 33-34, note q (both from Amelot), and the Reverend Thomas Hunter's hostile *Observations on Tacitus* (London, 1752), p. 100: "Some Apology is indeed offered by *Tacitus* for *Augustus*'s Conduct, but 'tis followed with all the Malice and Rancour imaginable; and his very domestick Affairs are ransacked, to expose him the more." Several years thereafter, Thomas Mercer berated Augustus' bloody proscription and "impious jealousy of future fame" that dictated the "foil" of Tiberius ("Of Poetry," in *Poems* [Edinburgh, 1774], p. 113). I owe this reference, and several others, to my colleague Eric Rothstein. For a useful analysis of these and comparable Tacitean pages, see Norma P. Miller, "Style and Content in Tacitus," in *Tacitus*, ed. T. A. Dorey, Studies in Latin Literature and Its Influence (London: Routledge & Kegan Paul, 1969), pp. 99-116.

making them love him for a Master, whom they before abhorr'd as a Triumvir" (1:7).[43]

The remarks of Amelot and Dryden ultimately stem from the Renaissance reaction to Tacitus' newly found works. Leonardo Bruni's *Laudatio Florentinae urbis* (1400), for example, used Boccaccio's discovery of the manuscript of Tacitus' *Histories* in about 1360.[44] As Hans Baron reports, "In the *Laudatio*, the criterion for judging the Roman Republic and the Roman Empire is the presumed effect of the rule of the emperors on the *virtus Romana*—the psychological impact of the Empire on the energies of the Roman people. The Republic," he continues, adapting Bruni, ". . . had seen eminent talents in every field of endeavor, but 'after the republic had been subject to the power of one man, those brilliant minds vanished, as Cornelius [Tacitus] says.' "[45] This information is drawn from the opening of the *Histories* and anticipates the *Annals'* discussion of the debilitating effects of flattery. The manuscript of the *Annals* reached Italy in 1509, was edited by Beroaldus for Pope Leo X in 1515, and ushers in the concept of Tacitus as enemy both to the empire and to the decay solidified by the Augustan settlement. Whatever their excellent personal traits, Julius Caesar and Augustus after him established tyrannic rule, thereby initiated the transformation of the Roman people,

---

43 From Amelot's *Tacitus*, 1:10, n. 1.

44 For valuable discussion of the several manuscripts, see Clarence W. Mendell, *Tacitus: The Man and His Work* (New Haven: Yale Univ. Press, 1957), pp. 256-348. See also the history of the printed texts, pp. 349-78.

45 *The Crisis of the Early Italian Renaissance: Civic Humanism and Republican Liberty in an Age of Classicism and Tyranny* (Princeton: Princeton Univ. Press, 1966), p. 58. Subsequent references are cited in the text. For support of Baron's views regarding the spread of the Renaissance libertarian spirit, see D. J. Gordon, "Giannotti, Michelangelo and the Cult of Brutus," in *Fritz Saxl 1890-1948: A Volume of Memorial Essays from his Friends in England*, ed. Donald James Gordon (London: Thomas Nelson & Sons, 1957), pp. 281-96; and Eric W. Cochrane, *Tradition and Enlightenment in the Tuscan Academies* (Chicago: Univ. of Chicago Press, 1961), pp. 186-87.

and "cleared the way for such evils and crimes as [their] successors . . . committed" (p. 61). The ideas of the *Laudatio* appeared in Bruni's later work and "remained characteristic of Florentine thought to the late Renaissance" (p. 66).

This eloquent belief was amplified by Bracciolini Poggio, Cino Rinucinna, Coluccio Salutati, and Pier Paolo Vergerio, among other "civic humanists" as Baron calls them (pp. 66-78): the Augustan solidifier of absolute rule is the creator of absolute decay and is responsible for the corruptions of government that followed.[46] The concept may have been carried into early Renaissance England by some of the traveling humanists themselves, their manuscripts and books, and quite surely by subsequent Italian heirs of humanism.[47] Whether by influence or accident, Poggio's use of Seneca's anti-Augustan *Controversiae*, his comments upon the loss of letters with the loss of liberty under Augustus, and his insistence that Augustus cannot take credit for the flowering of letters during his reign, all reappear in major English texts during the Restoration and eighteenth century.[48] In England, as on the Continent, Tacitus began to

[46] If the Florentine civic humanists looked to Tacitus for support of this vew, Tacitus may have looked to the senatorial writer C. Asinius Pollio, who remained neutral during the wars between Antony and Octavian, "devoting himself to literature and patronage, and writing a history of the civil wars between Caesar and Pompey, whose beginning he firmly placed in the year of the so-called First Triumvirate (60 B.C.). The lesson that the seeds of destruction were sown precisely at the moment of seeming peace was not lost on Tacitus when he came to look for a starting point for his *Annals*." Bruni and his followers, it would seem, had long precedent for their hypothesis. See R. H. Martin, "Tacitus and his Predecessors," in *Tacitus*, ed. Dorey (n. 42, above), p. 121 (referred to hereafter as Dorey).

[47] See Roberto Weiss, *Humanism in England During the Fifteenth Century* (Oxford: Basil Blackwell, 1957).

[48] For example, see Poggio's use of Seneca (Preface to *Controversiae*, bk. v, and perhaps bk. i) in Baron, pp. 66-67 (and p. 478, n. 41) and Arthur Murphy, trans., *The Works of Cornelius Tacitus*, 4 vols. (London, 1793), 4:348. Seneca's remark is also the basis for the *Craftsman*,

replace Livy both as a stylist and as a historian of practical use for one's age. According to Beatus Rhenanus, that substitution had taken place in Basel by 1532, just 17 years after the first printing of the *Annals*.[49] In 1574 Justus Lipsius published his important edition of Tacitus and in 1581 his political commentary that, with the comparable work by Carolus Paschalius in the same year, initiated the vogue of discourses and commentary upon Tacitus as a contemporary "politick" historian whose *Annals* were "quasi theatrum hodiernae vitae."[50] Tacitus became enormously fashionable.[51]

---

no. 4 (1726), an attack upon Augustus for perverting the law and for setting an example for Tiberius "to prosecute the most *innocent Books*, and destroy entirely that *just liberty*, which is the greatest Blessing of a free People." Poggio anticipates the argument of Thomas Blackwell (and others) that the growth of letters under Augustus was really the final flowering of republican virtue: see Baron, p. 27, and Blackwell, *Memoirs of the Court of Augustus*, 3:467. These Renaissance and eighteenth-century views are consistent with Sir Ronald Syme's *The Roman Revolution* (1939; rpt. Oxford: Clarendon Press, 1968), p. 487, et passim. It is a pleasure to acknowledge my debt to Baron and Syme.

[49] Arnaldo Momigliano, "The First Political Commentary on Tacitus," in *Contributo alla storia degli classici* (Rome: Edizioni di storia e letteratura, 1955), p. 38. According to James Burnett, Lord Monboddo, "No body ever thought of setting [Tacitus] up for a model of style, till Justus Lipsius brought him into fashion." Monboddo laments that influence: *Of the Origin of Language*, 6 vols. (Edinburgh, 1773-1792), 3:210-11. For further discussion of Tacitus' stylistic influence in Europe and England, see Morris W. Croll's several essays reprinted in his *Style, Rhetoric, and Rhythm*, ed. J. Max Patrick et al. (Princeton: Princeton Univ. Press, 1966), and George Williamson, *The Senecan Amble*, primarily chap. 5.

[50] Momigliano, op. cit., p. 39. Momigliano is quoting from the Preface to Lipsius' commentary in 1581.

[51] For the spread of Tacitus' works see Peter Burke's two essays, "A Survey of the Popular Ancient Historians 1450-1700," in *History and Theory*, 5 (1966): especially pp. 148-51, and "Tacitism" in Dorey, p. 150. In the latter, for instance, he shows that "in the sixteenth century the *Annals* and *Histories* went through at least forty-five editions; in the seventeenth century, 103 more. The earlier seventeenth century is the critical period: sixty-seven editions in the period 1600-49, compared with thirty-six for the period 1650-99. The fashion for Tacitus spread across Europe, East and West."

By about the middle or end of the sixteenth century, however, he began to blend with the pro-absolutist politics of the day, and also became the historian of monarchy and a guide to the preservation of strong princes and the progress of courtiers.[52] Tacitus apparently was behind Machiavelli's *Prince* and often was leagued with him as a politic counselor who protected the ruling power. But this association, says Trajano Boccalini's Apollo, really belongs to those "who neither study him nor understand him," since Tacitus teaches Machiavelli's techniques to the people, and thus warns them of princely machinations.[53] In England Tacitus

[52] This dual view has been epitomized by Mary Frances Tenney: "He served as guide to success at court; he became counsel for the theory of Divine Right; yet he fended for Parliament and the people, and vindicated tyrannicide" ("Tacitus in the Politics of Early Stuart England," *Classical Journal*, 37 [1941]: 155). The bibliography of Tacitism is extensive. In addition to those works already cited, see: Felice Ramorino, *Cornelio Tacito nella storia della cultura* (Milan: Hoepli, 1897); F. J. Haverfield, "Tacitus During the Late Roman Period and the Middle Ages," *Journal of Roman Studies*, 6 (1916): 196-201; Giuseppe Toffanin, *Machiavelli e il "Tacitismo"* (Padua: A. Draghi, 1921); Tenney, "Tacitus in the Middle Ages and the Early Renaissance and in England to about the Year 1650," Diss. Cornell 1931; Tenney, "Tacitus Through the Centuries to the Age of Printing," *Univ. of Colorado Studies*, 22 (1935): 341-63; Georgio Spini, "I trattatisti dell'arte storica nella Controriforma italiana," in *Contributi alla storia del Concilio di Trento e della Controriforma* (Florence: Vallechi, 1948), trans. and slightly abridged by Eric Cochrane, as "Historiography: The Art of History in the Italian Counter Reformation," in *The Late Italian Renaissance 1525-1630*, ed. Cochrane (London: Macmillan, 1972), pp. 91-133; Jürgen von Stackelberg, *Tacitus in der Romania: Studien zur literarischen rezeption des Tacitus in Italien und Frankreich* (Tübingen: Max Niemeyer, 1960); Kenneth Charles Schellhase, "Tacitus in Renaissance Political Thought," Diss. Chicago 1969. Schellhase's book, with the same title, has recently appeared (Chicago: Univ. of Chicago Press, 1977).

[53] *I Ragguagli Di Parnasso: or Advertisements from Parnassus; in Two Centuries*, trans. Henry Carey (London, 1656), p. 179 (misprinted as p. 169): Century 1, Adv. 86. Neverthless, Boccalini himself was criticized for appearing to think Tacitus a guide to tyrants. Thomas Gordon, in high dudgeon, claims that such censure by Boccalini and other

was more the republican than monarchic historian and was, in fact, often considered dangerous to the establishment. In 1627 courtiers were appalled by the Dutchman Isaac Dorislaus, suspiciously "bred in a popular air." The young scholar from Leyden was the first lecturer in history at Cambridge, and had the ill fortune to accept the advice of Fulke Greville, founder of the post, that he speak on Tacitus. Matthew Wren quickly wrote to (then) Bishop Laud that the foreigner's first performance "seemed to acknowledge no right of Kingdomes, but whereof the people's voluntary submission had been the Principium Constitutionum." The second was "stored with such dangerous passages . . . and so applicable to the exasperations of these villainous times" that Dorislaus was soon dismissed.[54] In 1637 an unnamed Stuart zealot spent part of a holiday reading "the *Annals* of Tacitus with the Annotations of Lipsius, published in small 4to in 1619 at Geneva." As a result, he "points attention to certain passages which he termed seditious, and wishes the book to be suppressed."[55] It is no wonder that Milton called Tacitus "a noble writer most opposed to tyranny."[56]

Niccolo Machiavelli was one Italian prop for the antityrannic Tacitus. Though often damned for *The Prince*'s grim advice on solidifying rule, he was admired for championing republican virtues in his *Discourses* on Livy. For James Harrington, Machiavelli was "the republican advisor and spokesman" and guide to preventing "Caesarism." Henry Neville, Machiavelli's translator in 1675, regarded

---

commentators is absurd. "Tacitus represents Tyrants as odious to all men, and even to themselves" (*Works of Tacitus*, 1:28).

[54] James Bass Mullinger, *The University of Cambridge*, 3 vols. (Cambridge: At the University Press, 1873-1911), 3:86-88.

[55] As in Tenney, "Tacitus in . . . Early Stuart England" (n. 52, above), p. 158.

[56] *A Defence of the People of England*, ed. Don M. Wolfe, trans. Donald Mackenzie, in *Complete Prose Works of John Milton*, 6 vols. to date (New Haven: Yale Univ. Press, 1966-), 4:443. Tacitus, Milton wrote originally, was "scriptoris boni, et tyrannis adversissimi" (*The Works of John Milton*, ed. John Mitford, 8 vols. [London, 1863], 6:109).

him as the republican "divine Machiavel." Algernon Sidney and Walter Moyle were also his admirers and would have read numerous anti-Caesarian and anti-Augustan remarks in Neville's version.[57]

In *Discourses*, i. 52, for example, Machiavelli epitomizes many of the attacks upon Cicero's folly and Octavian's ambition. The latter induced the vain orator to help him in his rise to power and destruction of the senate he was charged to defend: "Which might have been easily foreseen; nor ought *Cicero* so imprudently to have reviv'd the name of *Caesar*, by whom the whole world was brought into servitude, and especially *Rome,* nor have persuaded himself that a Tyrant or any of his race would ever restore that liberty which his Predecessor had suppressed."[58] The "classical republicans" I have mentioned—and others, like Bolingbroke—may have seen that "Machiavelli carried on and developed Bruni's [and thus the "new" Tacitus'] conception that a wealth of human energies was stifled by Rome's universal Empire."[59]

[57] As quoted in Felix Raab, *The English Face of Machiavelli* (London: Routledge & Kegan Paul, 1964): Harrington, pp. 188-89; Neville, p. 219; and Sidney and Moyle, pp. 218, 222-23. For Harrington—or John Hall, according to the 1737 text—Augustus is a usurper whose acquisition of power, as "every one knows, that knows any thing of the *Roman Story* . . . was as fraudulent and violent as could be." See *Grounds and Reasons of Monarchy Consider'd,* in *The Oceana and Other Works of James Harrington,* coll. by John Toland (London, 1737), p. 8. For further discussion of Machiavelli and this group of political thinkers, see Zera S. Fink, *The Classical Republicans: An Essay in the Recovery of a Pattern of Thought in Seventeenth Century England,* Northwestern Univ. Studies in the Humanities, no. 9 (Evanston: Northwestern Univ. Press, 1945); and J.G.A. Pocock, "Machiavelli, Harrington, and English Political Ideologies in the Eighteenth Century," *William and Mary Quarterly,* 22 (1965); 549-83. Isaac Kramnick's essay, with a somewhat different focus, is also valuable: "Augustan Politics and English Historiography: The Debate on the English Past, 1730-35," *History and Theory,* 6 (1957): 33-56.

[58] *The Works of the Famous Nicholo Machiavel* [trans. Henry Neville], 3rd ed. (London, 1720), pp. 321-22.

[59] Baron, *Crisis,* p. 70. See also Schellhase, "Tacitus in Renaissance Political Thought," diss., p. 134. Machiavelli appears often in opposition

Julius Caesar and Octavian after him destroyed the vigor and creative energy of the Roman people.

The Florentine Tacitus was not limited to Machiavelli. Trajano Boccalini was praised in Moréri and Bayle, and in the translations of the former by Jeremy Collier and of Bayle by Pierre des Maizeaux and then Thomas Birch.[60] His popular *I Ragguagli di parnasso* was Englished as *Advertisements from Parnassus*, appeared in 1656, 1657, 1669, 1704, and 1706, helped Trenchard and Moyle's argument against a standing army in 1697, and was referred to by the bookseller in *A Tale of a Tub* (1704); by Steele in *Spectator*, no. 54 (1712); by Addison in *Spectator*, no. 291 (1712) on *Paradise Lost*; by the *Craftsman*, no. 329 (1732); the *Daily Gazetteer*, 23 May 1739; and by others, including Samuel Johnson, throughout the Restoration and eighteenth century.[61]

Like so many of the historians and commentators, Boccalini is concerned with Augustus' cruelty, his corruption or

---

works. See the *Craftsman*, nos. 219, 220, 419, and 436, for example, as well as *Fog's Weekly Journal*, 13 June 1730.

[60] Louis Moréri, *Le Grand dictionnaire historique*, 4 vols., 8th ed. (Amsterdam, 1698); Jeremy Collier, *The Great Historical, Geographical, Genealogical and Poetical Dictionary*, 2 vols., 2nd ed. (London, 1701), based on Moréri's 8th edition; Pierre Bayle, *Dictionnaire historique et critique*, 2 vols. (Rotterdam, 1697); Pierre Des Maizeaux, *An Historical and Critical Dictionary*, 4 vols. (London, 1710), 5 vols. (London, 1734-1738); Thomas Birch, *A General Dictionary Historical and Critical*, 10 vols. (London, 1734-1741).

[61] John Trenchard and Walter Moyle, *An Argument Shewing that a Standing Army is Inconsistent with a Free Government* (London, 1697), p. 24. For the other, and additional, references, see Richard Thomas, "Trajano Boccalini's 'Ragguali di Parnasso' and Its Influence upon English Literature," in *Aberystwyth Studies by Members of the University College of Wales*, 3 (1922): 73-102. More recently, William Henry Irving has also studied some of Boccalini's English dress in "Boccalini and Swift," *ECS*, 7 (1973-1974): 143-60. For further aspects of his role in Renaissance political thought, see Claudio Varese, *Traiano Boccalini*, Biblioteca di Cultura (Padua: Liviana Editrice, 1958), and Schellhase, pp. 279-86 (diss.).

eradication of republican leaders and government, the precedent of autocracy and assassination, and the grim consequences for Rome. In the *Advertisements* Boccalini's Brutus
berates Caesar for teaching Augustus to reward his former
enemies, allow them to reap more benefits from servitude
than freedom, and thus finally make them "instruments to
Tiberius" by encouraging the tyranny they should have
resisted. Caesar, enraged, challenges Brutus to single combat
and assures him that his earlier wounds "were very well
cured by his Nephew *Augustus*, and by the whole Triumph-
erate, with the corrosive of proscription."[62] Several other
Advertisements make a similar point—Augustus' illegal acquisition of military force allowed him to destroy his opposition and Roman liberty and "transmit the Roman Empire, as Hereditary, into the Person of *Tiberius*" (p. 274:
2:30).[63]

For Boccalini—and the several nations who read his
Ragguagli—there is no distinction between Octavian and
Augustus. The princeps is "*Augustus*" or "*Octavianus Augustus*" and is the archetypal despot who inherited Julius'
name, talent for oppression, and ability to pass that talent
to his heirs. The destruction of Rome's genius follows and
is sadly displayed in one of the longest and most seriously
affecting of the Advertisements. It begins with an attack
upon the harshness and ingratitude of the *Pax Romana* and
ends with an attack upon the Caesarean succession and
those senators who foolishly aided their own destroyers.
Each scene is played out before Apollo's literati collected in
Melpomene's theater. Apollo commands that two groups

[62] All quotations are from the 1656 Carey translation (n. 53, above).
Citations are hereafter given in the text with page, Century, and Advertisement number. This is from pp. 136-38: 1:7.

[63] This is criticism of Brutus and stems from Cicero's epistles to Atticus, Books xiv, xv, and xvi. It also was adapted by Gibbon in his "Di-
gression on the Character of Brutus" (1765-1766) (*The English Essays
of Edward Gibbon*, ed. Patricia B. Craddock [London: Oxford Univ.
Press, 1972], pp. 96-106). For other anti-Augustan Advertisements in
Boccalini, see p. 164: 1:78 and pp. 309-10: 2:51.

appear: all the senators who assisted the tyranny of Caesar and Augustus out of ambition or avarice, and all those "who were wickedly slain in the cruel Proscriptions made by the Triumviri . . . in *Augustus* his long reign," and by Tiberius, Caligula, and Nero.

This was the most sad and lamentable spectacle that was ever seen represented in the memory of man in any place whatsoever; for then all *Pernassus* broke forth into deep sighs, and shed tears in abundance, when those that had assisted *Caesar* in his Tyranny, saw that not onely *Tiberius, Caligula, Claudius,* and *Nero,* but even *Augustus* himself, forgetting the obligations which they ought to their posterity who had ayded them in atchieving their Tyrannical power were by them destroyed and cruelly put to death. For . . . many of the sons of those Senators, who following *Caesars,* and *Augustus* his Colours, had appeared enemies to publike liberty, were afterwards cruelly slain by the insuing Tyrants, onely for that they discovered too much their love to live free; others for proving more vertuous Senators, then would stand with Tyrannical Government: and an infinite number by the meer bestiality of those that governed. . . . Those unfortunate Senators, who to make *Caesar,* and *Augustus* great, had with their swords in hand, and with so much effusion of blood, banisht liberty from out their Country, ran as if they had been mad, to embrace their children, grandchildren, and great grand-children who had been so Tyrannously treated; but being by them driven away with reproachful speeches, those Senators more afflicted then ever, said; You have reason to look upon us your Progenitors, with an incensed eye, and to drive us like enemies out of your sight; for you may truly say these your wounds were occasioned by these our hands, the Tyranny which hath made you so miserable by our imprudency, your calamities by our foolish Ambition, all the inhumanities whereinto we have most imprudently hurried you, by our unfortunate jars, and deplorable discord.

41

The senators conclude that "supreme Magistracies in a free Country" ought to be conferred upon and sought for only by honorable public servants, and not by the kind of man who seeks preferment from a tyrant "out of vain hopes of bettering his condition, and Family in publike slavery" (pp. 331-32: 2:61).[64] With this unhappy display in mind, one is hardly surprised that Boccalini, who also wrote discourses on Tacitus, embodies and propagates the view of that historian as a politic but essentially antityrannic historian. Apollo glorifies Lipsius, one of the commentators most influential in spreading "Tacitismo" among "the Flemish, Germans, English, French, Spaniards and Italians" (p. 178: 1:86), and later hears and dismisses the charges of several "*great Princes*" (p. 347) who claim that Tacitus should be arrested because he educates the people regarding the true nature of princely tricks of government. He makes "the people sharp-sighted," and so the rulers can no longer "throw dust in their Subjects' Eyes, . . . but that they would be aware of their being abused" (p. 348: 2:71).

Machiavelli and Boccalini were not alone in spreading Italian anti-Augustanism in England. The works of the Marchese Virgilio Malvezzi were also known and respected: all were translated, and several enjoyed two or more editions.[65] *Romulus and Tarquin* (1637, 1638, 1648), for example, was translated by then Lord Carey, and dedicated to Charles I; it included commendatory verses by William D'Avenant, Thomas Carew, and Robert Stapylton. Malvezzi's *Discorso sopra Cornelio Tacito* (1622) was translated by Sir Richard Baker in 1642 and was soon bound with Grenewey's translation of the *Annals* and *Germania*, and Savile's of the *Histories* and *Agricola*.[66] It was among the "Ouvrages ingénieux" that Moréri mentions in his praise of

[64] Thomas Gordon makes similar remarks in his *Works of Tacitus*, 1:88-89.

[65] For bibliographic details, see Rodolfo Brändli, *Virgilio Malvezzi politico e moralista* (Basel: Tipografica dell' USC, 1964), pp. 108-14.

[66] Such a copy is preserved in the Beinecke Rare Book and Manuscript Library of Yale University.

Malvezzi, and was of sufficient interest to have been read by John Milton in the mid-seventeenth century, and to have been in Samuel Johnson's library late in the eighteenth century.[67] These Discourses are more affectionate toward Augustus and monarchy and more hostile to the decaying republic than Machiavelli or the Florentine civic humanists could allow. They are nonetheless valuable for showing the inroads those commentators had made in the reading of Tacitus: anti-Augustanism had been indelibly stamped upon the European consciousness and had forced its way into Malvezzi's uncertain defense of absolutism. Indeed, as the later comparison between the versions of Dryden and Gordon will make clear, that stamp grew darker and bolder as the eighteenth century progressed.

For Malvezzi, Augustus avoided another civil war by wisely leaving the senate "some little authority" so that it would rest "satisfied and contented."[68] Although he hoped to restore the republic, it was so corrupt that (he twice tells us) the citizens were not fit for liberty and it was necessary for one "sole Lorde" to govern. He provided "half a liberty; leaving a great authority in the Senatours; and not a little in the people." Though the tyrant Tiberius created a "halfe-servitude," that is not the fault of Augustus, but "the ill fortune of his successours," whereas Augustus himself maintained the peace of Rome and the world (pp. 359-60).

Malvezzi also insists upon the good fortune, prudence, and wisdom that brought Augustus to the throne; his valor in battle and virtue that "brought himself forward by desert" (p. 93); and his wise governance, protection, enlargement of the state, and cunning in using "those that shewd themselves most ready to do him service" (pp. 97-98).

[67] For Milton, see *Of Reformation in England*, ed. Don M. Wolfe in *Complete Prose Works*, 1:573; and Johnson, *A Catalogue of the Valuable Library of . . . Samuel Johnson* (London, 1785), p. 6, item 72, as "Baker's discourse on Tacitus." A copy of Baker's translation of Malvezzi, "with annotations alleged to be by Milton or his secretary, is in the New York Public Library" (*Prose Works*, 1:573, n. 10).

[68] *Discourses upon Cornelius Tacitus*, trans. Sir Richard Baker (London, 1642), p. 9. Subsequent citations are given in the text.

Thus far we have a conventional monarchic view of Augustus and the later republic. But there has been a significant change in the post-Bruni world. In the *Laudatio*, we recall, a wicked Augustus is responsible for his successors' crimes because he "cleared the way" for them. If we look at Malvezzi once again, we shall see awareness both of Augustus' evils on his way to the throne, and of the dangers of absolute rule. These Discourses, I suggest, have absorbed the argument that Gibbon was also to use many years later—the ruler who destroys liberty yet rules well himself is responsible for the bad rulers after him.[69]

Though Augustus made himself princeps by fortune, virtue, and desert, he "brought himself forward by wickedness and perfidiousness, also." He attacked the nation with arms given him to defend it, and "there cannot be a greater wickedness, than when benefits are turned against him of whom they are received"—so great that God Himself disapproves of this as a model for either Christian or pagan (p. 94). Several Discourses thereafter, Malvezzi repeats the other accepted facts of Augustus' "thousand kinds of wickednesse" and his murder of "many [opposition] Senatours" in order to reform the nation by governing alone (pp. 358-59). However benevolent such despotism may be, Christians must reject it and "set Religion before Country and life, and Common-wealth and all: . . . and rather than imitate *Augustus*: follow the course of *Marcus Aurelius*," who refused to kill an evil companion (p. 371).

In spite of Malvezzi's attempt to exonerate Augustus from the moral collapse of the later Caesars, his responsi-

[69] The danger of precedent was urged most forcefully in the eighteenth century, but it was commonplace in the Renaissance as well. See Jonson's *Sejanus* (1603), I. ii, where Tiberius refers to Augustus' "pleasing precedent." The argument that Augustus' negative precedent destroyed Rome's future remained alive on the Continent. See Linguet's *Histoire des révolutions . . . romain* (n. 37, above), 1:16-19; and Jean-François de la Harpe's attempt to deny Augustus' responsibility for later imperial collapse: *Les Douze Césars . . . de Suétone*, 2 vols. (Paris, 1770), 1:306-7, 310-11.

bility is clear. Hence we see that Livia "besotted the old man" and "perswaded him to leave *Tiberius*, his successor, a cruell man," and that Tiberius, in turn, "also was able to elect a successour after him" (p. 362). But it is worse yet, since Malvezzi accepts the view of Tacitus (and Dio Cassius) that Augustus knowingly chose a malevolent heir so that he might appear the more glorious by comparison. That, he says, "I cannot indeed deny," and again warns Christians to avoid such practice (p. 372). A truly wise prince must disinherit an unworthy heir and select a prudent and virtuous stranger instead (p. 373). Malvezzi thus agrees with Tacitus' judgment: "though a Prince by chusing a wicked successour, make his own actions to seeme good; yet this is so farre from making him praiseworthy, that it brings him more dishonor, *as being a concurrent cause, of all the Evill the successour doeth*" (p. 375, my italics). This is a startling reversal of his earlier judgment that Tiberius' turning of half-liberty into half-servitude "is not to be attributed" to Augustus; and it makes plain that by the earlier seventeenth century on the Continent and the middle of the century in England, even monarchists reading Tacitus faced the moral issue of the culpability of Caesar Augustus for the destruction of Rome's genius and energy.

I will soon suggest some of the ramifications of such hostility to Augustus, hostility that approached the pandemic during the opposition to Walpole, when firmly entrenched anti-Augustanism was used by both political persuasions. Meanwhile, however, we can sense the rising fever by comparing relevant portions of Dryden's and Gordon's Tacitus, published respectively in 1698 and 1728, the former a money-making proposition for Dryden and his colleagues, the latter a skirmish in the battle of Whig and Tory, court and patriot, to claim the high ground of moral rectitude and hatred of tyranny.[70]

[70] Gordon's edition was later adapted by republicans. Peter Burke observes: "Josiah Quincy left Gordon (together with books by Algernon Sidney and Cato) to his son with the comment, 'may the spirit of

All for Love (1677; pub. 1678) had, of course, already drawn a frigid, manipulative, and rapacious Octavian, a character scarcely more amiable than his literary ancestor in *Antony and Cleopatra* (1606-1607). By 1698 Dryden was not likely to be friendly toward Augustus himself, though he is more restrained than Gordon. .Dryden, for example, says that the first triumvirate's power was "transferr'd" to Caesar and the second "gave place" to Augustus (1:4); for Gordon, "The Authority of Pompey and Crassus was quickly swallowed up in Caesar; that of Lepidus and Anthony in Augustus" (1:1).[71] Dryden says that authors under Augustus were only "hinder'd by the Growth of Flattery" (1:6); but for Gordon, with no authority in his text, under Augustus "the prevailing spirit of fear, flattery, and abasement . . . check'd" authors of distinction (1:1). Dryden shows that Augustus used different devices "that he might thereby strengthen the Succession" (1:11); Gordon shows that "it was the study of AUGUSTUS, to secure himself and the succession by a variety of stays and engraftments" (1:4). Dryden

---

liberty rest upon him'. The republican poet Vittorio Alfieri, 1749-1803, admired Gordon's work, as his book *On Tyranny* (1777) shows; and Gordon's book was reprinted at Paris in the second year of the republic. It is not surprising that Napoleon hated Tacitus" ("Tacitism," in Dorey, p. 169). We recall that John Clarke praised Gordon's Discourses, as did the opposition *Craftsman*, no. 220 (1730), though Gordon was a protégé of Walpole. Gibbon also read Gordon's volumes (*Miscellaneous Works* [1814], 1:41). But Gordon did not receive universal approbation. The *Biographia Classica* (n. 26, above) reports that Gordon "has most wretchedly acquitted himself in the Translation," and has overpraised his author (2:214-15). All quotations are from vol. 1 of Dryden's *Tacitus* and vol. 1 of Gordon's *The Works of Tacitus*.

71 Here, and in other places, Gordon is heightening his text, which lacks the monstrous connotations of "Swallowed up." Tacitus says that the power was *given over*: "et Pompeii Crassique potentia cito in Caesarem, Lepidi atque Antonii arma in Augustum cessere." See Julianus Pichon, *C. Cornelii Taciti opera omnia . . . in usum delphini*, 9 vols. (London, 1821), 1:26: i. 1 (originally, 4 vols. Paris, 1682-1687). For a study of Dryden's Octavian, see J. W. Johnson. "Dryden, His Times, and *All for Love*," in *Essays in Honor of Richebourg Gaillard McWilliams, Birmingham-Southern College Bulletin*, 63 (1970): 21-28.

says that few "had seen the times of Liberty" (1:13); Gordon laments that after a while "how few were then living who had seen the ancient free state!" (1:4).[72] Dryden's "Equality and Freedom were at once distinguish'd" (1:13) becomes Gordon's "the equality of the whole was extinguished by the sovereignty of one" (1:4). The relative modesty of the two preceding changes disappears when we see that Dryden believes Augustus had "establish'd the Succession against the Common-Wealth, by a large Provision of Heirs, and those in power" (1:26), whereas Gordon tells us that Augustus "even provided against a relapse into liberty, by a long train of successors" (1:9).[73] Dryden's partisans of Augustus say that "he sometimes made use of Severity and Force, but very rarely" (1:29); Gordon's claim that "in a few instances, he had exerted the arbitrary violence of power" (1:10). Dryden's (and Murphy's, and Tacitus', *Annals*, i. 10) detractors of Augustus mention nothing of the law; Gordon's argue that "in defiance of Law [he] levied an Army" (1:10). Dryden's Augustus "extorted [the role of praetor] from the Senate" (1:30); Gordon's "usurp'd the honours and authority of the Pretorship" (1:10). Dryden's Augustus has merely committed grammatically unmodified "Treason" in the death of Hirtius and Pansa (1:30); Gordon's is "the black contriver of this bloody treason" (1:10). Dryden's malicious Augustus selects Tiberius because he hopes for glory "by the Foyl of that Comparison" (1:33); Gordon's more malicious Augustus names Tiberius in order to gain "future glory from the blackest opposition and comparison" (1:11).

Most, if not all, of these and comparable changes reflect Gordon's fervent belief that Augustus destroyed Roman

[72] Tacitus merely says: "quotusquisque reliquus, qui rempublicam vidisset?" (Pichon, 1:37: i. 3). Both translators are using their own denotations for whatever connotations "rempublicam" had. Arthur Murphy's later translation (1793, n. 48, above) is more muted, but also interpretive: "Who had seen the constitution of their country?" (*Works of Tacitus*, 1:9).

[73] As one final example of the translator's coloring, compare Tacitus: "provisis etiam haeredum in rempublicam opibus" (Pichon, 1:53: i. 8). For Murphy, Augustus "left a long train of Heirs" (1:15).

47

virtue and that "the best of his Government was but the sunshine of Tyranny" (1:48). Overheated translation, he might have felt, is a small price to pay for the defense of freedom. Paradoxically, the classical legacy of Augustus Caesar included a post-mortem codicil that bequeathed a tarnished name to its maker; and it was further tarnished by loyal Walpole-Whig as well as the opposition.

The classical historians; republican polemics from Renaissance Italy; a few comparable, if muted, polemics from Renaissance France;[74] support from commentators, editors, and contemporary historians writing in Latin; the native English movement away from absolute and toward limited monarchy; and the reading of Tacitus as enemy to Augustus, the destroyer of Roman genius—all these combined and encouraged a formidable voice against the myths of Augustan virtue and performance.[75] To make clear how substantial and practically useful the anti-Augustan impact was, we should examine the uses of it in Britain during the Restoration and the eighteenth century, though for purposes of contrast and development it will be valuable to start somewhat before 1660 and end after 1800.

[74] Amelot, for example, notes that "Tacite oppose toujours la liberté à la Roïauté" (1:2, note b), and supplies this and other antiabsolute reflections for Dryden. But as Burke points out, Amelot's "own ethic was one of 'accommodation': A subject, he wrote, cannot avoid flattering princes" (Dorey, *Tacitus*, p. 158).

[75] From Bruni onwards, there has been an important group of classical historians who have challenged the view of the positive significance of Roman, including Augustan, history. Gordon and the other anti-Augustans belong to that group, which is alive today in works like Eric Badian's *Roman Imperialism in the Late Republic*, 2nd ed. (Ithaca: Cornell Univ. Press, 1968). For a recent discussion of such contemporary research, see Chester G. Starr, "The Roman Place in History," in *Aufstieg und Niedergang der Römischen Welt: Geschichte und Kultur Roms im Spiegel der neueren Forschung: von den Anfängen Roms Bis Zum Ausgang der Republik*, ed. Hildegard Temporini (Berlin and New York: Walter de Gruyter, 1972), 1:3-11. Starr's own *Civilization and the Caesars: The Intellectual Revolution in the Roman Empire* (Ithaca: Cornell Univ. Press, 1954) is also useful along such lines.

CHAPTER 2

The Legacy Improved, Part I.
Augustus Praised and Blamed:
His Personal Weaknesses and Destruction of Art

THE CLASSICAL LEGACY OF AUGUSTUS CAESAR INCLUDES some real and some factitious praise, together with abundant blame, both for his actions and for those who approved of them. Eighteenth-century and other "Augustans" who wished to find parallels and happy instruction in the career of the emperor were free to do so and did. One finds partisans of Augustus and numerous remarks in his favor from the Renaissance on. Ben Jonson's *Poetaster* (1601), for instance, characterizes Augustus as a model of much that is good in the monarch and the state. Dryden praises Charles II as Augustus in *Astraea Redux* (1660); the author of *Augustus Anglicus* argues that Charles II "was justly stiled, The *English Augustus*" who restored England "to its Primitive Happiness, Peace and Tranquility"; Sir Edward Sherburn's translation (1696) of Blondell's *Comparison of Pindar and Horace* paints Augustus and his age as "the most Gallant, the most Polite, and the most Illuminated of all that preceded, or since succeeded it." Sir Thomas Pope Blount calls him "one of the Happiest and Greatest *Princes* that the Sun ever saw"; Pope celebrates Augusta-Anne's present and wished-for accomplishments in the England of *Windsor Forest* (1714); Edward Biddle's unproduceable *Augustus. A Tragedy* (1717), shows us a pre-Actium Octavian, nobly concerned with the fate of the world and Rome's liberty: "I'll live *Rome*'s Friend, or dye her Sacrifice, / Be free or cease to be, Liberty or Nothing" young Caesar emotes in the unlikely manner of an ur-Patrick Henry. Anthony Blackwall knew that Augustus was a

49

patron in "the *Golden Age* of *Learning*"; somewhat later, Goldsmith assumed that during the Roman Augustan age "language and learning arriv'd at its highest perfection," and he considered the period in England that might be so labeled.[1]

There must be hundreds of comparable observations between 1660 and 1800, many of which have been pressed into service by those who read eighteenth-century literature in light of genial Augustan backgrounds. When we look closer, however, much, though certainly not all, of the apparently concrete bulk of this edifice turns out to be balsa wood. Blount, like the writer of *Augustus Anglicus* and other "Augustans," is a professed monarchist and thus aligns himself with a political system already collapsing and nearly flattened by 1727.[2] Biddle, whose honesty is more impressive than his talent, tells us that his present publication is a sign of his loyalty to George I (p. 1). Much praise of the Augustan age is by those seeking patronage and using the old myth of royal support as an ad hoc argument. Dryden is sublimely overt when he tells John Sheffield, to whom *Aureng-Zebe* is dedicated (1676), that he admires Virgil's times "because he had an Augustus for his patron. And to draw the allegory nearer you, I am sure I shall not want a

[1] For these, see *Poetaster*, iv. 3; v. 1; *Astraea Redux*, ll. 320-23; *Augustus Anglicus* (London, 1686), sig. a11ʳ; Blondell (1673) Sherburn (London, 1696), p. 85; Blount, *Essays on Several Subjects* (London, 1697), p. 68; *Windsor Forest*, ll. 335-36 et passim; Biddle, *A Poem on the Birth of the Young Prince. Born at the Royal Palace. . . . To which is Added, Augustus. A Tragedy* (London, 1717), p. 22; Blackwall, *An Introduction to the Classics* (London, 1719), p. 42; Goldsmith, *The Bee*, in *Collected Works of Oliver Goldsmith,* 5 vols., ed. Arthur Friedman (Oxford: Clarendon Press, 1966), 1:498.

[2] *Essays on Several Subjects:* "*Pure* and *Unmixt* [monarchy] would please me best (it being *that* by which the *Almighty* governs the *Universe*" (p. 87). Blount is aware that "*Kings* are but *Men*" (p. 88) and thus should not have divine power without divine attributes. However felicitous the Emperor Augustus' reign was, Blount berates the murderous cruelty "of *Octavianus Augustus* . . . after the taking of Perusia" (p. 148).

Maecenas with him. 'Tis for your Lordship to stir up that remembrance in his Majesty." That eminent poet Laurence Eusden celebrates George II's coronation with an equally obvious, but less elegant, bow, scrape, and Roman nod, as he proclaims that Britain's "own AUGUSTUS reigns," and new Virgils and other poets will give Albion "another, sweeter, *Classic* Age!"[3] Goldsmith's remark is less interested and less committed as well. It does not approve of Augustus or his values, and means only that art flourished during a certain number of years. Goldsmith, like Joseph Warton, who also used the "Augustan age" as a synonym for an epoch of great art, ultimately disapproved of the princeps, his political and moral values, and his debilitating influence upon Roman letters.[4] Finally, it is probable that in the eighteenth as in the twentieth century the terms *Augustus* and *Augustan*, when used positively, often meant nothing more than vague approbation of national strength, stable government, and support for the arts, and that on the whole *Augustan* was used as imprecisely then as, say, *democratic* is now.

It is difficult to provide closed periods when Augustus was or was not a hero of government or culture; but the evidence does support certain broad conclusions. Augustanism rises and falls with royalism and absolutism; it reaches one normative peak as Charles is restored and certain historical parallels seem appropriate; it loses force later in the century, especially after 1688, but regains some vigor under Anne, the Peace of Utrecht in 1713, and apparent strength by a Stuart monarch. For example, however favorably young Dryden regards Augustus, the

[3] Dryden, *Of Dramatic Poesy and other Critical Essays*, ed. George Watson, 2 vols. (New York: Dutton, 1962), 1:191 (referred to hereafter as *Essays*); Eusden, "A Poem on the happy Succession and Coronation of His Present Majesty," in *Three Poems* (London, 1727), p. 11.

[4] For Goldsmith's disapproval, see the discussion of his *Roman History* (1769), chap. 3, at n. 10ff in text, below; and for Warton, see his discussion of Pope's *Epistle to Augustus*, chap. 6, at n. 16 in text, below.

later "Discourse on . . . Satire" (1693) depicts him as a cunning and pernicious scoundrel; however noble young Pope thinks Anne as "Augusta," the *Epistle to Augustus* (1737) disowns the princeps as a tyrant. It also seems fair to say that the many streams of anti-Augustanism—whether literary, political, or historical—flow into the great Walpolean quarrels, between about 1726 and 1742, when each side and its journalistic appendages, not just the "Tory opposition" and the *Craftsman*, focus on Augustus as an emblem of a bad, un-British, tyrannic ruler.[5] Thereafter, classical and modern texts offered an attractive and open armory from which anti-Augustan weapons frequently were drawn, sometimes to attack an aberrant British politician, sometimes to attack the revolutionary French and their Napoleon, and commonly to indicate the bad, the false, and the ugly. A reasonable but wrong case can be made for Augustus as a norm early (and briefly) in both the Restoration period and the eighteenth century. After the mid-1730s, one continues to find scattered affirmative remarks and the occasional genuine defense; but by those years to call the eighteenth century an "Augustan age," with any pretense to serious meaning, is to misrepresent British history and much of what that century said and thought of itself.

Nor, if one thinks even for a moment about the development of British and American political thought between 1660 and 1800, should that be surprising. It is a strange hypothesis that holds up an absolute ruler as a model for a century that established parliamentary superiority under the "Whig supremacy," and an even stranger one that attributes to the "Tories" the sole or dominant use of anti-Augustanism during the Walpole years. (I am assuming, for purposes of argument, that those terms have roughly definable meanings.) The Whig litany, after all, always included limitations on monarchic power, and it was the

[5] See below, chap. 3, sec. II.

Whig Thomas Gordon whose attacks on Augustus supplied the *Craftsman* with some of its best ammunition. Any Whig, whether in or out of power, was committed to theoretical anti-Augustanism, even though an occasional intemperate response to an opposition goad might briefly make one think otherwise. As the classical—and British—historians make clear, *Augustus* is often a code-word for *tyrant*, with the modifiers *crafty, bloody, fortunate, mild, benevolent,* or *savage* used where appropriate. As a symbol, he is infinitely adaptable. For many Whigs, James II is the archetypal English Augustus, and William III and thereafter the Hanoverians are the legitimate line, the protectors of limited monarchy, the people, parliament, the crown, and freedom. Augustus as usurper thus becomes the Jacobite Pretender with his Tory friends, and the name George Augustus is merely a historical accident of no importance. For Tories, the Augustan usurper is William III or George I and George II, and the Hanoverians become illicit rulers who threaten liberty. The Stuarts emerge as banished Virtue victimized by a power-grasping Walpole and his king. George Augustus is therefore not a matter of parental nomenclature, but an obvious and dangerous historical analogue. Of course, each side is talking its particular form of partisan cant, and, of course, for many citizens all this chatter—but not the issues behind it—was of little real concern. For those troubling themselves to see British history through Roman spectacles, however, the point is clear— for non-royalists (the vast majority), to be politically Augustan was, by definition, to be politically bad.

The genuine support for Augustus, then, tends to fall into one major category—the royalists, for whom faith in kingship and benevolent absolutism, and mistrust of the people and their elected officers, were complementary articles of faith. Yet, even the royalists were made aware of Augustus' weaknesses and the countervailing arguments on behalf of the constitutional balance. The main thrust of British political theory and history, and the argument by demonstration in the beheading of one king and the forced abdication of another, modified what was called "the fiery zeal of an antiquated royalist."⁶ Unrepentant zealot historians and commentators state the case most forcefully for a strong monarch as head of state, the happy consequences that result, the virtues of Augustus Caesar as the paradigm of such a ruler, and his innocence of any responsibility for subsequent events in the Roman Empire. They also admit some of his flaws and his usurpation and agree that the people must at least *seem* to be part of government. The essential difference between these and the more representative British remarks, however, is in that *seeming*, for their royalism pushes them into the farthest possible corner of respect for constitutional checks and balances.

I: The Partisans of Augustus

The best known of the royalist histories of Rome were Thomas Otway's translation of S. de Bröe's *History of the Triumvirates* (1686), Laurence Echard's *Roman History* (1695-1698), and Thomas Hearne's *Ductor Historicus* (1705-1704 [sic]).⁷ Echard, probably the most popular, was influ-

---

⁶ *A Short Review of Mr. Hooke's Observations & c. concerning the Roman Senate, and the Character of Dionysius of Halicarnassus* (London, 1758), p. 2. The anonymous author goes on to say, in defense of Dionysius and freedom, that if Dionysius "was hired to flatter either Augustus, or the Romans, he most certainly was not worthy of his hire, for he has there departed from his own character of mildness and humanity to censure both" (pp. 31-32).

⁷ de Bröe [Citri de la Guette], *The History of the Triumvirates. . . . The First that of Julius Caesar, Pompey and Crassus. The Second that of Augustus, Anthony and Lepidus. . . . Made English by Tho. Otway* (London); Echard, *The Roman History, from the Building of the City, To the Perfect Settlement of the Empire, by Augustus Caesar* (London), vol. 2, *The Roman History, From . . . Augustus Caesar, To . . . Constantine the Great* (London); Hearne, *Ductor Historicus: Or, A Short System of Universal History and An Introduction to the Study of it,* 2 vols., 2nd ed. (London); there is some overlap with the *Ductor Historicus* (1698) of Abel Boyer and "W. J.," translated in part from Vallemont's *Les Eléments de l'histoire* (1696).

enced by de Bröe (see 1:sig. A6ᵛ), subsequently influenced
Hearne, and exemplified the pro-Augustan view. Like de
Bröe, Echard underplays Augustus' culpability and insists
upon Octavian's successful effort at "gaining the Hearts and
Inclinations of the People" (1:394; de Bröe, p. 590). Like
de Bröe, he nevertheless must include material that the
prosecution would fasten upon as evidence for its own case.
He admits, for example, that the triumvirate's proscription
gave "the last Blow to the *Roman* Liberty" (1:370, 378) and
pictures the three who begin to "act as Sovereigns, and to
divide the *Roman* Dominions between 'em as their own by
Right of Conquest" (1:379; de Bröe, p. 459). He also admits
that Augustus used "Games and Exercises" to divert the
people from their former roles in free government (1:424),
that his mock resignation increased his power, and that his
surrender of the peaceful provinces to the senate's control
was a ploy to limit its strength as he "engross'd all the
Soldiers and Militia to himself" (1:426-27). Once he was
named Augustus, "all the Power of the People and Senate
was transferr'd" to him (1:428); he became an apparent
bounteous fountain while actually keeping all power in his
hands. In the royalist's vision of the well-oiled Augustan
wheel of state, the occasional "Assemblies of the People"
passed "nothing of Importance . . . contrary to the Pleasure
of the Emperor." Similarly, the tribunes' power to act for
the people was allowed, yet limited; the people were permitted to select some of the magistrates, but Augustus saw
"that no unworthy Persons advanc'd themselves by any
indirect Practices. And this was the general course of *Augustus*'s Administration of the Government; no Prince in
the World being more Judicious in the complying with his
People, or more skilful in the preserving his Authority"
(2:3-4).

Echard sees the posting of 10,000 praetorian and urban
guards as healthy protection for the city and emperor; he
applauds the loss of republican "elevated . . . Temper, . . .
Greatness of Genius," and "Force of the Soul" if Rome

could gain "something more Polite and Sociable." For him, under Augustus there "never were more glorious, or at least, more pleasant Times than now, all Wars and Contests ceasing, all Arts and Sciences flourishing, and all Riches and Pleasures increasing." In short, "*Augustus* made the World happy, and was happy in the World; he had nothing to desire of the Publick, nor the Publick of him" (1:430).[8] Rome was, "for many Years, believ'd Indissoluble and Immortal" (1:429). Echard admits Augustus' sexual irregularities with women and his cruelty during the triumvirate; but, his seduction of Livia excepted, the former were "not very excessive," and the latter "purely the effects of his exquisite Policy." Moreover, "his innumerable Acts of Wisdom and Vertue afterwards, sufficiently wip'd away those Blots and Imperfections" (2:51). Echard leaves us with a declamation of universal respect and love that was to reappear in Hearne's *Ductor Historicus*[9]—the work of so warm a nonjuring Stuart devoté that he was dismissed from his position as second-keeper of the Bodleian Library.

Echard clearly lacks respect for "the people" and their right or ability to share in their own government; he does not ascribe the guilt for Rome's decline to Augustus, as Tacitus

8 Compare Velleius, chap. 89: "Mankind could desire nothing from the Gods, nor could they grant any thing more to Men" (*The Roman History*, trans. Thomas Newcomb [London, 1721], p. 189); and St. Evremond, "*Of* Augustus, *his Government, and his Genius*": "He made the World happy, and was happy in the World: He had nothing to desire of the Publick, nor the Publick of him" (*Miscellaneous Essays*, 2 vols. [London, 1692], 1:103). Significantly, in order to praise Augustus' achievements, St. Evremond largely refuses to consider Octavian's early actions: "they were too *Tragical*" (1:85). Pedro de Mexia, among others, also borrowed happy sentiments from Velleius, but he is more willing than St. Evremond to discuss the horrors of the proscription. See *The Imperial History: or The Lives of the Emperors*, trans. W[illiam] T[raheron] (London, 1623), pp. 22-38.

9 For Hearne, see 2:7, and for Echard, 2:51. Hearne's praise of Virgil and the imperial function of the *Aeneid* (2:8) comes from Echard, 2:18. There is other borrowing—some, perhaps, from the Boyer-W. J. *Ductor Historicus* of 1698.

does; he looks back to seventeenth- rather than forward to eighteenth-century values; and, of course, his views were not unique. In 1636 Richard Braithwait confirms Augustus' wise governance and the people's love for him. Several years thereafter, Samuel Clarke's life of Augustus (1665) bemoans the proscription and the murder of liberty-loving Cicero; but like de Bröe, Clarke believes that "God in his secret Counsell, had reserved the Monarchy of the whole World" for Augustus. His acquisition of the empire was unjust, his administration of it exemplary. The royalists John Nelson and Philip Warwick regard Augustus as a properly strong and wise monarch who enhances the state. St. Evremond thinks that "the Senate did nothing that was Wise and Good, but what *Augustus* had Inspired into them." Hearne himself acknowledges but softens Octavian's vices, and urges that Augustus was "almost Matchless in his Government" and would have left Rome flourishing forever if Tiberius had not reversed his wise practices. Some years later, in 1741, Thomas Gent also describes the benevolent reign that allowed Jesus to be born. Echard and his approach are acknowledged and influential as late as 1782, when the Reverend Jerom Alley applauds Augustus as the liberator of the people from the factious senate. Alley also tells of the consoling and sublime post-Actium change from Octavian to Augustus and the universal peace and good government that follow. As king and "Patriot!" Augustus atones for his "former depravity and excess," and is regarded "as the hero who conquered but to bless! His usurpation was" either forgotten or considered "as a new epoch of the liberty of Rome."[10]

[10] [Braithwait], *The Exact Collection of all the Roman Emperors* (London), pp. 5-6; Clarke, *The Life & Death of Julius Caesar . . . As also the Life and Death of Augustus Caesar* (London), pp. 57, 63, 84-93, for the praise of Augustus; Nelson, *The Common Interest of King and People* (London), pp. 31, 58; Warwick, *A Discourse of Government* (London), pp. 102-3; St. Evremond, *"Of* Augustus," in *Miscellaneous Essays,* 1:96 (St. Evremond's essay illustrates the association of monarchism and Augustanism); Hearne, 2:7; 2:21-22 (Tiberius); Gent,

The emphatic Augustanism of Echard and the seventeenth century thus exists and remains alive later; but these advocates must meet some or all of the problems of Octavian's brutality, Augustus' centralized power, and Rome's post-Augustan political collapse. These same issues form the core of others' serious misgivings regarding Augustus or outright rejection of him as a norm. Moreover, the royalists were the superannuated rear guard of a defeated army. The dominant eighteenth-century attitude toward their thinking and historiography is exemplified in Fielding's *Journey from this World to the Next* (1743). There the shade of Livy commends "the judicious collection made by [the 'patriot'] Mr. Hooke which, he said, was infinitely preferable to all others; and upon my mentioning of Echard's," the narrator observes, "he gave a bounce, not unlike the going off of a squib."[11] We also remember that in *Tom Jones* (bk. vi, chap. 2) the old-fashioned and consistently wrong-headed Mrs. Western reads Echard. Somewhat later, Voltaire implies that Echard glosses over Augustus' vices, and says: "L'histoire de *Laurent Echard* a paru aux hommes éclairés aussi fautive que tronquée."[12]

Most readers and writers after the late seventeenth cen-

Historia Compendiosa Anglicana: Or, A Compendious History of England, 2 vols. (York), 2:280; Alley, *Historical Essays on the Lives of Augustus Caesar and Lewis XIV. Of Cardinals Richelieu and . . . of William III* (Dublin), pp. 1-94; for these lines from "A Comparative View of the Lives of Augustus Caesar, and of Lewis XIVth," see pp. 94, 93.

11 *The Works of Henry Fielding, Esq.*, ed. Leslie Stephen, 10 vols. (London, 1882), 4:390, the final paragraph of chap. 9.

12 *Questions sur l'encyclopédie* (Geneva [?], 1770-1772), 9 vols., 2:350. The *Questions* were published in London in 1771, again in 1771-1772, and were read in England. See R. S. Crane, "Diffusion of Voltaire's Writings in England," *MP*, 20 (1923): 267. See also Gilbert Stuart's sympathetic review of the *Questions* in the *Monthly Review*, 44 (1771): 525-33. The attribution is in Benjamin Christie Nangle, *The Monthly Review First Series 1749-1789: Indexes of Contributors and Articles* (Oxford: Clarendon Press, 1934), p. 105 (referred to hereafter as Nangle).

tury were not royalists, and even those who once were had, by the revolution of 1688 and other events, been turned into advocates or acceptors of mixed, constitutional monarchy. As an elderly gentleman won to the side of the *Craftsman* remarks in 1730, "The whole Bulk of the People hath been brought by the *Revolution,* and by the present Settlement of the Crown, to entertain Principles, which very few of us defended in my younger Days" (no. 219, 12 September 1730). Almost any reader, whether royalist, anarchist, or Venetian oligarchist, would have found much of Octavian's early career and Octavian-Augustus' private life utterly inappropriate for a head of state, who should be a model for his nation. Many object strenuously to his manipulation of the arts in bloom and his responsibility for their withering thereafter. Hence, even granting some dubious and positive uses of Augustus, his name is often used, by author and citizen, with strong negative connotations indeed. Much of the anger stems from the classical and British historical legacy and includes hostility to despotism, cowardice, deviant sexuality, incest, and like amiable topoi.

II: ARTS AND LETTERS: AUGUSTUS AS TYRANT AND BUTCHER

Probably the ugliest and least ambiguous part of Augustus' background was his role in the triumvirate's proscription, a role even his partisans had to admit or lamely excuse. The persistence of the image of Octavian as butcher was due in part to descriptions by the classical historians and in part to what Jean Ehrmann has called "Massacre and Persecution Pictures in Sixteenth Century France."[13] This genre commemorated the savagery visited upon civilians from about 1548 to 1562, especially in 1561-1562, when the Ducs de Guise, Montmorency, and Saint-André induced further strife and were labeled "the Triumvirate." The

[13] *Journal of the Warburg and Courtauld Institutes,* 8 (1945): 195-99, plates, pp. 46-49. Subsequent references are cited in the text.

massacre of worshipping Protestants at Vassy (1 March 1562) was memorialized later in Europe and England through Protestant polemic, historians of the French civil wars, Dryden and Lee's play *The Duke of Guise* (1683), Pierre Bayle's harsh article in his *Dictionnaire . . . critique* (1697), and the gruesome paintings, some of which left France: one, for example, was sold in The Hague in 1743 (p. 197). These paintings share several conventions, chief among them the Roman triumvirs' watching or, in Antoine Caron's effort, participating in the slaughter of defenseless civilians. One picture, perhaps by Jerome Cock, prominently displays well over 100 heads (sans accompanying bodies), with frenzied soldiers in search of more, and a mournful inscription from Cicero (p. 48). Another painting includes a palace with a Latin motto—which appears on yet another version, as well—that translates as: "when unfortunate Rome was governed by three tyrants, events such as you see here depicted took place" (p. 197). A comparable sixteenth-century woodcut at the Bibliothèque Nationale reads: "Pourtraict representant les massacres cruels & inhumains faites à Rome l'an 711 de la fondation, par le Triumvirat Octauius Caesar, Anthonius & Lepidus" (p. 46). Considering such a background, we can understand why Jabez Hughes, or his printer, selected the typical emblem for his Suetonius' "Augustus": the triumvirs making lists for the proscription. Similarly, when Thomas Gordon wishes to depict "*the vindictive spirit of Octavius, and his horrid Cruelties,*" he heightens the violent colors in the verbal portraiture of the proscription with reference to these paintings' dominant convention: "Nothing was to be seen but blood and slaughter: the streets were covered with carcasses: the heads of illustrious dead were exposed upon the Rostras, and their bodies upon the pavement, denied the mercy of burial. . . . No sort of men escape his cruelty."[14] We are not surprised to find men as different as Crébillon (père) and Voltaire

14 Hughes, *The Lives of the XII. Caesars*, 2 vols. (London, 1717), 1:57; Gordon, *The Works of Tacitus*, 2 vols. (London, 1728-1731), 1:45.

each writing plays about that triumvirate's proscription, and each highlighting Octavian's savage conduct. Even Crébillon's Octave cries: "Juste Ciel! . . . Cachons-nous à ses yeux."[15]

Other graphic representations of Augustus—some favorable—are not nearly so entertaining.[16] The best known, or at least the most often seen, Augustus in eighteenth-century Britain was that in Verrio's adaptation of the Emperor Julian's satire *The Caesars*, a work in which Augustus is judged as dangerously changeable, ambitious, blasphemous, and clearly inferior to the genuine stoic Marcus Aurelius.[17]

[15] Crébillon, *Le Triumvirat, ou la mort de Cicéron, tragédie* (1754; pub. 1755), p. 56. Voltaire's *Le Triumvirat* (1764; pub. 1766) was also called *Octave et le jeune Pompée ou le triumvirat*. See chap. 7, sec. I, n. 11 and text below, for further discussion of these plays and the Crébillon-Voltaire rivalry. For another gruesome French verbal portrait of the proscription, see Henri Ophellot de la Pause [J. B. C. Isoard Delisle], *Histoire des douze Césars de Suétone*, 4 vols. (Paris, 1771), 1:357-68.

[16] James II himself was sculpted by Grinling Gibbons and cast in bronze in the garb, it is said, of Augustus Caesar; Burlington's Chiswick House positions a bust of Augustus, solus, in a prominent place above the east portico's double doorway; in 1765 Carl van Loo portrayed Augustus closing the Temple of Janus—a common topic—for the salon of 1765 (much to Diderot's annoyance at Augustus' insipid expression: "Cela, un empereur!"). One suspects a comparable reaction to the comparably insipid Augustus in Jean-Joseph Tailasson's "Virgil Reading the *Aeneid* to Augustus and Octavia" (1787), now at the National Gallery, London.

[17] Julian's Menippean satire was propagated in England by the distinguished antiquary Baron Ezekiel Spanheim (1683, in French), Gibbon's friend the Abbé de la Bleterie (1748, also in French), and the solid English hack John Duncombe, who used his predecessors' work well and saw his own effort, *The Works of the Emperor Julian* (1783), go into a third edition by 1798. Julian as Emperor and satirist was long known to Gibbon, who recognized the less-than-flattering portrait of Octavian, but nevertheless thought Julian gave "too much honour to the power of philosophy and to Octavius," and implies that the latter's change is due to art rather than the teachings of the stoic Zeno (*The History of the Decline and Fall of the Roman Empire*, ed. J. B. Bury, 7 vols. [London, 1900], 1:71, n. 33 [noted also in Duncombe, 3rd ed.,

Verrio's mural (ca. 1700) was deservedly berated, on artistic grounds, by Pope and Horace Walpole, and was viewed by the many visitors to Hampton Court's dominant King's Staircase, which it decorates. As Edgar Wind has well shown, this work was in part a reflection of "the Protestant pamphlets against 'popery' " and James II.[18] Verrio is thus glorifying the Whigs, the Protestant succession, and William III, and criticizing the Church of Rome. The King-Alexander is introduced and protected by Hercules, "for the lion and lion-slayer were the favourite emblems of William III" (p. 129). Behind and to the right of Julius Caesar is Augustus himself with Zeno muttering in his ear and a vapid look on his face, all designed, Wind argues, "to suggest the figure of a 'priest-ridden' monarch," one presumably like James II (p. 130, n. 1).

Such characterization of Augustus was matched by British writers, who were especially indignant about his personal cruelty and private life. Abraham Cowley attacks him for spilling Rome's noblest blood in order to acquire the toys of greatness. He also laments that "The false *Octavius*, and wild *Antonie* / God-like *Brutus* conquer *Thee*." The latter comment reappears and is praised in Bysshe's *Art of English Poetry* (1702) and thus gained even more readers.[19] Dryden's

1:151n]). Gibbon discusses, and praises, the *Caesars* at the opening of chap. 24. *Decline and Fall*, 2:479-80. He is quick to observe the self-serving of Augustus and other emperors as opposed to the selfless "superiority of the Imperial Stoic" that gains the love of the gods (2:480). For a recent discussion of Julian and Gibbon see Robert J. Ziegler, "Edward Gibbon and Julian the Apostate," *Papers on Language and Literature*, 10 (1974): 136-49.

18 *Journal of the Warburg and Courtauld Institutes*, 3 (1939-1940): 128. Subsequent citations are given in the text. For Pope and Walpole, see p. 127. As if to show his zeal for the Protestant, "Greek" William, and his own more-than-Julian contempt for the Caesars, Verrio adds a small bizarrely constructed deity, with a fish's tail and bat's wings, apparently spitting on the exalted Romans beneath him.

19 "Of Greatness," in "Several discourses by way of Essays, In Verse and Prose," *The Works of Mr. Abraham Cowley*, 5th ed. (London, 1678), pp. 122-23; "Brutus," in *Pindarique Odes*, ibid., p. 33 (different

Preface to Ovid (1680) berates the obscenity in Augustus' poems and his vindictive nature and cowardice. In 1711 Pope calls Augustus a "severe & barbarous" tyrant in the proscription. By 1738 Bolingbroke outdoes Suetonius in portraying Augustan depravities: "when Rome was ransacked by the pandars of Augustus, and matrons and virgins were stripped and searched, like slaves in a market, to chuse the fittest to satisfy his lust, did Antony do more?"[20] Later in the century Joseph Wilcocks' school-text *Roman Conversations* (1763) shows a clergyman telling his young charges that Augustus' "former crimes" were never totally "effaced in the eyes of men. Mankind will always look on him with hatred and detestation, though mixed with admiration" and pity. A few years thereafter Gilbert Stuart's sympathetic review of Voltaire's *Questions sur l'encyclopédie* reproduces much of Voltaire's savage indictment of Augustus and claims that these remarks "will not be unacceptable to our readers." Augustus is a publicly ridiculed pathic and "a man who had neither modesty, honour, nor probity; whose avarice, ingratitude, and cruelty, were excessive."[21]

---

pagination from the reference above); Bysshe, 2nd ed. (London, 1705), p. 41. The heading in Bysshe includes, "*See* Liberty. Trust." On p. 82 of "Several Discourses," Cowley registers Brutus' annoyance with Cicero for helping Octavian, and adds: "This was spoken as became the bravest man who was ever born in the bravest Common-wealth." In the same section, on "the Government of Oliver Cromwell," he observes that in desperate times for a nation, God's will is mysteriously at work to chastise and correct. "The . . . errors and cowardice" of an Octavian are then rendered "harmless [to himself], by unexpected accidents" (p. 67), and the wisdom of the senate, Cicero, and Brutus are of no value.

20 Dryden, *Essays* (n. 3, above), 1:263-64; Pope, *The Correspondence of Alexander Pope*, ed. George Sherburn, 5 vols. (Oxford: Clarendon Press, 1956), 1:116; Bolingbroke, *The Idea of a Patriot King* (1749), ed. Sydney W. Jackman (Indianapolis: Bobbs-Merrill, 1965), p. 76; also conveniently found in *The Works of Lord Bolingbroke*, 4 vols. (Philadelphia, 1841), 2:422.

21 [Wilcocks] *Roman Conversations; Or, Historical Exercises: Being some of the Principal Characters in the Roman History . . . Compiled*

The men of letters also found objectionable Augustan cruel infringements of freedom, encouragement of slavery, and the consequences for art. Dryden's Preface to Virgil (1697) temperately calls Augustus the best of bad conquering despots, but much in need of wise and improving poetic counsels. The Third Earl of Shaftesbury agrees with those views and stresses that Augustus' sweet but "poisonous government" soon gave way to overt tyranny and miserable art.[22] Lewis Crusius' *Lives of the Roman Poets* (1726) observes that in spite of Augustus' apparent success in government and letters, the Romans had nearly "lost their liberties," and that with the end of Augustus' reign would come the end of art.[23] In the meanwhile, Augustus used the poets

---

for the Use of Places of Education, particularly Westminster-School, 2 vols. (London), 2:44 (the educational function of this book makes Wilcocks' remarks especially significant); *Monthly Review,* 44 (1771): 526, 528.

[22] Dryden, *Essays,* 2:239, for the poets' good influence upon Augustus in life and art. Watson has, unfortunately, excluded a long section of importance for understanding Dryden's politics and literary sources. For this section, see *The Critical and Miscellaneous Prose Works of John Dryden,* 3 vols. in 4 (London, 1800), 3:444-518, especially 449-59 and Malone's notes. See p. 453 (and also p. 449) for Dryden's observation that Virgil knew "this conqueror, though of a bad kind, was the very best of it." Watson's characterization of the passage as showing "support for Virgil's anti-republicanism" (2:234) is overstated. Dryden says: "I may safely affirm for our great author, (as men of good sense are generally honest,) that he was still of republican principles in heart" (Malone, 3:449). Dryden bases his remark on the praise of Cato —of Utica, he thought. For Pope's interpretation of that praise, and its consequences for his judgment of Virgil's politics, see chap. 4, n. 9 and text, below. For Shaftesbury, see Anthony Ashley Cooper, *Characteristics of Men, Manners, Opinions, Times* (1711), ed. John M. Robertson, 2 vols. in 1 (rpt. Indianapolis: Bobbs-Merrill, 1964), *Advice to an Author,* 1:144. Many of Shaftesbury's observations on Augustus (and Horace) were consolidated and reprinted in George Turnbull's *Three Dissertations; On the Character of Augustus, Horace, and Agrippa . . .* (London, 1740).

[23] 3rd ed., 2 vols. (London, 1753), 1:vi and xxii. Subsequent citations are given in the text.

for his own propaganda and shrewdly placed himself in the will of Virgil, among many others (1:57). The legacy-hunter encouraged humanity in those around him in order to be "thought and stiled the Guardian of the Republick, [rather] than, what indeed he was, its absolute Prince" (1:118). He tolerated public dissension among actors in order to divert the public from more serious matters. Hence, Bathylus the mime told him: "Nothing could happen better for *Caesar*, than that the people should always amuse themselves with the trifling disputes of two Players." Crusius then adds—"I leave the reader to make the application" (2:163).

Numerous readers did precisely that: Joseph Spence in several works, the compiler of the *Biographia Classica* (1740), Joseph Warton, and Christopher Pitt, all of whom attack Augustus—while granting his virtues. Pitt's life of Virgil, for instance, paints Augustus as an ugly spirit who required the softening and radically misrepresenting strains of the poets before he and his illegal government were tolerable to the recalcitrant nation. In 1768 Launcelot Grevelle, a character in John Cleland's *The Woman of Honour*, laments Antony's good treatment by dramatists, but consoles himself with the knowledge that Antony's suicide was brought about "by one of his own gang, that cowardly and cruel in cold blood, Augustus, whose successes, as they are called, were the ruin not only of his own family, . . . but of the greatest republic." As a result of "sinking into slavery" under Augustus, Rome's "annals, after that period, became . . . the reproach of humanity, the disgrace of history, and the scorn of curiosity."[24]

[24] Spence, his ninth lecture as Oxford's Professor of Poetry, read on 14 October 1730, "On Virgil's Aeneid. That it was a Political Poem," BM Add. MS 17281; *Polymetis* (London, 1747), pp. 18-20, 42, n. 38, 85-86; *Remarks and Dissertations on Virgil: With Some other Classical Observations: By the late Mr. Holdsworth, Published with Several Notes, and Additional Remarks, by Mr. Spence* (London, 1768), pp. 28, 208, 217, 227, et passim, with special emphasis, not necessarily hostile, on Virgil's poetry as support for Augustus; *Biographia Classica*, 2 vols. (London), 1:190, 196, 208-9, 212 (see also chap. 5, sec. 1 at n. 28

If Cleland had read Edward Gibbon's first published work, he might have had Grevelle do some translating to help his case. The *Essai sur l'étude de la littérature* (1761) includes this succinct judgment on the rise of young Octavian: "Tyran sanguinaire, soupçonné de lâcheté, le plus grand des crimes dans un chef de parti, il parvient au trône, et fait oublier aux républicains qu'ils eussent jamais été libre." Once firmly established, the milder Augustus supplied his people with chains that "on portait sans le sentir."[25] Comparable remarks appear in several other essays by Gibbon and, as we shall see, culminate in the third chapter of the *Decline and Fall* (1776).[26]

A sign of the consistent literary sniping at Augustus may be seen in the feline survival of the incipient anti-Augustanism in Canto 35, v. 26 of Ariosto's *Orlando Furioso*.

Augustus Caesar was not such a Saint,
As *Virgil* maketh him by his description,
His love of learning scuseth that complaint,
That men might justly make of his proscription;
Nor had the shame that *Nero's* name doth taint,
Confirm'd now by a thousand yeares prescription,
Been as it is, if he had had the wit,
To have been frank to such as Poemes writ.[27]

---

in text, below); Warton, ed., *The Works of Virgil*, 4 vols. (London, 1753), 1:ix-x; Pitt's "Life of Virgil," ibid., pp. 10-11, 19-23; Warton, *Essay on the Genius and Writings of Pope*, 2 vols. (1756-1782), 5th ed. (London, 1806), 2:341n; Warton, *The Works of Alexander Pope, Esq.*, 9 vols. (London, 1797), 4:146-47n; Cleland, 3 vols. (London), 3:55-56.

25 *Miscellaneous Works of Edward Gibbon, Esq.*, ed. John Lord Sheffield, 5 vols. (London, 1814), 4:89-90, 91. See also 4:91 n.‡, and "Extrait de trois mémoires de M. l'Abbé de la Bleterie," 3:171.

26 For some other remarks by Gibbon, see "On the Triumphs of the Romans" (1764), *Miscellaneous Works*, 4:378-80; ". . . a Catalogue of the Armies . . . of an Epic Poem," (1763), ibid., 4:328-29; "Extraits de mon journal," 26 September 1763, ibid., 5:327.

27 *Orlando Furioso*, trans. Sir John Harrington, 3rd ed. (London, 1634), p. 292. William Huggins adds an interesting note to his translation: "Ariosto here, and in the three following stanzas, banters the

The poem appeared in English in 1591 (John Harrington), 1755 (William Huggins), and 1783 (John Hoole, abridged). This particular section, however, was singled out as a gloss in the notes to Amelot de la Houssaye's translation of Tacitus (1690) and thus appeared as well in 1698 in "Dryden's" version of Amelot. Dryden must have read it by 1697, since he quotes the first four lines in his Preface to Virgil in that year and ambiguously adds, "whether they will pass for gospel now I cannot tell."[28] Any ambiguity was eschewed by subsequent commentators in the eighteenth century. William Bromley's 1698 note (from Amelot's Tacitus) tells us that Augustus deserved unhappiness in his own family because he violated sacred friendship in favor of pleasure, "and abused *Mecenas*'s Wife . . . which has given to *Ariosto* the Italian Poet, to say . . . *Augustus* was not so Virtuous, nor so Good, as *Virgil* tells us." The Huggins translation excepted, the lines were apparently dormant—though I suspect that they surfaced elsewhere—until the notes to Voltaire's *Octave . . . ou le triumvirate* (1766), and then his widely read *Questions sur l'encyclopédie*, when they were reinvoked as tokens of Augustus' debauchery and Virgil's folly in praising him. One year later, readers of the

---

falsehoods which the greatest poets have uttered, and yet have passed for true history among their admirers" (*Orlando Furioso*, 2 vols. [London, 1757], 2:61, new pagination and title page for the *Annotations*). For the Italian of this passage, see Huggins, 2:207. It is normally the first two lines that most impress Augustus' detractors.

Non fu sì santo, nè benigno Augusto,
Come la tuba [or tromba] di Virgilio suona.
L'aver avuto in poesia buon gusto,
La proscrizione iniqua gli perdona.
Nessun sapria, se Neron fosse ingiusto,
Nè sua fama saria forse men buona;
Avesse avuto e terra, e ciel nemici
Se gli Scrittor sapea tenersi amici.

28 See *Tacite avec des notes politiques et historiques*, 2 vols. (The Hague, 1692), 2:56 (note to *Annals*, iii. 25); Dryden, *Essays*, 2:239.

Monthly's review of Voltaire would see that "Ariosto has expressed himself with . . . propriety as well as grace," when he attacked Augustus and Virgil.[29] Ariosto's forgiveness has been jettisoned; Amelot's righteous indignation has been salvaged.

This fervor of condemnation among the literati is in part a function of the classical legacy already discussed. It is also a reflection of what scholars, artists, and poets were telling and showing one another, their readers, and viewers, so that several of the visual and verbal arts offered a common view of the uglier side of Augustus and his influence. Moreover, many others in the eighteenth century shared a willingness to reexamine the past, not as cliotherapists supporting a nation's ego by means of historical myth, but as Swiftean surgeons probing for a tumor that needed to be cut out for the patient's ultimate health. Even Augustus' apparently most brilliant and lasting achievement was subject to hostile examination.

III: AUGUSTUS AS THE ENEMY OF ART

No commonplace was more familiar than that which praised Augustus as patron of the arts, with results magnificently clear in the poetry of Virgil and Horace, the history of Livy, and the architecture of Vitruvius. Anxious novices and mature artists alike proclaimed the glories of the monarch and court in which talents like their own would not be wasted. "Sovereign of Science! Master of the Muse," Smart sang in his georgic *Hop Garden* (1752) while praising Augustus. As late as 1773, that eminent crank Percival Stockdale longed for a return to the halcyon days "When Caesar's taste inspired the poet's lays," even those of poets who were

[29] [John Dryden et al.] *The Annals and History of Cornelius Tacitus*, 3 vols. (London, 1698), 1:317, n. 2, Historical Notes to Tacitus, *Annals*, iii. 25; *Le Triumvirat*, in *Oeuvres complètes de Voltaire*, 70 vols. (Paris, 1785-1789), 5:173; *Questions*, 2:347; *Monthly Review*, 44 (1771): 582.

enemies to his "despotic reign."[30] But there was another song sung, one resonant with satiric, elegiac, and tragic notes that had its origin as early as the classical Augustan age itself and had a broadly based European, as well as British, cast and audience. This role portrayed Augustus not as the protector, but as the destroyer of art, the lucky inheritor of the last moments of republican vigor, which he annihilated where necessary, banished when expedient, and employed when possible. In the process, he turned the lingering arts into the agency of government propaganda and, thereby, the agency of Rome's accommodation to usurpation and slavery.

The view of Augustus as an enemy of the arts had distinguished classical precedent. Book five of Seneca the elder's *Controversiae*, for example, portrays Augustus as the first to burn books "when nothing in their writings affected the public." This policy "of punishing men for their literary merit was altogether new. Happily for the good of mankind, this species of tyranny was not devised before the days of Cicero." The just gods "took care that this method of crushing the powers of the mind, by illegal oppression, should begin . . . when all genius ceased to exist."[31]

As we recall, Tacitus also insists that Augustus hurt the quality of letters. The opening paragraph of the *Annals* tells us that the great events of the republic "are already recorded by Writers of signal renown." Even under Augustus there were distinguished historians who could "have composed his story, till by the prevailing spirit of fear, flattery, and abasement, they were check'd."[32] Book one of

[30] *The Collected Poems of Christopher Smart*, ed. Norman Callan, 2 vols. (London: Routledge & Kegan Paul, 1949), 2:151; Stockdale, *The Poet: A Poem* (London, 1773), p. 19.

[31] As in *The Works of Cornelius Tacitus*, trans. Arthur Murphy, 4 vols. (London, 1793), 4:348.

[32] Thomas Gordon, *The Works of Tacitus*, 1:1. Gordon's hostility to Augustus was common to both the anti- and pro-Walpole segments of his career. *Cato's Letters*, no. 65, 10 February 1722, depicts Augustus as a bloody proscriber who "had butchered Myriads, and enslaved all," and so debilitated his people that the legions were nearly worth-

the *Histories* is comparably indignant regarding Augustus and his malign influence. After Actium and Augustus' rule, "the historic character disappeared, and genius died by the same blow that ended public liberty. Truth was reduced to the last gasp. . . . Adulation began to spread her baneful influence, and a rooted hatred of their ambitious masters rankled in the breast of numbers. . . . The care of transmitting due information to posterity was utterly lost." Tacitus and his translator Murphy amplify this charge when they discuss biography in the *Life of Agricola*.[33] They no doubt gained support from the republican historian Asinius Pollio (77 B.C.-A.D. 5) who is characterized in Macrobius' *Saturnalia* as saying to Octavian, who had just attacked him in verse, "I shall keep quiet, for it is not easy to write against a man who can proscribe me."[34]

Knowledge of these sources was widespread. Seneca's observations were used in Quattrocento Florentine attacks on destructive absolutism and were turned to domestic political use in the *Craftsman*, no. 4 (16 December 1726), a quarrel with Augustus for perverting the law and thus encouraging Tiberius "to prosecute the most *innocent Books*, and destroy entirely" the great blessing of liberty. For almost 100 years, readers of Dryden's, Gordon's, or Murphy's versions of Tacitus would have been reminded of his indignation

---

less "As to Military Virtue, it was no more: The Praetorian Bands were only a Band of Hangmen with an Emperor at their Head." In no. 25, 15 April 1721, Gordon associates Octavian and Cromwell as tyrants who controlled the military and enslaved their people. Gordon and his colleague, John Trenchard, include many other anti-Julian and anti-Augustan attacks.

[33] Murphy, *Works of . . . Tacitus*, 3:5-6 (*Histories*, and see 461, note g); 4:52-53, 346-49, note c).

[34] "Temporibus triumviralibus Pollio, cum Fescenninos in eum Augustus scripsisset, ait: *At ego taceo non est enim facile in eum scribere, qui potest proscribere*." *Saturnalia* ii. 4. 21 in *Aur. Theodosii Macrobii . . . opera*, 2 vols. (Zweïbrücken, 1786), 1:343. The passage was quoted in Ophellot's *Suétone* (n. 15, above), 1:373, and in Martignac's translation of Horace, 2 vols. 3rd ed. (Paris, 1696), 2:393.

(as well as Seneca's in Murphy's work), and, as we have seen, the spirit of such remarks was entrenched in a general British hostility to despotism.

Both a cause and effect of this hostility was the persistent belief that the arts could flourish best only in freedom. Once the Roman republic collapsed, Roman arts would collapse as well, however impressive the dying-speeches might seem. Even the transplanted French royalist St. Evremond, who largely admired Horace and Virgil and once believed in the wisdom of Augustus as a governor, expresses this view. He argues that the later commonwealth, not the Augustan age, was the flowering of Roman genius, and he tells the Maréchal de Créqui that under Augustus, Roman "Parts as well as Courage began . . . to decay. Grandeur of Soul was converted to Circumspect Conduct, and Sound Discourse to Polite Conversation." What we see and hear of republican authors makes him believe "that we must search some other time than that of *Augustus*, to find the sound and agreeable Wit of the *Romans*, as well as the pure and natural Graces of their Tongue."[35] Basil Kennett is almost apologetic in narrating what, by 1696, was an often-thought and well-expressed view of why Rome's art collapsed. Oratory, he says, reached its peak "rather in the *Augustan* Age, than in *Augustus* his Reign, ending in *Cicero*, at the Dissolution of the Common-Wealth," when Rome lost "the ancient Liberty . . . which inspir'd him with all his lofty Thoughts, and was the very Soul of his Harangues."[36]

The equation of liberty and art was venerable in the later seventeenth century; it was not likely to founder during the eighteenth century and was accepted by Addison, Shaftesbury, Swift, Pope, Collins, Dyer, Gray, Goldsmith, and others. As one example among many, Thomson's *Liberty* (1735-1736) assumes that art flourishes under Liberty's pro-

[35] *Miscellaneous Essays* (n. 8, above), "To Monsieur the Marshall de Créqui" (1694), 2:9-10.

[36] *Romae Antiquae Notitia: Or, The Antiquities of Rome* (London, 1696), sig. a6r-a6v.

tection. The corruption of modern Rome, he tells Virgil, "First from your flatter'd Caesars . . . begun," and later adds that Augustus' apparently humane simulations of freedom merely serve "The Chain to clinch," further break the people, and destroy art. Art can live forever only when Liberty, not a temporary Maecenas, is the true patron.[37]

One point implicit in this commonplace had been made explicit as early as Tacitus—that is, Augustus' numerous poets were inherited, not created, and owed their genius either to peace itself and Maecenas' patronage, to the exciting times that brought out the best as well as worst in men[38] or, in the most familiar argument, to the greatness of the republic that Augustus destroyed. Partisans of these views, especially the last, insist that the "Augustan age" is radically misnamed if it denotes Augustus' responsibility for great art. Octavian's ungrateful acquiescence in Cicero's proscription and his overt expulsion of Ovid were often cited as particular examples of his malevolence to the muse.

Nat Lee's unintentionally comic masterpiece, *Gloriana or the Court of Augustus Caesar* (1676), uses accepted his-

[37] *Antient and Modern Italy Compar'd: Being the First Part of Liberty, A Poem* (London, 1735), pp. 29, 42, for the quotations. For liberty and art, see *The Prospect: Being the Fifth Part of Liberty* (London, 1736), pp. 29-30, where arts flourish in British soil, "planted, by the potent Juice / Of *Freedom* swell'd." Gray's *Bard* and *Progress of Poesy* (1757) are equally zealous, if less frenetic, in the cause. In *Roman Portraits* (London, 1794), Robert Jephson shares the faith, transfers some of his hostility to revolutionary France, and knows that however sweetly Augustus' caged birds might sing, "Good Cato, Tully, Brutus, liv'd no more; / Their names, like wrecks, bestrew'd th' ill-omen'd shore" (p. 228).

[38] For this argument, see Thomas Blackwell, *An Enquiry into the Life and Writings of Homer* (London, 1735), p. 65: "The abstract *Sciences* are generally the Product of *Leisure* and *Quiet*; but those that have respect to *Man,* and take their Aim from the human Heart, are best learned in Employment and Agitation." His example is Virgil, who twice saw Rome become "a Prey to lawless Power; her Constitution destroyed, and Prices set upon the Heads of her bravest Sons for opposing a Tyranny."

torical fact and myth and his own fertile wit. He portrays Augustus as an elderly, half-crazed, sexually famished tyrant and "black Usurper" who unfairly banishes Ovid and is still remembered for his share in Cicero's death.[39] Lee's melodrama exploited long-standing anger at those actions, an anger documented and communicated by Scaliger (and his translator), whose Ovid insists that he himself deserved banishment for his lies in praise of Augustus. John Gower's translation of "CLIO's complaint for the death of OVID" in 1640 also bitterly laments the exile, as do Dryden in 1680 and William King in 1761.[40]

[39] The play was reprinted in 1734—separately from Lee's *Works* of that year—and since it was not performed, may have been an attack upon George II. The opening couplet is spoken by Ovid and is worthy of *Tom Thumb*: "Vast are the Glories, *Caesar*, thou hast won, / To make whose Triumphs up, the World's undone." If the play was involved in political squabbles, it would not have been the first time for Lee's efforts, since *Lucius Junius Brutus* (1680) was "silenc'd after the third Day of acting it; it being objected, that the Plan, and Sentiments of it had too boldly vindicated, and might enflame Republican Principles" (*An Apology for the Life of Colley Cibber*, ed. B. R. S. Fone [Ann Arbor: Univ. of Michigan Press, 1968], p. 188). In 1703 Charles Gildon turned Lee's play into the more acceptable *The Patriot, or the Italian Conspiracy, A Tragedy* (London), and was obliged both to remove its attacks on monarchy and to change its scene from Rome to Florence in the time of Cosimo di Medici.

[40] *Ovids Tristia. Containinge five Bookes of mournfull Elegies*, trans. W[ye] S[altonstall] (London, 1633), sig. A5r. He adds that Augustus himself deserves banishment,

> For such foule deeds thy private roomes do staine,
> That men condemned ne're did act the same.
> . . . .
> I then did lye when as I praysed thee,
> For this my banishment was deserv'd by mee.

For Gower, see *Ovid's Festivalls, or Romane Calendar*, ed. Edward Alliston (Cambridge and London, 1640), sig. B6v: "*Thy name* Augustus well with thee agreed: / *'Twas given in flattery*; but by this all see, / *Thou wert* Augustus in *thy cruelty*"; Dryden, *Essays*, 1:263-64; King, *Political and Literary Anecdotes of his own Times* (London, 1818), pp. 165-68.

Cicero's execution was even stronger evidence against Augustus as benevolent patron; remembered as barbaric in its own right, it was compounded with the sin of ingratitude, with the symbolic quality of an illegal triumvir's murder of one who saved the republic from Catiline, and with dire consequences for literary history, whether read with opposition or administration bias. In 1728, for instance, Thomas Gordon dedicates his translation of Tacitus to his patron Robert Walpole and argues that under Augustus "Truth was treason." No one "would venture to speak it . . . and when Flattery bore a vogue and a price there were enough found to court it, and take it. Hence the partiality or silence of Poets and Historians."[41] Conyers Middleton, whose *Life of . . . Cicero* (1741) was heavily subscribed by the royal family, numerous peers, and men of letters, makes overt some of Gordon's assumptions regarding courtly silence. "The odium" of Cicero's death, he says, "fell chiefly on ANTONY; yet it left a stain of perfidy and ingratitude also on AUGUSTUS: which explains . . . why his name is not so much as mentioned either by HORACE or VIRGIL," or their contemporaries. Middleton also makes clear that "after CICERO's death and the ruin of the Republic," Roman oratory was fit only for "making panegyrics, and servile compliments to . . . Tyrants."[42]

41 *The Works of Tacitus*, 1:50.

42 *History of the Life of Marcus Tullius Cicero*, 2 vols. (London), 2:499-50, and 2:534-35. Middleton also says that the orator's death "was a triumph over the Republic itself; and seemed to confirm and establish the perpetual slavery of *Rome*" (2:497-98). Hence his name, though glorious, "was no subject for Court Poets; since the very mention of him must have been a satire on the Prince." Virgil even unjustly yielded the palm of oratory to the Greeks rather than praise Cicero (2:500). Middleton's popular life of Cicero went into a fifth edition by 1755, was translated into French—by the Abbé Prévost—in 1763, and Spanish in 1790. The Yale University 1741 copy in English includes French manuscript annotations. The subscribers to Middleton's work included Ralph Allen, Burlington, Colley Cibber, Samuel Johnson, Esq. (probably not *the* Johnson?), Lyttelton, Uvedale Price, Pope, Sir Robert Walpole (five large paper books), William Warburton, and Daniel

These last examples of anti-Augustanism appear among friends of the court of Walpole and George II, but that court hardly held exclusive rights to the franchise. In 1766 Robert Andrews bluntly states that liberty, like art, "had with the murder'd and immortal Cicero breathed her last, and left the world to Augustus now settled on a Tyrant's throne." Virgil was not inspired by Augustus, but only by his own previous education and the "inspiration of the gentle Muses." The "patriot" historian Nathan Hooke quotes Middleton's lines above, but nevertheless thinks that Middleton softened Augustus' "odium," however little the softening now appears. In 1794 Robert Jephson criticizes Horace and Virgil for ignoring Cicero, mentions and shares Middleton's opinion regarding the reason for their silence, and later concludes that Augustus' role in the orator's proscription was more despicable than Antony's.[43]

Augustus and his despotism thus killed Cicero, banished Ovid, and emasculated history and biography. According to Dryden, they also diminished the vigor, honesty, and quality of satire. In his Preface to the translation of Juvenal (1693), Dryden argues that Augustus knew his subjects could forget neither his "usurpation . . . upon their freedom," nor his violence and "slaughter" in the process. He therefore pro-

Wray. The Royal Family subscribed the large paper edition, and John Lord Hervey subscribed twenty-five large paper sets. For the relationship between Hervey, Middleton, and *Cicero*, see Robert Halsband, *Lord Hervey: Eighteenth-Century Courtier* (Oxford: Clarendon Press, 1973), pp. 242-44, 254-55, 264-71. For discussion of Prévost's *Histoire de Cicéron*, see Jacqueline de la Harpe, *Le Journal des Savants et l'Angleterre 1702-1789*, Univ. of California Publications in Modern Philology, vol. 20 (Berkeley and Los Angeles: Univ. of California Press, 1941), pp. 346, 350, 351.

[43] Andrews, *The Works of Virgil, Englished* (Birmingham), pp. 11-12; Hooke, *Roman History*, 4 vols. (London, 1738-1771), 4:364, note e; Jephson, *Roman Portraits*, p. 96, n. 3 (Middleton, Horace, and Virgil), pp. 173-75 and 174n, for the relationship between Cicero and Octavian. Jephson's portrait offers a convenient summary of much of the praise and blame of Augustus.

vided "for his own reputation by making an edict against lampoons and satires," and thus "for his own sake" re-invoked the dread *lex laesae majestatis,* in which death by whipping was the penalty for aspersing the broadly defined Roman majesty. Satirists could not accuse the plentiful adulterers "when Augustus was of that number." Hence, "though his age was not exempted from the worst of villanies, there was no freedom left to reprehend them, by reason of the edict."[44] At the end of the next century Alexander Thomson is even blunter regarding Augustus' reaction when satire was directed at the princeps himself: "he put to death, by the hand of Varus, a poet of Parma, named Cassius, on account of having written some satirical verses against him." That example, Thomson claims, helped to persuade Ovid that silence regarding his discovery of Augustus' sexual indiscretions was an act of prudence.[45]

These several instances of Augustus as enemy of the arts were obviously adaptable for or against Walpolean political purposes—and were used by both Gordon and Bolingbroke, among many others. They were also adaptable for different purposes—simple comment, historical inquiry, or general moral outrage—and they make clear that the politicians and their cronies used available commonplaces rather than in-vented new ones.

Specifically, the Abbé Jean Baptiste du Bos's popular *Refléxions critiques sur la poésie et la peinture* (1719) had a significant discussion of the Augustan age abstracted for British readers in 1740 and again in 1772; the work was wholly translated into English by Thomas Nugent in 1748. George Turnbull's *Treatise on Ancient Painting* (1740) turns to du Bos for support of his belief that peace is not

---

[44] *Essays,* 2:132-35. Many years later the Walpole *Gazetteer,* 27 October 1738, wished to reinvoke this law to punish Pope and other opposition satirists. See below, p. 144.

[45] *The Lives of the First Twelve Caesars, Translated from Suetonius* (London, 1796), p. 236.

adequate to perfect the fine arts. "The great Men who composed what is called the *Augustan* Age, were already form'd before the more peaceful Days of that Reign commenc'd." Though Augustus "encouraged the great Poets and Genius's of every kind, yet the best Authors were already become great Men before that Encouragement."[46]

These writers on either side of the Channel were joined by others of warmer temper. James Harris' *Hermes* (1751) admits that Augustus was patron to many fine writers, but insists that they "were bred and educated in the principles of a free Government. 'Twas hence they derived that high and manly spirit" that induces admiration. Octavian's legacy of government soon stopped the growth of liberty and letters. In 1762 an unknown author published *Letters to a Young Nobleman*, which the *Monthly Review* praises, "though few of the Author's observations are new" (26 [1762]: 13). In his long discussion of "the Influence of Liberty upon Taste," he insists that those Augustus protected "were formed in the time of liberty," that half of the putative Augustans "died before ever the name of Augustus was heard in the world," and that Augustus, "so far from creating a genius, or correcting taste, . . . certainly put a stop to their improvement" and induced their decline when he changed the Roman constitution.[47] Joseph Warton makes a similar point regarding the irrelevance of Augustus to many of the "Augustan" writers. In 1785, however, the contentious John Pinkerton went even further than his predecessors who, at least, granted the "Augustans'" greatness, if not the label itself. He urges that the entire nonsense of Augustan ages is a weed to be rooted out, for the observation that genius

[46] For du Bos' comment, see *Refléxions critiques*, 2 vols., 6th ed. (Paris, 1775), 2:193-94; Turnbull (London), p. 107; Ralph Griffiths' review of Charles Cameron, *The Baths of the Romans* (1772), in the *Monthly Review*, 47 (1772): 371. Griffiths is quoting Cameron on du Bos. Attribution in Nangle, p. 71.

[47] Harris (London), pp. 419-20n; *Monthly*, William Rose (Nangle, p. 146); *Letters* (London), pp. 137-38 (wrongly printed as p. 237), p. 147 (the constitution).

reached its peak in those periods is a "remark of superlative futility." As for Rome in particular, "where is Tacitus, almost their only original writer?" The "superior good sense and observation of the English" allow them to know better; they "fix no Augustan age for their country."[48]

This insistence upon the non-Augustanism of the best Augustan art appears in several other British texts unconnected with political squabbling of the 1730s. It also appears in many writers on the Continent—Voltaire among them—whose works are quoted at length in the pages of the *Monthly Review*.[49] These writers are really attempting to resolve the paradox of a prince who diminished letters yet lived in an age famous for them. Perhaps the best such attempt is that by Thomas Blackwell, whose *Memoirs of the Court of Augustus* was popular in Britain and France. He includes hostility to Augustus and an attempt to put as good a face as possible on the court-poets, who were, he believes, really republicans manqués.

[48] Warton, see note 24, above; Robert Heron [pseud. for Pinkerton], *Letters of Literature* (London), pp. 159-60. Unfortunately, Pinkerton is not altogether correct. An English "Augustan Age" when used, however, often is debunked. Swift says that Charles II's reign is "reckoned, although very absurdly, our *Augustan Age*" ("Thoughts on Various Subjects," in The Prose Writings of Jonathan Swift, vol. 4, *A Proposal for Correcting the English Tongue, Polite Conversation, etc.*, ed. Herbert Davis with Louis Landa [Oxford: Basil Blackwell, 1964], p. 249). As late as 1790 William Enfield, reviewing *The Works . . . of Leonard Welsted* (1789), added another complication: "The author . . . flourished in what is sometimes, though perhaps with no great propriety, called the Augustan Age of English Literature" (*Monthly Review*, second series, 3 [1790]: 149). Attribution in Benjamin Christie Nangle, *The Monthly Review Second Series 1790-1815: Indexes of Contributors and Articles* (Oxford: Clarendon Press, 1955), p. 224. The consistent disclaimer is at least as significant as the infrequent label.

[49] Voltaire has already been cited. See also the review of Henri Richer's *The Life of Maecenas* (1746), trans. Ralph Schomberg (1748; 2nd ed. 1760), in the *Monthly Review*, 35 (1766): 97 (by John Langhorne, Nangle, p. 192); and J. J. W. Munnich, *Versuch über die Gränzen der Aufklärung, & c . . . An Inquiry into the State of Morals and Science among the Antient Romans*, in *Monthly*, second series, 15 (1794): 566-68 (by Benjamin Sowden, Nangle, *Second Series*, p. 232).

What we loosely term the *Stile of the Augustan Age,*
was not *formed* under *Augustus.* It was formed under the
Common-Wealth, during the high struggles for Liberty
against *Julius Cesar,* and his Successors the Triumvirs,
which lasted upwards of fifteen Years. The Men who had
been *formed* under *Augustus shone* under *Tiberius,* and
strictly, spoke the Language of his Age. *Cinna,* therefore,
and *Varus, Gallus,* and *Pollio, Junius Calidius, Virgil,*
and *Horace,* with all their contemporary Poets, learned
the Language of *Liberty,* and took the masterly Tincture,
which that Goddess inspires both in phrase and Sentiment. This gave them that Freedom of Thought and
Strength of Stile, which is only to be acquired under *Her*
Influence; which, when joined to the Politeness that accompanies the slippery Transition from Freedom to blind
Obedience, produced the *finished Beauty* we admire in
their Works. . . . Let not therefore *Virgil* or *Horace,* or
Valgius or *Varus,* be looked upon as *courtbred* Poets under
Augustus: no more than *Milton, Waller,* or *Cowley* were
under Charles II. They were free-born *Romans,* some of
them early venturing Life and Fortune in the Cause of
Liberty, who were called to Court, and protected and encouraged by the Prince's Ministers; in return for which
they did him and them the greatest of all services. The
Roman Model copied by *Virgil* was *Ennius,* as *Lucilius*
did by *Horace.*

The *Roman* Composition began to degenerate even
under Augustus.[50]

IV: The Vision of Augustan Truth

Lest these commonplaces should become tiresome, several
anti-Augustans couched their attacks in a genre that puts us
in a world at once removed from familiar reality and familiar
error—the genre of the historical or personal dream or vision
in which, as the convention has it, truth may be seen. According to the *Gazetteer* for 9 July 1737, "History . . . takes off the

[50] Three vols. (Edinburgh, 1753-1763), 3:467-68.

Mask" of dissemblers and shows reality. We know that this form was used by the fourth-century Emperor Julian, and the seventeenth-century Boccalini and Verrio, to Augustus' detriment. In some cases, however, Augustus was a benign force. Addison's *Tatler*, no. 81 (1709), narrates a dream of the temple of fame that includes Virgil and others (but not Horace) already seated when Augustus enters. He "appeared, looking round him with a serene and affable Countenance upon all the Writers of his Age, who strove among themselves which of them should shew him the greatest Marks of Gratitude and Respect."[51] On the whole, however, the vision genre gives us more of Boccalini's despotic than Addison's benevolent Augustus, and at one point turns upon itself and criticizes the Addisonian dream. It also suggests how the artists' and scholars' generalized anger toward Augustus for his destruction of liberty could be turned to practical political use for the moment.

If young Alexander Pope had doubts about Augustan virtues, they must have been reinforced by 1721, when he edited the works of John Sheffield, Duke of Buckinghamshire, which include the "Dialogue Between Augustus Caesar, and Cardinal Richelieu." This masterful performance begins with the myth of Augustus that modern students think the eighteenth century believed, and promptly shows its absurdity. Richelieu praises Augustus as "the wise, the happy AUGUSTUS! the perfection of prudence, the pattern of Princes, and admiration of all the world for these seventeen hundred years!"[52] The cardinal has only two objections to

[51] One also sees "Great *Augustus*" in Pope's *Temple of Fame* (1715), line 229. John Dyer, *The Ruins of Rome* (London, 1740), evokes the image of "Happy Augustus!" who was inspired by the poets he encouraged in those days "Auspicious to the Muses" (p. 20).

[52] *The Works of John Sheffield, Earl of Mulgrave, Marquis of Normanby, and Duke of Buckingham* [ed. Alexander Pope], 2 vols., 2nd ed. (London, 1729), 2:154. Subsequent citations are given in the text. Ignorance of eighteenth-century anti-Augustanism has led a recent historian of the English dialogue into an error regarding Sheffield. Frederick M. Keener thinks that Richelieu "plays so small a part that

raise regarding that distinguished shade—"ingratitude and cruelty" which, when joined, "I, and all mankind abhor." Augustus agrees that if he is guilty of these faults all of his greatness "was not worth the buying it at so dear a rate" (2:155). He insists that he can purge himself of these severe accusations by confessing "a thousand [lesser] follies" (2:156) in order to show that he is innocent of the major crimes. Unless Augustus is acquitted of the admittedly horrible charges, his strategy will be self-defeating. That is precisely what he cannot do, however, for after indicting himself from his own mouth—he admits, for example, that he selected Maecenas as his minister because he wanted his wife (2:159)—he invents a palpably false story regarding the proscription of Cicero. The suspicious cardinal says: "You would make me believe that he is yet alive, if I did not see him here every day shaking his head (which you cut off) at your going by him so confidently." Alas, Cicero himself is wrong to shake his severed head. Augustus was tricked by Antony, who assured him that he would spare Cicero if Augustus would seem to proscribe him, "and so at once cunningly satisfied his revenge, and blacken'd me to all posterity." Augustus could not tell the world that he was fooled, his friends told him he would not be believed, and

---

almost any other person, including Brutus [from a dialogue by John Hughes] would have served as well." Hughes, though, is properly historical, whereas "Sheffield distorts and fabricates history to an extent unmatched by any other British dialogue-writer." Keener concludes that "it is not at all to Alexander Pope's credit that he prepared Sheffield's *Works* for publication" (*English Dialogues of the Dead: A Critical History, an Anthology, and a Checklist* [New York: Columbia Univ. Press, 1973], pp. 52-53). See also p. 54, where Sheffield is, among other things, "sensational and irresponsible." Surely, however, we regard the monarchist Richelieu's condemnation as more impressive than that of either republican Brutus. Virtually everything that Sheffield put into Augustus' mouth was available to him in historical commentary—as Pope, to his credit, well knew. The exception is Augustus' justification (2:161) of Cicero's proscription, an outrageous fabrication intended to show Augustus' duplicity.

Lepidus, the only person present, "durst not disoblige MARK ANTONY . . . for which I was reveng'd of him also" (2:161-62). Augustus took away Lepidus' army and made war on Antony—all to avenge Cicero's death.

It is here that the Dialogue, already beyond Augustus' control, makes its obvious turn. Richelieu will never trust history or, on Augustus' advice, its commentators. In the process he has learned not to trust Augustus, for like Gulliver somewhat later, he has seen historic truth: "when once a prepossession is over, how one's eyes are open'd. I begin now to recollect a thousand things, which might have before convinc'd me of your being no such SOLOMON." He recalls that Augustus illicitly married Livia; called his daughter whore in the senate as "the very gravest Senators sneer'd at me to my very face"; was led about by his lower protuberance by Livia, who led about many younger men by their comparable protuberances as well; was called murderer by Maecenas, whom he cuckolded; and made Tiberius his successor. Indeed, Richelieu says, "when I admir'd you most, I could not excuse it." Augustus, now drawn from defense to admission of guilt, concludes the Dialogue with his own shame. "Neither can I do it now. What would you have more? I confess myself impos'd on all my life; most commonly well, but at my death so ill, that I am yet asham'd of it" (2:163-65). Richelieu begins the discussion with respect for Augustus and reluctantly mentions his flaws; he ends with an awareness of the lies of the Augustan reign, new insight into its depravity, and a recalled and justified outrage at a bad choice of successor. This Dialogue, condemning Augustus on many grounds, was written by one of the most important of Restoration and earlier eighteenth-century literary aristocrats. It was read and edited by Alexander Pope, and appeared in 1721, a suppressed edition, 1723, and several times thereafter in London (4th ed., 1753), and The Hague (1726 and 1727).

Gulliver's Travels (1726) was even more popular and again offered a brief character of Augustus. In Glubbdubdrib, Gulliver is allowed to call up any spirits he wishes and is informed "that they would certainly tell me Truth; for Lying was a Talent of no Use in the lower World." Since the patriotic Briton chiefly saw "the Destroyers of Tyrants and Usurpers, and the Restorers of Liberty to oppressed and injured Nations," Augustus is absent—in fact, but not in comment, for "the Court of *Augustus*" is depicted as corrupt in rewarding the unworthy and punishing the just and the brave.[53] Gulliver's surprise at the rapid spread of corruption under that monarch applies to Georgian Britain, since Swift's work was intended and accepted as both political and moral satire; but the attack must have been regarded as appropriately rooted in real Augustan history, especially since Swift had made an even more hostile attack on Octavian in 1701.[54]

Walpole could not permit the opposition or the uncommitted to monopolize the cant of freedom, liberty, and virtue. On 5 November 1735, his newspaper the *Gazetteer*, anticipating the birthday of William III, reprints much of Mr. Tatler's dream of the temple of fame. Parson Stretcher is especially unhappy with the temple's occupants and quarrels with Addison's judgment and Augustus' politics. "What *Augustus* did there, unless to pry and dissemble, he could not see, and as little of his Favourite *Virgil*'s Business, but to flatter the former and all of his Tribe." If Virgil and Addison really wanted "to celebrate *Beneficence to Mankind*" and the virtues praised in the temple, one man alone combines them, "on whose POLITICKS, AUGUSTUS [might have built] a *firmer Empire*." For the *Gazetteer*, as for Ver-

[53] The Prose Writings of Jonathan Swift, vol. 11, *Gulliver's Travels*, ed. Herbert Davis (Oxford: Basil Blackwell, 1965), pp. 195, 196, 201 (bk. iii, chaps. 7-8).

[54] See his remarks in the *Contests and Dissentions*, chap. 3, sec. 1, at n. 1, below, and Bertrand A. Goldgar, "*Gulliver's Travels* and the Opposition to Walpole," in *The Augustan Milieu: Essays Presented to Louis A. Landa*, ed. Henry Knight Miller, Eric Rothstein, and G. S. Rousseau (Oxford: Clarendon Press, 1970), pp. 155-73.

rio a generation earlier, William III is superior to Augustus.[55]

In 1761 the arch Tory William King wrote his *Political and Literary Anecdotes of his own Times* (published London, 1818). This aged enemy of Walpole was an admirer of Virgil, Horace, and Ovid; but he had only contempt for the poets' master. George II and Walpole were dead (1760, 1745), and King, who was 76, expected to die shortly (p. 165); he is thus not likely to have had an old topical target in mind for his portrait of Augustus, one communicated by the "humane and gentle" Ovid, who was unjustly banished and who, in the manner of shades, gives King "the real character of the emperor" (p. 165). Ovid heartily repents of his flattery to that despicable man, who deserved nothing of the veneration apparently paid him. Ovid sounds as if he has had the benefit of ghostly discussion with Suetonius and Tacitus as he characterizes a "false, cruel, and inexorable" butcher whose proscriptions must permanently "stain his memory" (p. 166). Moreover, he probably lacked courage, certainly lacked "fortitude of mind," was miserly, and depended on Maecenas to reward Horace and Virgil. Augustus, he concludes, "was every day guilty of some base and mean action, either to gratify his lust and avarice, or to discover the real sentiments of the Roman people" (pp. 167-68).[56]

[55] For another, seditiously harsh, portrait of a usurping Augustus, see *Fog's Weekly Journal*, new series, no. 7, 16 July 1737 (p. 111, below). As we have seen in chap. 1 (see text at n. 18, above), in 1760 Lyttelton, long out of opposition, published his *Dialogues of the Dead*, the ninth of which labels Messala "a deserter from the republick, and an apologist for a tyrant" named Augustus.

[56] Such historical conversations took place in France as well—with similar results. In 1771 Henri Ophellot de la Pause records an "Entretien d'un Despote & d'un Philosophe, sur Auguste." The despot is Cromwell, an admirer of Augustus; the philosophe is "Sidney," who happens to have a manuscript lecture on Augustus which, of course, is read to Cromwell and convinces him that Augustus is everything that is wrong in a governor. Sidney also places Horace and Virgil in their true light—talented poets and political flatterers—and makes clear

Whether one looks at the "truths" of a fourth-century Roman emperor and his adapters in Britain, a seventeenth-century Italian and his English translations, an eminent native aristocrat and his more eminent poet-editor well before the "patriotism" of the 1730s, involved members of that opposition, the government's own organ of defense and attack, or writers no longer personally or chronologically involved in opposition, a common picture of Augustus emerges—"he was every day guilty of some base and mean action." Those actions took place during and after his rise to power, and were offensive in their own right, doubly so in a monarch, who should be an example to his people; they also included manipulation of his inherited artists and destruction of the arts thereafter through destruction of freedom. The latter point would evoke even more hostile reaction of immediate use for British history and politics of the eighteenth century.

that by 1771 the French rightly assumed that England's earlier despot was "Augustan," and that her essential genius was anti-Augustan, libertarian, and philosophe in spirit. Somewhat later, in his own voice, Ophellot says that the banished Ovid "mourut dans son exil detestant son tyran & faisant sans cesse des vers en son honneur." See *Histoire des douze Césars de Suétone,* 1:330-44 (the Entretien), and 4:69 (Ovid). The French association of Augustus and Cromwell is overt, as well, in S. N. H. Linguet, *Histoire des révolutions de l'empire Romain,* 2 vols. (Paris, 1766), 1:13-14.

~~~~~~

CHAPTER 3

The Legacy Improved, Part II. Augustus in Theory and Practice: Constitutional Balance and Political Activity

THE MOST IMPORTANT OBJECTION TO AUGUSTUS WAS NOT that he was a butcher, or a torturer, or a pathic, or a lecher, or incestuous, or a legacy-hunter, or a censor, or even a book-burner. Nobody is perfect, as the nation successively ruled by Oliver Cromwell and Charles Stuart no doubt remembered. The dominant objections were to his destruction of the balanced constitution of the Roman Republic, the fatal precedent he set for other rulers, and the establishment of the empire whose slavery and fall were inherent in its creation. Moreover, as either rhetoric, or genuine belief, or both had it, Augustus was consciously and maliciously guilty of murdering the republic. As Tacitus and Dio Cassius taught the eighteenth century, Augustus selected Tiberius knowing that he was evil, knowing that he would further ravage the empire, and hoping that his own memory would be further enhanced as a result of the contrast. Augustus' rule, then, served British theoreticians, historians, and politicians as a practical guide: it showed them what not to do in their own nation, and they saw what happened in Britain and France when Augustus' ways were followed.

I: AUGUSTAN PRECEDENT AND THE CONSTITUTIONAL BALANCE

Swift's early *Contests and Dissentions . . . in Athens and Rome* (1701) offers a pre-Walpole example of the eighteenth-century concern with constitutional balance. So long as the "Balance of Power is equally held," all sides will be restrained; but once different factions are forced to unite under the victor's banner, "at last both are Slaves." That is how a boy like Octavian came to power and "entailed the vilest Tyranny that Heaven in its Anger ever inflicted on a Corrupt and Poison'd People. . . . Here ended all Show or Shadow of Liberty in Rome."[1]

Thomas Gordon's "Discourses on Tacitus" (1728) also deal with some of these issues. Gordon argues that Augustus' reputation was higher than it deserved because of "the badness of his Successors; and for his posthumous lustre he was indebted to the extreme misery of the Roman people." Yet it was Augustus himself who was responsible for the "entailed" "monsters of cruelty" like Tiberius and Caligula. He could have ended his usurpation with his life and returned the liberty he stole from his fellow-citizens, but "his power and name were dearer to him than the Roman people or human race: he made provision by a long train of successors against any possible relapse into liberty." This makes clear "that he meant to perpetuate slavery."[2]

Whether or not Gordon's judgment was accurate, it certainly was a familiar one, and was often expressed in the image of Augustus as a nobly togaed riveter of his countrymen's chains. Like Gordon, Aaron Hill both discusses the princeps' undeserved reputation and portrays a man so self-centered that only the subjection of the world could satisfy him. Hill's *Enquiry into the Merit of Assassination* (1738) regarded the first Caesar as the real (hopeful) preserver of liberty. Unlike his uncle, Augustus was incapable of reforming Rome or restoring the republic, and so he established his own authority. To praise Julius would have implied dispraise for Augustus, which that "artful, double-dealing"

---

[1] *A Discourse of the Contests and Dissentions Between the Nobles and the Commons in Athens and Rome with the Consequences they had upon both those States*, ed. Frank H. Ellis (Oxford: Clarendon Press, 1967), pp. 110-11.

[2] *The Works of Tacitus . . . Containing the Annals. To which are Prefixed Discourses upon that Author*, 2 vols. (London, 1728-1731), 1:50.

man would not allow. Since he determined to appropriate the sovereign authority for himself and his family, he permanently changed "the Old free Constitution of *Rome* into absolute, and hereditary, *Monarchy*." This gave "Place to a horrid, *New Period*, of Subjection, and Slavery."[3]

Edward Wortley Montagu, Jr., is comparably disenchanted and sees Augustus' reign as a historical lesson for his own countrymen. Augustus prepared the Romans "for the yoke of slavery" by keeping them "constantly intoxicated by one perpetual round of jollity and diversions."[4] He thereby "rivetted [the chains of slavery] beyond a possibility of removal." Montagu sees a parallel in James II and his insistence on a standing army and consequent disarming of the people (p. 384). Several years thereafter, George Wilson Meadley again uses historical parallels, now between Augustus and the younger William Pitt, and damns Pitt with both the comparison and contrast. Augustus founded "an efficient despotism in every department of the State" and soon prepared his debilitated countrymen "for the yoke." In the process, he at least encouraged arts and letters. Pitt is all too like Augustus in leading Britain down the same path, but has "no corresponding claims to the applause of the historian and the poet."[5]

Such a ruler and expert riveter had modern exemplars more powerful than Pitt. Augustus was not only the enslaving tyrant, but also the paradigm of the Augustanism that France under Louis XIV and England under Oliver

[3] *An Enquiry Into the Merits of Assassination: With a View to the Character of Caesar: And His Designs on the Roman Republick* (London), pp. 92, 94.

[4] *Reflections on the Rise and Fall of the Ancient Republicks. Adapted to the Present State of Great Britain* (1759), 4th ed. (London, 1778), p. 290. Subsequent citations are given in the text.

[5] "Two Historical Portraits: Octavius Caesar and William Pitt, Rienzi and Buonaparte, Compared," in *The Pamphleteer*, 18 (London, 1831): 131, 132, 134. The composition was written more than twenty years earlier.

Cromwell experienced. Edward Burnaby Greene provides examples of each abundant comparison. He observes that "the character of AUGUSTUS" would surely have suffered if his poetic flatterers had not "warped" our attention "from his public guilt to his private munificence. . . . Such too is the fate of a modern AUGUSTUS [Louis XIV], who possessed not one good quality of the former." Some pages later he remarks that by and large Augustus "may be declared a CROMWELL with a portion of *literary* endowments." Each man enslaved his country while increasing its prestige. The despotism of Augustus made Roman arms more feared than ever, just as "English arms were never more greatly dreaded than under the usurpation of CROMWELL."[6]

These concerns with the future as a projection of the past, with political precedent and the constitution, were very much part of the conventional baggage of British historians of Rome. History, commentators frequently insist, is valuable for displaying proper or improper examples, and thus has the force of what Bolingbroke, borrowing from Dionysius of Halicarnassus, calls philosophy teaching by examples. Indeed, in his *Letters on the Study . . . of History* (1752) Bolingbroke virtually likens ancient events to a classical poem imitated by a modern author. Both the concerned political thinker and poet carefully examine the

6 "The Influence of Government on the Mental Faculties" in *Critical Essays* (London, 1770), pp. 176, 227. For other discussion of Augustus and Louis XIV, see William Rose's review of Voltaire's *Age of Lewis XIV*, in the *Monthly Review*, 7 (1752): 176, and the beginning of chap. 7, sec. 1, below. For Cromwell as Augustus or Caesar, see Thomas Blackwell, *Memoirs of the Court of Augustus*, 3 vols. (Edinburgh, 1753-1763), 1:141-42; Owen Ruffhead on *The Parliamentary or Constitutional History of England*, vols. 21 and 22, in the *Monthly Review*, 22 (1760): 378. The attributions are in Benjamin Christie Nangle, *The Monthly Review First Series 1749-1789: Indexes of Contributors and Articles* (Oxford: Clarendon Press, 1934), pp. 55, 171 (referred to hereafter as Nangle). For French discussion of Augustus and Cromwell, see chap. 2, n. 56, above.

earlier text, determine what can best serve contemporary purposes, adapt, and, where possible, improve the past in the living present.[7] Non-royalist historians and political commentators agreed that imperial Rome induced its own decline by destroying the republic's balanced constitution and transferring power into the emperor's hands. Isaac Kramnick quite properly states that "praise of the virtuous British . . . mixed government and balanced constitution is found in virtually all" eighteenth-century political writing. Harringtonian commonwealthman, nostalgic Tory reactionary, opposition Whig, administration court Whig, and the informed, literate citizen shared "the fundamental assumption" that mixed government was essential to Britain's constitution and liberty.[8] As Lord Monboddo puts it in 1776, "there can be no government truly free which is not so mixed." Of course, men of varying political persuasions would assign varying weights to each branch. Samuel Johnson and Goldsmith's Vicar of Wakefield saw the king as the unifying force and check upon the power of the other branches. Gibbon thought the peers "a body of nobles, whose influence may restrain, while it secures, the authority of the monarch." Still others regarded the commons and the "people" as the dominant force;[9] but all agreed that absolut-

[7] Two vols. (London), 1:61, 67. On the latter page, for example, he says that "History is the ancient author: experience is the modern language. . . . we translate the sense and reason, we transfuse the spirit and force: but we imitate only the particular graces of the original; we . . . are far from affecting to copy them servilely."

[8] *Bolingbroke and His Circle: The Politics of Nostalgia in the Age of Walpole* (Cambridge, Mass.: Harvard Univ. Press, 1968), pp. 137, 140. Both chapters 5 and 6 are useful for purposes of this study. Kramnick rightly stresses that whatever the authority of Aristotle, Polybius, and Cicero for the mixed constitution, "a much more important influence was the legacy of English political and constitutional experience" (p. 139).

[9] James Burnett, Lord Monboddo, *Of the Origin of Language*, 6 vols. (Edinburgh, 1773-1792), 3:241; Johnson, in *Boswell's Life of Johnson: Together with Boswell's Journal of a Tour to the Hebrides and Johnson's Diary of a Journey into North Wales*, ed. George Birkbeck Hill,

ism in any branch of the balanced government was tyrannical
and bad, moderate rule was good, the people had a right to
determine their governors and, the cementing force of these
venerable clichés, limited constitutional monarchy insured
the rights of the nation's king, aristocrats, and commoners.

We can see several of these beliefs in the *Roman History*
(1769) of Oliver Goldsmith, an author who has been called
a positive "Augustan," who has praised the letters of the
Augustan age, and who in fact has many good things to say
about Augustus and the happiness of Rome under his tute-
lage. Goldsmith has limited affection for the republic, is
aware of the virtues of the first two Caesars, and believes
that "could we separate Octavius from Augustus, he would
be one of the most faultless princes in history."[10] But we cannot make that separation, and Goldsmith insists upon constitutional safeguards, the value of precedent, and the simple
decency of men who rule the state.

Antony and Octavian, allies in the "infernal" (2:42) triumvirate, were "usurpers of their country's freedom" (2:40)
and invaders of their city, which felt "all the deliberate
malice of cool-blooded slaughter" (2:42). The constitutional
balance, moribund before Julius, died under the triumvirate; the victory at Philippi made liberty impossible and
an absolute sovereign necessary (2:50). Goldsmith sees Augustus' reign as a brilliant attempt to embalm the corpse

---

rev. L. F. Powell, 6 vols. (Oxford: Clarendon Press, 1934-1950) 1:423-
24; 4:117 (subsequent references to the *Life* are from this edition);
Goldsmith, *Vicar*, chap. 19; Gibbon, *The History of the Decline and
Fall of the Roman Empire*, ed. J. B. Bury, 7 vols. (London, 1900), 2:165;
for the "people" as important, see Hooke, text and n. 14, below. The
student of eighteenth-century politics, especially Johnson's, will want
to read Donald J. Greene, *The Politics of Samuel Johnson* (New Haven:
Yale Univ. Press, 1960).

[10] *The Roman History, From the Foundation of the City of Rome,
To the Destruction of the Western Empire*, 2 vols. (London), 2:119.
Goldsmith is among a group of historians ambivalent toward Augustus
but, finally, at least as aware of his negative as of his positive achievements. Subsequent citations to this edition are given in the text.

before it rots; the princeps appears to have succeeded in his time, but was actually too late and even enhanced the process of decay. Goldsmith now quietly invokes the joint concepts of the balanced constitution and the value of precedent.

Augustus' only check in acquiring power had been the threat of competition from Antony. Upon his death, however, the process of unbalancing continued under the guise of separation of powers and a clever confusion of appearance and reality. Goldsmith often urges us to notice these developments: once on the throne Augustus "seemed totally divested of suspicion" (2:98); "the people's interests and his ambition seemed to co-operate, and while he governed all, he let them imagine that they were governing themselves" (2:99); "he pretended to preserve to himself a very moderate share of authority" (2:100); there might have been permanent happiness "under such a monarch as Augustus now appeared to be" (2:100); while pretending to resign from office, he had "previously instructed his creatures in the senate how to act" and only showed "seeming generosity" (2:103); and during his long and peaceful reign "the happiness of the people seemed to conspire with his own" (2:110). This collection of warnings regarding apparent virtues is paralleled by examples of real evils, all based upon the danger of making inroads upon the constitution. The brutality of the proscription was dreadful and overt; but such brutality when covert had even graver implications. Goldsmith thus modifies his initial judgment regarding Augustus' political virtue in establishing order—or, he says, with full awareness of the fragility of institutions, "rather permanent servitude; for, when once the sovereignty is usurped in a free state, every transaction on which unlimited authority can be founded is called a regulation" (2:98-99).[11] Although Au-

[11] Goldsmith borrows this either from Montesquieu's *Considérations sur les causes de la grandeur des romains et de leur décadence* (1734), or the Chevalier de Jaucourt's adaptation of Montesquieu in his article

gustus preserved the old names, he destroyed the old functions: "he caused himself to be styled emperor, . . . he made himself to be created tribune, . . . and prince of the senate" (2:99). In the process of "uniting in his own person so many different powers" (2:99) he *seemed* to preserve all interests as equal under his benign protection, and the "misguided people" began to believe that they lacked only the liberty to disrupt the state. Goldsmith rejects the principate by invoking the lesson of precedent: The Romans "were taught to change their sentiments [regarding Augustan order and freedom] under his successors, when they found themselves afflicted with all the punishments that tyranny could inflict or sedition make necessary" (2:100). The senate and people, whose "Roman spirit was entirely eradicated" (2:119) under Augustus, soon become incapable of decent public or private lives. The senators lost their authority, integrity, and honor and wished only to flatter the emperor and torment his presumed enemies. The people were even more corrupt and exchanged their freedom for the emperor's dole. "Too effeminate and cowardly to go to war, they only railed against their governors; so that they were bad

___

on the Roman Empire in the *Encyclopédie* (Neufchâtel, 1765), 14:334. For Montesquieu, see chap. 7, sec. 1, at n. 8 in text, below. Goldsmith's achievements—or lack of them—as a historian still need study. It is not commonly known, or at any rate not commonly appreciated, that in 1769 he succeeded Gibbon as the Royal Academy's Professor of Ancient History. As he told his brother Maurice on or about 21 September, "there is no sallary, anex'd and I took it rather as a compliment to the institution than any benefit to myself" (*The Collected Letters of Oliver Goldsmith*, ed. Katharine Balderston [Cambridge: Cambridge Univ. Press, 1928], p. 84). Johnson praises Goldsmith the historian in Boswell's *Journal of a Tour to the Hebrides* (1785), Wednesday, 25 August 1773, 5:108-9, in *Life of Johnson* (see n. 9, above). See also *Life*, 2:236-37, 3:82 (Johnson's epitaph for Goldsmith), 4:312, and The Yale Edition of the Works of Samuel Johnson, vol. 1, *Samuel Johnson: Diaries, Prayers, and Annals*, ed. E. L. McAdam, Jr., with Donald and Mary Hyde (New Haven: Yale Univ. Press, 1958), p. 171.

soldiers, and seditious citizens" (2:156-57). Thomas Black-well had already argued that the real Augustan poets were not Horace and Virgil, born in earlier times, but the luxurious, licentious Ovid and the punning Manilius.[12] Goldsmith suggests that the real Augustan ruler was Tiberius (2:157), and that his own limited admiration for the achievements of the Augustan tenure should be seen through the larger perspective of the collapse of constitutional government.

Even historians as different as Nathan Hooke and Thomas Blackwell shared a basis for indignation regarding Augustus. Hooke was a childhood friend of Pope's and, upon the appearance of the first volume of his *Roman History* in 1738, an opposition literary ally as well. He dedicates that volume to Pope and proclaims his political bias in this "*Attempt towards a History of* Roman Virtue *and* Patriotism."[13] Since the patriots drew much of their opposition to Walpole from the country squirearchy, Hooke emphasizes Rome's diminution of the role of the "people" in the government and its elevation of the aristocratic and executive

---

[12] *Memoirs of the Court of Augustus*, 3 vols. (Edinburgh, 1753-1763), 3:467-68.

[13] *The Roman History, From the Building of Rome to the Ruin of the Commonwealth*, 4 vols. (London, 1738-1771), 1:sig. A2r. Subsequent citations are given in the text. Hooke's bias toward the people meant a correspondent hostility to aristocracy—in contemporary political terms, the court. In later volumes—1745, 1764, 1771—he engages in running debates with Conyers Middleton's hagiographic *Life of . . . Cicero* (1741), in part because it praises Cicero's oligarchic senate as the glory of Roman freedom and achievement. Middleton, Hooke objects, flattered the court and royal family that controlled his point of view (4:363-64, note e). The antiaristocratic Hooke regards the usurpation of Caesar as providing more true liberty to the people than the senate had allowed (4:208). Many readers were so sensitive to Rome's political relevance for England that such observations were noticed and censured. Owen Ruffhead, for example, largely approves of Hooke's third volume, but reacts harshly to his defense of Julius Caesar and his view that the declining constitution excused Caesar and his successors' hastening of its subversion and establishment of monarchy: great men should have preserved the constitution and the state (*Monthly Review*, 30 [1764]: 111; attribution in Nangle, p. 128).

94

branches.[14] Rome's decline began when Sylla, the leader of the aristocratic party, rose to dictatorial power through murder of the Gracchi, the advocates of agricultural reform on behalf of the people. Thereafter, different senatorial factions warred with one another until these bloody contests ended "in the subjection of *Rome* to an absolute and confirmed Monarchy" (2:560). Excessive power in the hands of the aristocratic senate led to the senate's suppression of the people and then to the monarch's suppression of both. Liberty and equality depend upon an *"Equilibrium* of power" (3:5), which is impossible where most citizens are denied everything except the right to sell their votes. Sylla's tyranny induced subsequent revolutions that finally allowed Octavian to *"Ruin . . . the Commonwealth,"* as Hooke's title puts it. That ruin is directly related not only to Octavian's duplicity, treachery, force, and cruelty, but to his abolition of constitutional restraints. Even his soldiers recognized this and therefore treated him with "contempt and indignation as a lyar and a traitor to his companions" (4:377). Moreover, Augustus ruled "with no other legal title than that odious one of the *Triumvir,* which he had promised to resign" (4:445). Yet worse, his precedent of executive control of all offices "was afterwards conferred upon his successors at once by one single instrument, and despotic monarchy established by a law, called afterwards *lex regia*" (4:447). Octavian was not the beast who killed a thriving beauty; he was merely the natural outcome of almost one

14 By the "people" Hooke no doubt means what Goldsmith's Vicar of Wakefield does in chap. 19. There he tells the Whiggish butler, masquerading as his own master, of "those men who are possest of too large fortunes to submit to the neighbouring man in power, and yet are too poor to set up for tyranny themselves. In this middle order of mankind are generally to be found all the art, wisdom, and virtues of society. This order alone is known to be the true preservers of freedom, and may be called the People" (*Collected Works of Oliver Goldsmith,* ed. Arthur Friedman, 5 vols. [Oxford: Clarendon Press, 1966], 4:101-2). The vicar, of course, is a country curate and a "husbandman," one of "the three greatest characters upon earth" (Advertisement, 4:14).

hundred years of disruption of the people's rights, grasping for power by the aristocracy and ultimate monarchic despotism as the constitution was overthrown. When Augustus' armies illegally made him consul, "from this moment neither Senate nor people ever recovered so much as the appearance of liberty" (4:352, note u).

If anti-Augustanism were peculiar to the "Tory opposition," we should expect a court historian to favor Augustus; yet Conyers Middleton does not; nor does Thomas Blackwell (the younger), whom on 7 October 1748 George II appointed Principal of the Marischal College in the University of Aberdeen. Ingratitude was not among his faults, and in his *Memoirs of the Court of Augustus* he praises his Hanoverian king, blames the opposition and its satellite poets, and portrays a flourishing British world very different from that of the *Dunciad*, a poem written by a member of a dangerous "squint-ey'd faction."[15]

Blackwell's affection for the patriots' favorite enemies was no barrier to his book's popularity or reception as a libertarian document: its first two volumes were reissued in 1760 and 1764, and had already been translated into French in 1754 and 1759; the three-volume set was translated in 1768 and 1781 and may have contributed to anti-Augustanism in France. Samuel Johnson objected to Blackwell's "furious and unnecessary zeal for liberty," but the *Monthly* more positively noted its "warm regard to liberty and the British constitution."[16] Blackwell was politically pure

---

[15] *Memoirs*, 1:151. Subsequent quotations are cited in the text. He also calls the opposition "a factious Opposition" led by a "pretended Patriot" (1:153), and he later claims that Pope, unlike Lucilius, only "*effected*" the character of being "*To* VIRTUE *only*, and its Friends, a Friend" (3:51).

[16] Johnson reviewed the second volume of Blackwell's work in *The Literary Magazine*, 1 (1756): 41-42, 239-40. See also *The Works of Samuel Johnson*, 9 vols. (Oxford, 1825), 6:9-16 (p. 12 for the remark quoted). Johnson sees little need for Blackwell's frequent warnings regarding danger to British freedom. William Rose (Nangle, p. 64) reviewed vol. 1 of Blackwell in the Whiggish *Monthly*, 8 (1753): 420-38 (p.

enough to be on radical young Shelley's reading list in 1814 and 1816.[17] The reasons for this largely favorable reception are clear enough: Blackwell supports several of the commonplaces dominant in eighteenth-century theories of limited monarchy,[18] and he often does so through the contrasting example of Augustus. Blackwell's work is in fact distinguished by its scrupulous attempt to be fair to Augustus' achievements and change in personality once his supremacy had been assured. As a result, we are aware that it is the devil who is being given his due.

For our present purposes, however, we need not discuss Blackwell's Augustus as traitor, murderer, coward, or manipulator, nor as post-Actium Jekyll to his earlier Hyde (even though "all the Policy and Cunning of thy after-Days cannot wash out the Stains of thy *early Perfidy*" [1:359]). We do need to reiterate Blackwell's concern for "the British constitution." His portrait of Augustus' achievements thus is

---

420 for the quotation) and vol. 2 in 14 (1756): 223-37. Rose disapproves of Blackwell's prose style, but likes him as a "zealous advocate for liberty" (14:232). The "Tory" *Critical Review*, 1 (1756): 66-67, also grumbles about grammatical, philological, and stylistic infelicities in the second volume; it does not deal with content, perhaps because it agrees with Blackwell's conventional enthusiasm, though it certainly would prefer more power, or respect, for the monarch. The *Critical* thus is more appreciative of Hooke's *Roman History* and his other historical-political tracts: see 5 (1758): 469, and 6 (1758): 80. Johnson makes useful distinctions between the two journals in the *Life*, 2:40 and 3:32. For another appreciative comment on the *Memoirs*, see Robert Jephson, *Roman Portraits* (London, 1794), p. 257. Johnson's harsh review was also read for many years. In 1806, for example, Henry Stewart praises its "spirit of sound criticism" (*The Works of Sallust*, 2 vols. [London, 1806], 1:xxviii-xxix). For discussion of the translation, by A. R. J. Feutry, see Jacqueline de la Harpe, *Le Journal des Savants et L'Angleterre 1702-1789*, Univ. of California Publications in Modern Philology, vol. 20 (Berkeley and Los Angeles: Univ. of California Press, 1941), p. 422.

17 *Mary Shelley's Journals*, ed. Frederick L. Jones (Norman: Univ. of Oklahoma Press, 1947), pp. 30, 73.

18 See Caroline Robbins, *The Eighteenth-Century Commonwealthman* (Cambridge, Mass.: Harvard Univ. Press, 1959), p. 212.

hedged by suggestions of the transcience of good times under arbitrary power, and is used as a contrast to British hereditary, constitutional monarchy:

> If any Thing can palliate, for certainly nothing can justify, the Woes which *Augustus* made his Country suffer, it may, perhaps, be the mixt Form of Government which he introduced; a Form useful to the Prince, and, at least, not less so to the Nation, which thereby enjoyed, whilst he reigned, the Advantages of Freedom, joined to tranquility, and good Order; for the *Romans*, equally secured against the tumultuous Licentiousness of a Democracy, and the Oppression of a tyrannical Power, had a proper Degree of Liberty under a Monarch to whom they were not Slaves, and tasted the Sweets of a popular Government, without the deadly Consequences of internal Feuds. (3:555)[19]

As enlightened despots go, Augustus "may boldly be proposed as a Model and Example to all the Princes in the World" (3:406). But the *if, palliate, nothing can justify, woes, suffer, may,* and *perhaps* remind us that he was a despot, and the phrase *whilst he reigned* recalls Britain's constitutional balance and virtuous hereditary kingship. There can be no question of the preservation of her mixed government headed by the meritorious King George II, a supreme magistrate who governs his free people according to law (1:146). On the other hand, Augustus ruled by show of law over an apparently free people, and had temporarily enhanced, but permanently destroyed, the grandeur of his na-

---

[19] Blackwell borrows this paragraph from the largely pro-Augustan J. B. L. Crevier, *Histoire des empereurs romains depuis Auguste jusqu'à Constantin*, 12 vols. (1749-1755). The work was translated by John Mills, 10 vols. (1755), and 10 vols. (1814); see (1814) 1:347, for the relevant section. Since Mills completed this volume on Blackwell's behalf (d. 1757), that source is not surprising. Much of the final volume in fact takes a friendlier attitude toward Augustus than the first two volumes suggest. For a hostile comment on Crevier's politics, see chap. 7, n. 3, below.

tion. Augustus emerges as tainted, though praised. He may have anticipated the British system, but is a model of what not to do to preserve it.

The relationship between British king and British citizen is one of respect, because each knows that he is governed and controlled by a constitution larger than either, and that the king's greatest glories are his adherence to law and the freedom of his people.[20] Blackwell's limited monarchy is a closely woven fabric that had been loomed since the Magna Charta. There is a clear contrast with his portrait of the relationship between Augustan princeps and Augustan slave:

> That *Cesar* endeavoured to make the Republic flourish, after . . . [Actium], is undoubtedly true; and now that he was become the Master of *Romans*, he had the same Affection for them, as a *West India* Planter has for his Negroes, whom he wishes to thrive, to behave orderly, and procreate, that they may increase his Property. But it was as much beyond his Power to restore it to its former State, as to put the Head upon the bloody Corse of any of the great Men he had formerly murdered. The sole Measure that could have been any Species of Atonement, 'To restore LIBERTY to *Rome*,' when pressed to it by the nobleminded *Agrippa*, he utterly rejected. . . . But all his boasted Marble Structures put together were not worth the Life of one brave Inhabitant of the old brick Buildings, of whom he had massacred Thousands; and far less of the exalted Spirit that animated them, which his Cruelty first helped to break, and his cunning finally extinguished. (3:376-77)

Blackwell later portrays felicities under Augustus' reign and is not perfectly consistent with this outburst. Unlike Gibbon and others, he does not fully act on the implications of Augustus' usurpation or on the hollowness of artistic

[20] See also Goldsmith's *Citizen of the World*, Letters L and LXXX (1760): the remark was a commonplace.

achievement if it comes at the cost of honesty to one's self for the moment, to the history of one's nation, and to stability and art for the future. Blackwell does, however, show Augustus as a ruler who provided his country and the world with an early, if inadequate, form of mixed government; he also shows the readers what may happen in a nation that, paradoxically and foolishly, depends on absolutism to preserve constitutional limitation: the people become the slavish property of their owner.

Goldsmith, the historian biased toward monarchy in the balanced state; Hooke, the opponent of George II; Blackwell, the protégé of George II—all discuss Augustus' violation of the constitution and all regard him as either the father or settler of tyranny and the fall of Rome. There were, of course, several other British (and Continental) historians of Rome during the eighteenth century, but the prevailing attitude of most of them toward Augustus is summed up in the first three chapters of Gibbon's great work.[21] Here, more

[21] The historians of Rome fall into three large and sometimes overlapping classes as regards Augustus: those who favor his rule and overlook or excuse his faults in the cause of a royalist's monarchy; those who are ambivalent, recognize and respect Augustus' achievements, but also recognize his personal defects and destruction of the constitutional balance necessary for freedom; and, those who have less, little, or no ambivalence and see his reign as generally bad for Rome and the world she governed. The first class includes de Bröe, Echard, Hearne, Crevier, and the several others cited in chap. 2, sec. 1, above. The second includes Peter Heylin, *Augustus. Or an Essay of those Meanes and Counsels whereby the Commonwealth of Rome was altered and Reduced into a Monarchy* (1632); Joseph Wilcocks, *Roman Conversations* (1763); Goldsmith; [?] Frederick, *Roman History* (1774); and Adam Ferguson, *History of the Progress and Termination of the Roman Republic* (1783). The last includes Gordon, Hooke, Blackwell, Gibbon, [Charles Hereford] *History of Rome* (1792), and several others mentioned throughout this study, including many of the philosophes. Although incomplete, the list does suggest that the further one moves from seventeenth-century royalism, the further one moves from positive Augustanism. Even Crevier was conservative, and perhaps outmoded and archaic, when his first volume appeared in 1749. David P. Jordan is correct when he reminds us that "Gibbon himself did not increase our knowledge of

than in any other Roman history of the period, we see a clearly laid out indictment of the violation of constitutional checks and balances, a topic so important that Fielding interpolates his gypsy episode in *Tom Jones* (1749: bk. vii, chap. 12) as a comment upon the '45 and the threat of absolutism, and Henry Brooke, the "patriot" author of *Gustavus Vasa* (1739), includes a long, tiresome, constitutional lecture in *The Fool of Quality* (1764-1770: chap. 17).

Gibbon begins the *Decline and Fall* by painting a salutary picture of Rome during the Age of the Antonines (A.D. 98-180), when the empire was at its fairest, most civilized, and unified; but he also introduces strands that will later become part of the solid fabric of the republic which serves as a foil to the tatters of the empire. For example, it was only the "image of a free constitution" that "was preserved with decent reverence," and the Roman senate only "appeared to possess the sovereign [executive] authority" already "devolved on the emperors."[22] Moreover, he makes clear that the empire's expanse was a function not of imperial but of republican virtue, and carefully distinguishes the three parts of the tensely unified state that were responsible for Rome's "rapid succession of triumphs" during her first seven centuries. New dominions "had been acquired by the policy of the senate, the active emulation of the consuls, and the martial enthusiasm of the people" (p. 1). In spite of the surface felicity described in the first two chapters, Rome's "long peace, and . . . uniform government . . . introduced a slow and secret poison into the vitals of the empire" (p. 56). Gibbon adapts the opening of Tacitus' *Annals* and *Histories* and says that under the absolute monarchs "the minds of men were gradually reduced to the same level, the fire of

Roman history, but he synthesized all that European civilization knew of her ancient past" (*Gibbon and His Roman Empire* [Urbana: Univ. of Illinois Press, 1971], p. xiii). I suggest that Gibbon also synthesized political attitudes toward Augustan absolutism.

[22] *Decline and Fall* (n. 9, above), 1:1. Subsequent citations are given in the text.

genius was extinguished, and even the military spirit evaporated." In arts as in arms and government, authority led to a slackening of the will to excel and "precluded every generous attempt to exercise the powers, or enlarge the limits, of the human mind," as was possible "under a popular government" (p. 58).

Gibbon is preparing us for the discussion of Augustus immediately thereafter. At the end of chapter 2 we move from the description of servitude, to the results of servitude, and then to chapter 3 and the cause of servitude. Chapter 2 ends with a lamentation for the decay of genius due to the decay of republican independence; chapter 3 begins with a definition of monarchy, "in which a single person . . . is entrusted with the execution of the laws, the management of the revenue, and the command of the army." Without the sternest safeguards, "so formidable a magistrate will soon degenerate into despotism" (p. 59)—precisely what happens during the Augustan age. As Gibbon was to say in the opening of chapter 8, "from the reign of Augustus to the time of Alexander Severus, the enemies of Rome were in her bosom—the tyrants, and the soldiers" (p. 195). Chapter 3 thus appropriately begins with a discussion of Octavian's solidification of power, even though it is entitled "Of the Constitution of the Roman Empire, in the Age of the Antonines." The Antonines were benevolent despots, but their reigns were temporary reprieves from real tyranny. Marcus Antoninus recommended Brutus "as a perfect model of Roman virtue" (p. 71, n. 34), but he could not restore the republic that Augustus' depredations upon the constitution had destroyed. This violation of equipoise is at the heart of the ensuing discussion of the princeps.

Augustus has many of the nastier (nonsexual) traits described by Tacitus, Suetonius, and Dio Cassius. He is an untrustworthy, insincere, "crafty tyrant," who perpetrates a "comedy" in appearing to limit his tenure in office, and in preserving the forms of the institutions he destroys (p. 61).

He is a clever hypocrite with "a cool head, an unfeeling heart, and a cowardly disposition." Moreover, the name Octavian was so "stained with the blood of the proscriptions" that he hoped, "had it been possible, to erase all memory of his former life" and thus accepted the title "Augustus," which the senate offered (p. 70).

Gibbon's attack has more than the force of classical authority; it has also the weight of British outrage, first at the executive's usurpation of power and destruction of a limited monarchy, and next at the pernicious precedents that were set in the process. We recall the tripartite distribution that helped make the republic great. After Actium, however, "with its power, the senate had lost its dignity," the people "demanded only bread and public shows" (p. 60), and the consuls had their authority subsumed under that of Augustus, until only the forms of republican government and senatorial dignity remained.

Acquisition of power began with the military and extended to the civil and religious sectors, so that Augustus soon became censor, proconsul, and imperator: by degrees, examiner of morals, governor of the city, general of the army, and then the hitherto unknown title of consul with tribunitian powers, a blending of the offices of highest magistrate in the state and head of the senate, with the authority of the people's representative, who could oppose the senate and veto its legislation. The offices of consul and tribune were previously held for one year; the senate conferred both upon him for life. During the republic each branch was restricted by the others and by its own brief term in office; but, as Gibbon makes clear, such harmonious discord disappeared under the new order: "when the consular and tribunitian powers were united, when they were vested for life in a single person, when the general of the army was, at the same time, the minister of the senate and the representative of the Roman people, it was impossible to resist the exercise, nor was it easy to define the limits, of his imperial prerogative." As supreme pontiff and censor, Augustus also super-vised religion and the "manners and fortunes, of the Roman people" and senate (p. 65).

As all the authority was moving ever inward toward "the *Imperial magistrate*," the spiritual sloth that had become institutionalized by the time of the Antonines already be-comes evident: "the ordinary magistrates of the common-wealth languished in obscurity, without vigour, and almost without business" (p. 66). By playing out the charade of pop-ular elections to the consulship, Augustus humbly sought the people's votes, permitted "all the inconveniences of a wild democracy" and thereafter encouraged the transfer of such elections to the more temperate zone of the senate. Hence in Tiberius' reign "the assemblies of the people were for ever abolished." Even in his own time, however, Augus-tus apparently ruled by means of the degraded and dis-armed senate, which "*seemed*," in Gibbon's italics, to deal with major issues of war and peace, but actually controlled only "the exercise of the judicial power" (pp. 66-67). Au-gustus had a "tender respect . . . for a free constitution which he had destroyed" (p. 70). In its place he created "an absolute monarchy disguised by the forms of a com-monwealth." He and his successors "professed themselves the accountable ministers of the senate, whose supreme de-crees they dictated and obeyed" (p. 68).

As the term *successors* denotes, Gibbon impales Augus-tus for his settlement of autocracy. He not only removed the people's vote, but also established the show of senato-rial ratification of his tenure. Augustus agreed to accept the titles of proconsul and imperator only for ten years, hoping that, long before then, he could retire from a posi-tion so dangerous to the state. To no one's surprise, yet more such terms were necessary and yet more confirma-tions: "The memory of this comedy . . . was preserved to the last ages of the empire by the peculiar pomp with which the perpetual monarchs of Rome always solemnized the tenth years of their reign" (p. 61). The title of consul with tribunitian powers was similarly "continued to all his successors" (p. 64), beginning with Tiberius, on whose behalf he "dictated a law" investing future princes "with an authority equal to his own over the provinces and the armies" (p. 73).

Again and again in reading the Tacitean Gibbon, we are aware of the quiet anger regarding Augustus' effect upon subsequent generations, for whom freedom and a free constitution were "irrecoverably lost" (p. 60). The perfect settlement of the empire meant that "the Romans, after the fall of the republic, combated only for the choice of masters" (p. 118). The combat was due in part to Augustus' inception of the praetorian guards as his personal bodyguard, since he knew that the army itself could be corrupted. "How precarious was his own authority over men whom he had taught to violate every social duty!" (p. 72). Long after Augustus' death (A.D. 14), the senators gained a chance to restore liberty; but it evaporated when, after the murder of Caligula (A.D. 41), they busied themselves in sloganeering and libertarian debate. "While they deliberated, the praetorian guards had resolved," and they installed "the stupid Claudius" as emperor: "The dream of liberty was at an end; and the senate awoke to all the horrors of inevitable servitude" (p. 72). Within 200 years the guards of Augustus were to go from resolvers to vendors of empire, and at a public sale made a very good bargain with Didius Julianus (A.D. 193), who outbid his competitors and was—briefly, before his murder—emperor of the marketplace called Rome.

Gibbon breaks the chronological order of his narrative to indicate that the blame for the praetorians' act rests with Augustus. "That crafty tyrant, sensible that laws might colour, but that arms alone could maintain, his usurped dominion, had gradually formed this powerful body of guards, in constant readiness to protect his person, to awe the senate, and either to prevent or to crush the first motions of rebellion." In order to avoid offense and alarm,

Augustus prudently kept most of his troops in surrounding towns; but Tiberius, more confident of Roman servility, moved them into the city, and "for ever riveted the fetters of his country." Gibbon will not let us forget that the guards "derived their institution from Augustus" (pp. 103-4).

As we near the end of chapter 3 we have a new appreciation of the complexities and price of Roman grandeur, and a new insight into the empire under the Antonines. As Harold L. Bond has pointed out, and as the entire third chapter has made clear, the vision of the reign of the Antonines is tinged with unhappiness.[23] Those noble princes must have been melancholy when they "recollected the instability of a happiness which depended on the character of a single man." Some "licentious youth, or some jealous tyrant, would abuse . . . that absolute power which they had exerted for the benefit of their people." The army "was a blind and irresistible instrument of oppression," and "the corruption of Roman manners would always supply flatterers" to applaud and ministers to serve "the fear or the avarice, the lust or the cruelty, of their masters." Indeed, "these gloomy apprehensions had been already justified by the experience of the Romans." This decadent, autocratic, oppressive, and unstable system was due to the revolution of government by Augustus. "It is almost superfluous to enumerate the unworthy successors of Augustus" (pp. 78-79).

By now it is almost superfluous for Gibbon to reiterate that Augustus himself was unworthy; but he does so, nonetheless, and in a context that reminds us of the vanity of human wishes and the ironic end of even the greatest

[23] *The Literary Art of Edward Gibbon* (Oxford: Clarendon Press, 1960), pp. 26-27. For other useful discussions of Gibbon, see the several essays in *Daedalus*, 105 (1976). This volume concerns "Edward Gibbon and the Decline and Fall of the Roman Empire." See also J. G. A. Pocock, "Gibbon's *Decline and Fall* and the World View of the Late Enlightenment," *ECS*, 10 (1977): 287-303.

achievements. The Romans were rendered miserable by their leaders for two reasons: aside from death, the universal power of the empire made escape impossible. But, more important, "the exquisite sensibility of the sufferers" made them feel their shame intensely (p. 79). In spite of complicity in their own fall, the Romans "preserved the sentiments, or at least the ideas, of their freeborn ancestors. The education of . . . Tacitus and Pliny, was the same as that of Cato and Cicero. From Grecian philosophy they had imbibed the justest and most liberal notions of the dignity of human nature, and the origin of civil society." Gibbon then reaffirms his belief (long anticipated by Walpole's client Thomas Gordon) that the Romans had no love for their first imperial masters. "The history of their own country had taught them to revere a free, a virtuous, and a victorious commonwealth; to abhor the successful crimes of Caesar and Augustus; and inwardly to despise those tyrants whom they adored with the most abject flattery" (p. 80).[24] It is reasonable to assume, as Gibbon might have seen it, that every compliment to the achievements of the divine Augustus was an inverted curse on that tyrant who gained authority first by his own vile nature and the army he controlled, and then by the gradual destruction of the balanced constitution that once made Rome great.[25]

[24] For a corroboration of Gibbon's view, toward a different end, see the discussion of Pierre-Charles Levesque's history of the Roman Republic, chap. 7, sec. 1 and notes 15-17, below. Gordon makes a relevant remark in *The Works of Tacitus*, 1:94. Julius and Octavian were loaded with "all sorts and every excess of Honours, while they who conferred them abhorred" those lies and their recipients, whom they hoped to destroy. Gibbon long believed in the Romans' physiological subjection and psychological republicanism. See his "Inquiry whether a Catalogue of the Armies sent into the Field is an essential part of an Epic Poem" (1763), in *The Miscellaneous Works of Edward Gibbon, Esq.* ed. John Lord Sheffield, 5 vols. (London, 1814), 4:328-29.

[25] In manuscript notes for revision of the *Decline and Fall* Gibbon lamented that he had not made plainer the implications of Augustus' changes: "Should I not have deduced the decline of the Empire from the tyranny which succeeded the reign of Augustus? Alas! I should"

Gibbon probably would have agreed that the only appropriate "Augustan age" for his nation would have been the interregnum of Oliver Cromwell, for he too violated the constitution and brought all power into his own hands. Eighteenth-century Britain was not likely to wish a return to such Augustanism.

There can be little doubt regarding the bipartisan breadth of the hostility to Augustus throughout the eighteenth century, for nearly all persuasions shared a love for the sort of constitution he destroyed. Examination of representative newspapers for the administration and opposition from about 1726 to 1742 suggests both its bipartisan depth and its utility in daily political life. The political press of those years serves as a convenient positive force for much abundant negative anti-Augustanism, and helps to mold his unattractive traits into powerful verbal armaments. These common weapons came from a common factory and were delivered through a common medium. It was a battle the present generation was likely to be moved by, and one future generations were not likely to forget.

II: Practical Implications—The Shared View of Augustus in the Political Press

We might expect the administration to set itself at the far end of the opposition's schemes and beliefs. If, for example, the *Craftsman* praised Queen Elizabeth, the *London Journal* would admit that she was a great monarch but arbitrary, independent of her parliament, and vastly improved upon by the present ministry and reign. If the *Craftsman* urged that the Spaniards be smitten hip and thigh,

---

(1:xxxv, note). That "Alas!" seems unnecessary, however. For a useful study of these notes, see Patricia B. Craddock, "Gibbon's Revision of the *Decline and Fall*," *Studies in Bibliography*, 21 (1968): 191-204, especially 197, 200. Craddock reprints those notes in her edition of *The English Essays of Edward Gibbon* (Oxford: Clarendon Press, 1972), pp. 338-52.

the *Gazetteer* would insist upon the values of Christian peace and charity, tranquil trade, and the paths of international diplomacy. If the opposition demanded vigorous particular satire that named scoundrels for what they were, the government would advocate nonlibelous general satire that rewarded virtue rather than illicitly punished presumed vice. But this pattern is broken regarding Augustus, for the administration was irrevocably committed to parliamentary limitations upon the crown. Walpole's journals thus consistently berate real or would-be absolute rulers, whether the Gracchi, Marius, Julius Caesar, Cromwell, or modern Jacobites. For all Julius' manifold virtues, he destroyed the tottering but still balanced constitution of Rome. His grand-nephew, namesake, and successor carried on and perfected Julian policies, especially the channeling of power into the grasp of the princeps. Some defense of Augustus is present in the *London Journal* and the *Gazetteer*'s support for the administration's battles against the (alternately or inclusively) Papist, Jacobite, Tory Bolingbroke and associates; but to paint Augustus in glowing colors would be to support the arbitrary royalism they opposed in the Stuarts and thus would undermine their own ideological and practical planks.

It should be no surprise that the opposition is fiercer in its attacks on Augustus, for it has the handy nomenclatural accident of a George Augustus to belabor and does so with pleasure and gusto. Like the historians, the journalists sometimes are ambivalent regarding Augustan history, even in the opposition press. The *Craftsman*, no. 182, 27 December 1729, for example, praises Augustus' wisdom in not prosecuting Horace for covert criticism in the Damasippus (*Satires*, ii. 3). That *"wise Prince"* only grew tyrannical "towards the latter End" of his reign. On the whole, however, it is that latter end, together with Octavian's bloody rise to power, that most exercised the *Craftsman*. In no. 219, 12 September 1730, Octavian encouraged destructive faction, and Augustus instituted "such a Succession of Monsters . . . as God never sent in his Wrath to execute Vengeance on any other Nation." The following number, on 19 September, berates Augustus for later bad emperors and for "the Violence, the Treachery, and the bloody Massacres, on which‍ this *absolute Monarchy* was founded." In no. 437, 16 November 1734, the *Craftsman* argues that "the *Tribunitial Power*," originally designed to preserve the Romans' liberty, "confirmed their *Slavery*" when illegally placed "in the Hands of *Augustus*."

The themes of Augustus as violent usurper, greedy acquirer of power, and creator of subsequent tyranny, are unified in the *Craftsman*'s outrage regarding possible censorship of the press. Augustus provides all too obvious a paradigm for the similarly inclined court party of Walpole and George II.

Drawing upon Tacitus, the *Craftsman*, no. 4, 16 December 1726, explains how Augustus "was the first Person in *Rome*" who interpreted the *lex laesae majestatis* to allow punishment of words as well as deeds. This action was both bad in its own right and supplied the precedent for Tiberius "to prosecute the most *innocent Books*, and destroy entirely" Rome's freedom. Consequently, all the arts declined, and the *Craftsman* quotes Seneca's familiar lines from the *Controversiae* claiming that all genius died after Cicero's death due to *"such Methods of punishing* ingenious Men." Neither liberty nor letters can flourish under rules in which words are considered high treason. *"Scribere est agere* will always be esteem'd, by Men of Sense and Probity, as a most unjust, arbitrary and tyrannical Interpretation."

Augustus does not get off with these few censures. As one further example, in no. 21, 17 February 1727, the *Craftsman* also turns to Tacitus and also portrays the princeps as a Walpolean figure lusting for authority: "He grew *insolent* by Degrees, and at length *engrosssed* the whole Power of the Empire in his own Hands."

The *Craftsman*'s reasoned anti-Augustanism pales next to *Fog's Weekly Journal* for 16 July 1737, an issue so savage that, according to a contemporary hand in the British Library's Burney Collection copy, "For This Impudent paper with its audacious parallel the Printer was, Deservedly taken into Custody." This virtual call to revolution was couched under sometimes confused historical parallels and the dream or voyage convention that promises "truth." Augustus, first seen kicking a football, is soon invited by the traveler to practice on more-tempting matter, and gladly kicks the flattering courtiers out of his apartment. Shortly thereafter, the traveler and his companion discuss the failings of Augustus and his wife "Julia" (also properly called Livia at times), who is the bawd for her cruel, cowardly, and adulterous husband. The companion finds Augustus' vices inexcusable, but praises Julia-Livia's wisdom in pimping for him and thus helping to preserve Rome. "By this Method she kept him at Home, and prevented his leaving the Management of the Publick Affairs, to some *Blood-Sucker* of a *Minister*, while he went in Search of Foreign *Bona Robas*, squander'd the *Roman* Treasures, and oppress'd the *Roman* People with innumerable Taxes, to support not only his own Vices, but those of his Minions and Favourites, and to satisfy the Avarice and Ambition of his Minister, as did his Successor, *Tiberius*." The companion recognizes that the traveler, in his envy of Livia, may attribute her generosity with other women's charms to self-interest and policy. In fact, she was aware "that *Augustus* was an Usurper upon the Rights of the Commonwealth, and that she might apprehend, had others minister'd to his Pleasures, and he had to avoid shocking her Sight, withdrawn from *Rome*, the *Romans* might have taken the Opportunity of his Absence, to shake off the Yoak, notwithstanding the Authority of a dissolute, corrupted, adulating Senate, which she must know, was contemptible in the Eyes of all *brave, generous, and Publick Spirited Romans*." The traveler and companion take slightly different paths to the same anti-Augustan goal.

Old England, a post-Walpole opposition journal, is a few years beyond the heat of battle and is less militant, though still vigorous, in its attacks. Walpole remains a target but Augustus really is an enduring emblem of absolutism. Issue no. 60, 24 March 1744, is kind to Augustus. On the whole, no reign was so successful and no monarch "better beloved by his Subjects, notwithstanding all the Exceptions to his Title." The handsome praise thus concludes with a reminder of Augustan blemishes. Perhaps the writer recollects that no. 53, 4 February 1744, had discussed Augustus' creation of a Roman civil list, by which he hoped to give "a kind of Atonement to his Country, for depriving her of her Liberty: But in the Event, it prov'd the Cause of all the miseries and Calamities she afterwards suffer'd." As with so many things Augustan, the plan destroyed governmental balance, for it put large sums of money into the hands of corrupt rulers who followed: the senate and emperor kept the people "within an inextricable Circle of Slavery." On 18 August 1744, the same journal (no. 81) is even more critical of Augustus and the pernicious succession for which he was responsible. Philo-Camoens believes that the vain, cowardly, cruel Augustus deliberately selected Tiberius so that he himself would look better by comparison. He leaves the reader to determine whether a highly placed man recently removed from office had consulted this tale to gain comparable glory.

Such onslaughts could not be ignored or they would seem to offer genuine parallels to the reign of George Augustus and thereby give away more than the administration felt prudent. Walpole's friends often insisted that the opposition's parables, allegories, oracular encounters, and, especially, "parallel History" were spurious, dishonest, inaccurate, ignorant, malicious, obscene, libelous, and a variety of other epithets of similar force and purpose, all subsumed under the general head of "*compleat Villainy* and consummate Malice against the Government" (*London Journal*, 29 June 1734).[26] Like the opposition press, the government's *London Journal* and *Daily Gazetteer* gave Augustus credit for his virtues, and like political organs and writers of other times, were sufficiently fluid in their principles to praise yesterday's scoundrel as today's wise prince. On the whole, however, when they defended Augustus, they did so within carefully defined limits and after having been goaded, as two significant dialogues between the *Craftsman* and the *London Journal* make clear.

On 14 September 1728 the *London Journal* criticizes the *Craftsman* and opposition libel in general. In the process, it says that "*Augustus Caesar*, as *Tacitus* tells us, made all kinds of Libels High Treason; not only such as were written against the State or the Imperial Family, but such as concerned the meanest citizen." The *Craftsman* reacts like a greyhound to a hare, quotes the offending passage in its own no. 117, and argues that Tacitus told this tale "with Indignation, as the worst Action of that Prince's whole Reign, and the Forerunner of all that horrid Tyranny, which followed in the next." The *Journal* replies on 19 October, insisting that Tacitus was not indignant and that Horace (*Epistles*, i. 7) shows that such laws were long in effect and not peculiar to Augustus. The *Craftsman*, not to be outdone in virtuous outrage, uses the Postscript to

[26] Ridicule was one of the administration's weapons against such malice. On 6 February 1731 the *London Journal* printed John Lord Hervey's "*Journalists* Display'd. A New Ballad. To the old Tune of Lullibullero," in which opposition rhetoric is reduced to mindless formulaics like "*Ribbledum, Scribbledum, Fribbledum, Flash*," and "*Satyrum, Traytorum, Treasondum, Trash*." (Robert Halsband questions the attribution. See his *Lord Hervey: Eighteenth-Century Courtier* [Oxford: Clarendon Press, 1973], p. 119.) The *Gazetteer* for 26 August 1738 is more subtle in its attack on Pope and the *Essay on Man*:

> . . . by consequence, within the Plan,
> There must be somewhere, such a thing as Man:
> 'Tis full as plain a Consequence, *I hope*,
> There must be somewhere, such a Man as *P—pe*.

its no. 122 to insist that Tacitus shows "the strongest Marks of his Indignation," that Augustus committed a "tyrannical Act . . . in perverting the *Law of Majesty*," and that the section from Horace actually defends the sort of personal satire the administration abhorred.

Since Tacitus had already been enrolled on the side of "liberty" as opposed to "tyranny," and Thomas Gordon, the administration's Tacitean translator and commentator, was an enthusiast for such a view, the *Journal* probably lost this skirmish. But it intended to keep up the war with some of the same veteran troops and weapons, and in the process blundered and forced itself to retreat. On 4 July 1730 the *Journal* offered a familiar attack upon the *Craftsman* for encouraging the sort of faction that tortured Rome and encouraged the people (the "rabble") to usurp the power of the magistrate. Chaos ensued: "Even Anarchy was almost as Good; and a Man of Sense who would make the most of Life, had much rather have liv'd under the Pacific Reign of Augustus, tho' cloath'd with all Power, then under *a Mob Government*, always quarrelling at Home, or fighting *Abroad*."

Bolingbroke could scarcely have found a better opening if one of his own operatives had written those lines. In the *Craftsman*, no. 220, 19 September 1730, Humphry Oldcastle twists the *Journal*'s words to suit his needs:

> Mr. *Osborne* . . . hath been pleas'd to let us know that He prefers the *absolute Monarchy of Augustus* to the *free State of the Roman Commonwealth*. He prefers likewise, I suppose, (at least his Discourse leads one to think so), the violence, the Treachery, and the bloody Massacres, on which this *absolute Monarchy* was founded, to the civil Disorders, which were occasioned by establishing and maintaining an *equal Commonwealth*. I should desire him to compare the Reigns of a *Caligula*, a *Nero*, a *Domitian*, an *Heliogabalus* (which had never happen'd) with the glorious *fourth* and *fifth Centuries* of

the Republic of *Rome*: .... I hope you, Mr. *D'Anvers*, will . . . make Him ashamed of having prophaned the Language of a *free People* in so prostitute a Manner, and to such slavish Purposes! Advise Him to learn better Notions of Government from Mr. *Gordon's* excellent Discourses, prefix'd to his Translation of *Tacitus*; in which He will find his Favourite *Augustus* set in a true Light, and prov'd to be an infamous Tyrant, though somewhat more artful than his *Successors*.

Osborne must have found it especially galling to be chided with the wisdom of a work dedicated to Robert Walpole; and especially galling to have his paper wrenched into a meaning that only the most antiquated royalist could have supported. In his response on 18 July, he thus outlines the miserable result of the factions—of course comparable to those of the opposition today—of the falsely glorious commonwealth, argues that it was held together only by expansionist wars that ravaged innocent nations, and that disruption and splintering ensued once those wars, jealousies, and fears were brought to the heart of Rome and her institutions. It was that and only that, he argues, that made him praise the years of peace after Augustus was settled and "made the best use of Power of any Man that ever lived." Osborne angrily denies that admiration of the later Augustan peace implies praise of his earlier usurpation, and by implication damns such usurpation as soundly as had Oldcastle himself.

That is, because OSBORNE *likes the Good* which AUGUSTUS did after he was fixed in Power, therefore *he likes all the Evils* which he did to obtain that Power; and because *he hates the lesser Evils* which happen'd under a factious and seditious Commonwealth, therefore *he approves the greater Evils of Rapine and bloody Massacres*, under the Tyranny of a few Men who contended for the Government of the World; and because he look'd upon

AUGUSTUS's Reign to be the best of all absolute Monarchies, therefore he *likes all the Causes* of that absolute Monarchy, and *all the Consequences of it too,* even a NERO and CALIGULA. Miraculously argued!

Osborne's anger has partially blunted his wit. He is forced to grant that the Octavian forerunner and Caesarean successors were brutal, and that Augustus himself was absolute, however good a monarch—that is, much of the core of opposition (and administration) attack. He can defend Augustus only on the basis of his good reign for the relatively few years of power—again, an argument that the opposition could in part accept and then build upon, as Oldcastle did, to insist that no such narrow view can be held by an honest, far-sighted man. Such dubious defenses of Augustus could not last long and generally disappear (there are exceptions) when the *Daily Gazetteer* takes over much of the administration polemic in 1735. Indeed, on 9 September 1735 the *Gazetteer* utterly rejects the *Journal's* argument on the temporary fruit of benevolent despotism.

Charles I may have desired the happiness of his people—in his own way, "in the Way of Servitude, in the Manner of Slaves." The *Gazetteer* illustrates such slavery with the example of Augustus, for "No Man ever disputed" that he too sought the welfare of his country, and did so "successfully; yet *Augustus* was a Tyrant, and it would have been happier in the End, if he had held a contrary Conduct; since the Spirit of Liberty not being quite Extinct, would then, in all Probability, have been rouzed to a Re-establishment of its ancient *Palladium,* and the Slavery of the World had been prevented." By 1735, in short, Walpole's administration argues that Augustus is responsible for subsequent slavery and should not be praised for his temporary achievements.

Given the essential dogma of Whig policy, this reasoned rejection of the earlier tenuous stance is predictable. "To oppose arbitrary Power, and to resist Oppressors, is what all the Friends to Revolution Principles have always contended for, and will always think right," the *Gazetteer* argues on 29 February 1740. Hence, though Augustus is often praised for pleasant personal and family traits, intelligent patronage and political organization, he normally (but not always) is characterized as an absolutist who, of course, only an opposition Tory and Jacobite could admire. Julius Caesar originated tyranny in Rome, but it was "completed and continued under the succeeding Emperours" who enervated the minds and corrupted "the Manners of the *Roman* Senate and People" (27 December 1737). To do so, those emperors overturned the balanced constitution that the "Revolution Principles" had established. On 12 May 1738, "R. Courteville" argues that "no sooner was *Augustus* free from Competitors, than he assumed the tribunitian Power, which thence forwards belonged to the Emperours. Thus a Power created for the Preservation of Liberty, became an Engine of Oppression; and the Protector of the People against the Nobles, became the Master of both." In an exchange with the *Craftsman* for 7 April 1739, the *Gazetteer* again invokes the exploded Augustan constitution as a synonym for oppression. The opposition need not fret about a fancied parallel between Tiberius' enslaved Rome and modern Britain. "There is not, there cannot be any Parallel drawn between the People of *Britain* and of *Rome* after the Establishment of *Augustus*; because that very Establishment destroyed the Constitution."

Aside from the individual compliments to Augustus between 1735 and 1742, there is only one significant number of the *Gazetteer* in praise of that ruler. That is by "R. Freeman" and appears on 26 August 1741, when Walpole's resignation was simply a matter of time. In this issue the question is not whether Augustus and Maecenas are bad or good, but how the administration writers can most graciously pay homage to the first minister and king who subsidized them for so long. This *Gazetteer* is a nostalgic cry, a thank-you card and tribute to the endurance of the myth of Augustan and Maecenean virtue. Walpole emerges as the personally unambitious patron, pure of heart, in service to his nation and his prince. Indeed, both men are "generally commended and universally admired."

The handsome tribute to Walpole and his king does not seriously diminish the essential findings of this and the preceding chapter. The appeal of Augustus as an emblem of stable government and noble achievements in arts and arms is gravely, perhaps fatally, undercut and often rejected. Artists, scholars, poets, ordinary citizens throughout the century, and men actively involved on either side of the quarrels of the Walpole years shared the belief that Octavian was a coward and was ungenerous, bloody, perhaps sexually aberrant, and certainly a usurper. They also believed that as Augustus turned the commonwealth into his private satrapy he soon enervated arts and arms, established slavery by ruining the balanced constitution, and made the Tiberian succession inevitable and the Romans inevitably servile. There was praise of Augustus, though less and less as royalism waned; but there was much condemnation based on the most serious of moral and political issues.

It seems reasonable to hypothesize that such widespread discussion would have practical implications for literary history and literary texts, as well as for the views of historians and the needs of practicing politicians. If, after all, the Augustan is not the Good Thing (or even "neutral" shorthand) many modern students have supposed it, perhaps those Roman authors and genres associated with it in the eighteenth century are not so good either. To offer an extreme, but I hope illuminating, analogue, let us suppose—*incredulus odi*—that Hitler had won; that in order to buttress his nightmarish regime he found several great living poets of a previous generation who had not fled to saner climes; that one wrote a stunning epic on Hitler's triumphs at Moscow, Paris, London, and New York, the purpose of which was reconciling modern Germany to the legitimacy of the new Adolphan age; that another poet, of alternating sexual preference, wrote satires, which included one telling Hitler's cronies not to take up with another man's wife when there were willing *zimmermädchen* and boys for their pleasure; and that when Hitler asked this poet to write and publish an epistle to him, lest posterity think him ashamed of being known as his friend, this satirist complied with a virtuoso performance urging Hitler to select only the best poets to sing his praises and to patronize those poets willing to serve the state and Hitler's "image." Let us also suppose that in the course of events Hitler's successors began to lose control of the Third Reich and a new satirist arose, one who attacked the present age and its rulers with indignation, and who suggested—at the possible cost of his life—that the man who created this Reich in the first place was the despicable beast to whom the present generation should look with hatred. Let us finally suppose that some 1700 years later a society has evolved in which words like *liberty, freedom, limitation of power, constitutional checks,* and *mixed government* are not only in constant use but, in spite of disagreements regarding their specific applications, are also deeply felt and believed as essential to the nation's history, identity, and civilizing role in an expanding world. Granting a certain degree of compartmentalization, variations of taste, and recognition of technical greatness, which poet, shall we assume, would be more congenial, more "relevant," more respected, and more representative of that free nation's genius?

It is at least conceivable that so far-fetched an analogue might cast some light upon Augustus Caesar, Virgil, Horace, and Juvenal in the eighteenth century, and perhaps upon one of Pope's greatest works.

CHAPTER 4

"Let Horace blush, and Virgil too":
The Degradation of the Augustan Poets

> HEROES, and KINGS! your distance keep:
> In peace let one poor Poet Sleep,
> Who never flatter'd Folks like you:
> Let Horace blush, and Virgil too.

THUS ALEXANDER POPE PROUDLY WRITES IN HIS EPITAPH, AS an act of dissociation from the Horatian and Virgilian fawners.[1] That view of the blushing court-poets was a long time in building, and was familiar when Pope used it for possible marmoreal purposes. It was, in fact, a simple inversion of the positive royalist association of court and letters of (roughly) the seventeenth century. Virtually all commentaries on those poets stress their support of Augustus' reign. As Thomas Hearne says of Virgil, "under the Name of *Aeneas* he made the Noblest, the most Exquisite and most Compleat Panegyrick upon *Augustus* that ever was made in any Age of the World; and is generally believed to have much promoted that Veneration the Senate and People had for him."[2] This concept was accepted with hardly a grumble, and so in 1800 Edmond Malone, commenting on Dryden's "Discourse on Epick Poetry," says: "That the ÆNEID was written with

[1] The Twickenham Edition of the Poems of Alexander Pope, vol. 6, *Alexander Pope: Minor Poems*, ed. Norman Ault and John Butt (London, 1954), p. 376. The date of publication is 1738; the date of composition is unknown. The title includes this line: "*For One who would not be buried in Westminster Abbey.*" The Twickenham editors believe that "this epitaph was obviously never meant to be taken too seriously" (p. 376). The opposite seems true.

[2] *Ductor Historicus: Or, A Short System of Universal History, and an Introduction to the Study of it,* 2 vols., 2nd ed. (London, 1705-1704 [sic]), 2:8-9. The remark was already a commonplace.

a view of reconciling the Roman people to a monarchical
form of government, was originally suggested by Bossu
(Traité du Poème Epique, 1. 1. c. xi) and his notion was
afterwards enlarged on by the Abbé Vatry. . . . With these
Frenchmen, Pope, Spence, and the ingenious and learned
Dr. Joseph Warton concur"—as do Samuel Cobb, Joseph
Trapp, Joseph Addison, and numerous others.

The pastorals and georgics were also long seen as aids to
the Augustan settlement and as repayments of personal obligations. As early as 1589 A. F. tells the Archbishop of Canterbury that the *"principall occasion of writing these Pas-
toralls was the maiesteie of* Iulius Caesar *and* Augustus his
sonne," and that Virgil *"doth magnifie* . . . Augustus *for
restoring him to his lands in* Mantua." By 1628, when the
Tacitean dawn had come up, there were misgivings about
Virgil's support of the morally suspect monarch. William
Lisle's note to the first eclogue's use of "my freedom" (lines
32-33) says that *"Virgil* could not have . . . flattered more
artificially, than by confessing to have gained liberty by his
meanes, who was suspected to have aimed at the destruction
and usurpation of the general liberty and immunities of
Rome."[3] So long as a strong monarch is the norm, so long
will the demanded blushes be put off: Lisle is, after all,
complimenting Virgil for his skill in dealing with a delicate
situation, for the Augustan usurpation was still often

[3] "Discourse" (Preface to Virgil; 1697), in *The Critical and Miscel-
laneous Prose Works of John Dryden*, ed. Edmond Malone, 3 vols. in 4
(London, 1800), 3:454; Addison, *A Discourse on Antient and Modern
Learning. . . . Published from an Original Manuscript of Mr. Addison's*
(London, 1734), p. 8; A. F., *The Bucolicks of Publius Virgilius Maro*
(London), sig. A2r-A2v; W[illiam] L[isle], *Virgil's Eclogues* (London,
1628), p. 18; see p. 13 as well. Lisle is translating the commentary of
Lodovicus Vives. The gloss of the section regarding "liberty" (lines 27-
35) took a variety of related forms. Père François Catrou observes:
"Virgile fait ici une Déesse de la Liberté. . . . C'était Octavien César,
qu'il vouloit représenter par cette divinité propice. Il flatte ce jeune
Triumvir en le marquant sous l'idée de la *Liberté*" (*Les Poësies de Virgile*, 4 vols. [Paris, 1729], 1:8).

thought of as the happy shift from a chaotic democracy to a stable monarchy. By the later seventeenth century, however, the full implications of the re-vision of Augustus were taking hold, and we find Virgil in need of defense for what was once a matter of praise. Hence Dryden argues that though Augustus certainly was a tyrant and conqueror, he was the best alternative at the time, and so Virgil, seeing that there could be peace if the people were only quiet under the new power, "concluded it to be the interest of his country to be so governed; to infuse an awful respect into the people towards such a prince; by that respect to confirm their obedience to him; and by that obedience to make them happy. This was the moral" of the *Aeneid*. But Virgil himself, "as men of good sense are generally honest . . . was still of republican principles in heart." Nevertheless, Dryden is aware that both Virgil and Horace have distorted history, and knows that "the Triumvir and Proscriber had descended to us in a more hideous form than they now appear, if the Emperor had not taken care to make friends of" the poets. More than a half-century later Christopher Pitt, in Warton's Virgil, echoes and embellishes Dryden's statement: "we should have entertained a far different Notion of *Augustus*, who was in reality no better than the Enslaver of his Country, and the Person who gave the last Word to expiring Liberty, if *Virgil* and *Horace* had not so highly celebrated him, and gain'd us . . . over to his party."[4]

Others were not won over and were even more deeply troubled by the court-poets' decision. Dryden is dealing with a matter of high and lasting ethical concern, one as applicable to the twentieth century as to classical or English "Augustan" ages—how to use one's own power, here the power

---

[4] "Discourse on Epick Poetry," in Malone, *Prose Works*, 3:453-54, 449 (republican), 525 (proscriber). For the latter remark, see also *John Dryden: Of Dramatic Poesy and other Critical Essays*, ed. George Watson, 2 vols. (New York: Dutton, 1962), 2:239. Pitt, *The Works of Virgil, in Latin and English*, ed. Joseph Warton, 4 vols. (London, 1753), 1:19. See also 1:21-22.

of public voice and private counsel, to influence a bad man's greater power. After years of turmoil and the death of the best of Rome's men and institutions, stability was finally possible under a scarcely legitimate and certainly cruel young prince. But he was also a prince willing to listen to the advice of Maecenas and others, and willing, if given utter submission, to govern "decently." Virgil could have divorced himself from all contact with the tyrant and retreated to silence and self-approbation, or chastized his aberrations and perhaps have died a martyr to a noble cause. He chose, instead, to accept Maecenas' invitation and a third path—whatever his personal feelings, Rome needed peace and order now, and so needed a model for what the new Caesar should be.

That theme is overt in Dryden's and Pitt's discussion and appears, commonly with obviously defensive tones, throughout the eighteenth century. The Third Earl of Shaftesbury notes that Horace and Virgil changed the nature of their naturally barbarous prince and "taught him how to charm mankind." In the process they "made his usurped dominion so enchanting to the world, that it could see without regret its chains of bondage firmly riveted." But the world soon also saw the miserable fruits of "this specious machine of arbitrary and universal power." Samuel Cobb's *Clavis Virgiliana* (1714) stresses that in the georgics "VIRGIL was no arbitrary Man: Oblig'd he was to his Master for his Bounty, and he repays him with good Counsel, how to behave himself in his New Monarchy, so as to gain the Affections of his Subjects, and deserve to be called the *Father of his Country*." In 1738 Henry Pemberton, writing on epic poetry and the opposition poem *Leonidas*, disagrees with those who "attribute to Virgil the impious design of assisting the establishment of universal slavery" by flattering Augustus with the picture of Aeneas, so that "the tyrant would be pleased . . . and might delude his countrymen into a base acquiescence under the new bondage." The strength and clarity of the argument Pemberton resists are at least as impressive as his rebuttal. That is true in 1766 as well, when Robert Andrews argues that Virgil knew Rome had fallen, and that the only way for him to save his country from utter destruction was beautifully to sing "the oracles of political Wisdom, charming the Savage [Augustus] into Clemency." And in 1775 a country curate in Brentford urges that "the Poet by an elegant flattery taught his Patron his duty."[5]

Readers and critics of Virgil and of Horace also had a moral choice to make. They could accept the poet's sacrifice of "poetical conscience" in praising the tyrant, as that curate put it for himself and Dryden (p. xviii), yet insist that on balance, and under the circumstances, Virgil was a wise and good man (whereas Augustus was not). Another group, more concerned about the conflict between morality and expedience, thought Virgil was blemished but not beyond forgiveness. We recall that Joseph Warton and Christopher Pitt were among this number. Joseph Spence was as well. In 1730 his ninth lecture as Oxford's Professor of Poetry was entitled "On Virgil's Aeneid. That it was a Political Poem," written to confirm Augustus' power. In the tenth lecture, Spence urges that Virgil knew his master's true nature, and was "not eager to confirm tyranny." Hence the poet pictures him as he should be rather than as he was, and Aeneas emerges as "a good and pious King" devoted to his people

[5] Shaftesbury, Anthony Ashley Cooper, *Advice to an Author*, in *Characteristics of Men, Manners, Opinions, Times* (1711), ed. John M. Robertson, 2 vols. in 1 (rpt. Indianapolis: Bobbs-Merrill, 1964), 1:143-44; Cobb, *Clavis Virgiliana: or New Observations upon the Works of Virgil* (London), p. 8; Pemberton, *Observations on Poetry, Especially the Epic: Occasioned by the Late Poem upon Leonidas* (London), p. 23; Andrews, *The Works of Virgil Englished* (Birmingham), p. 12; curate, *Sentimental Fables* (Brentford), p. xviii. I hope it is clear that in reporting these severe judgments in this and the following chapter, I am describing a historical, not my personal, judgment. One need not share it to recognize its validity within its context. For discussion of some aspects of Augustan literary politics, see Gordon Williams *Tradition and Originality in Roman Poetry* (Oxford: Clarendon Press, 1968), pp. 43-49, 76-88.

and his gods.[6] Spence elaborates on these remarks in
Polymetis (1747) but, perhaps owing to the earlier opposition's influence, is then harsher regarding Virgil's role: he
"was not so highly encouraged by Augustus and Maecenas
for nothing. To speak a little more plainly; he wrote in the
service of the new usurpation on the state; and all that can
be offered in vindication of him in this light is, that" any
ruler would have been a usurper as well and that Augustus
was probably more indulgent than the competition. These
and other "political" remarks were borrowed for the Warton Virgil of 1753 and for the Holdsworth-Spence Virgil
of 1768.[7]

Such misgivings, however, were not peculiar to London
and Oxford literati. In Scotland the eminent Thomas
Blackwell also thought it a "matter of Lamentation that
such Men should have been under a Necessity of stooping
to flatter a flagitious Youth.—Miserable was the Plight of
their Country, when it was *requisite* and *proper* to make
such Compliments." Never, he hopes and prays, will one
of Britain's major writers find it "fitting or prudent for him
to deify the Prince, who, after murdering our best and greatest Men, should finally strip us of our Liberty."[8]

[6] BM Add. MS 17281. Lecture nine was read on 14 October 1730;
lecture ten is undated but must have followed shortly thereafter. It
concerns the principle truth or plan of the *Aeneid*: "Ne quis vero eum
tyrannidi confirmandae studere, temere Opinetiur, aequum est osten-
dere Regem eum talem voluisse, qualem quisque patriae suae
Amator lucro publico apponeret. . . . In Aenea vero exemplum Regibus,
quos commendaret, delincare voluit. Rex in illo pius bonusque
depingitur, populi amandissimus deorum cultor egregius" (MS pp.
14-15). Quoted by kind permission of the British Library Board.

[7] *Polymetis* (London), p. 20; Warton's Virgil, 1:21-22; Edward Holdsworth and Joseph Spence, *Remarks and Dissertations on Virgil* (London), p. 208. These remarks are also alluded to in Malone's notes to
Dryden's Preface to Virgil, but "as POLYMETIS is not an uncommon
book," he will not transcribe Spence's familiar arguments (Dryden,
Prose Works, 3:454, n. 1).

[8] *Memoirs of the Court of Augustus*, 3 vols. (Edinburgh and London,
1753-1763), 3:376. As we shall later see, Blackwell shifts the onus from
the court-poets to Augustus, who evoked their song.

The third group looked at the evidence and concluded that the only choice for an honest man was moral separation from the enemy. Indeed its judgment, though severe, is implicit in the positions of the other groups and is, if not more realistic, perhaps the dominant opinion of those in the eighteenth century concerned with the relationship between letters, the throne, and political virtue.

This concern was apparent by 1717, when Wicksted distinguished between his benevolent George I and the malevolent Augustus in their respective nurturing of poetry. Once "*Augustus* grasp'd the Helm of State," he found that his "infant Tyranny requir'd; / The great Encourager of Arts." He helped his poets' inspiration and was, in turn, helped by them:

IX

Their Harps with flattering Sounds repay'd
Th'Imperial Patron's skillful Cost:
But whilst th'applauded Artists play'd,
The *Roman* Liberty was lost.

X

GEORGE Triumphs in a nobler Cause:
By Him reviving Patriots see
Religion flourish with their Laws;
Their Conscience, as their Country, free.

George I will help to preserve English liberty, and so "unalarm'd the Muses sing." Pope expresses comparable hostility in his conversations with Spence, conversations that were known, approved, and quoted by Warton. Probably sometime in the summer of 1739, Pope bluntly states his abhorrence of Virgilian flattery and then says: "The *Aeneid* was evidently a party piece, as much as *Absalom and Achitophel*. Virgil [was] as slavish a writer as any of the gazetteers. I have formerly said that Virgil wrote one honest line . . . and that, I now believe was not meant of Cato Uticensis."[9] The

9 Wicksted (the *British Museum Catalogue* does not provide a first name; a contemporary work immediately below it is by John Churchill

126

one honest line was *Aeneid*, viii. 670, alluded to in his *Epilogue to the Satires* (1738), ii. 120—but when Pope was convinced that it was not Cato the friend of the republic and enemy of Caesar, but Cato the censor whom Virgil praises, then *all* of the *Aeneid* becomes dishonest, and its author is as slavish "as any of the gazetteers." Virgil apparently sided with the administration and consequently was an enemy of the patriots and their "liberty."

Although this anger became overt during the opposition's noisiest moments, it flourished, like the anti-Augustanism to which it was linked, long after Walpole was but a memory. Hence John ("Estimate") Brown, writing in 1764, complains that the *Aeneid* suffers as a result of its obeisance to "the *ruinous Policy* of the Times." The subjects peculiar to Rome's greatness, "the *Glories* of the *Republic,* the *Achievements* of its *Heroes,* . . . are cast into *Shades,* and seen as through a *Veil*: while the *strongest Lights, and highest Colourings* of his Pencil are prostituted to the *Vanity* of the *ruling Tyrant.*" The noblest of Roman poets has become slave and whore. Edward Burnaby Greene rejects the argument that Aeneas was a model for Augustus and sees, instead, a miserable lie, for Augustus-Aeneas lacked "a genuine affection for his country, which he effectually enslaved." In another place he adds that the princeps rewarded only those who followed his cause, and would have

---

Wicksted, perhaps the same man), *An Ode for the Year MDCCXVII. To the King* (London), pp. 2-3; *Joseph Spence: Observations, Anecdotes, and Characters of Books and Men: Collected from Conversation,* ed. James M. Osborn, 2 vols. (Oxford: Clarendon Press, 1966), 1:229-30. Shortly before that, Pope illustrates eighteenth-century literary compartmentalization—admiration for Virgil's art together with scorn for its content: Virgil's georgic begins with "the grossest flattery to Augustus that could be invented. The turn of mind in it [is] as mean as the poetry in it is noble" (1:229). See 1:160-61 for Pope's pride in his refusal to flatter or accept reward for his verses, further evidence of the seriousness of his epitaph. I suspect that Spence was Pope's tutor regarding Cato, but he could have found the same information elsewhere—in Catrou's *Virgile,* 3:57, for example. Virgil would not mention Cato of Utica: "il fut trop odieux aux Césars."

appeared far uglier "had not *flattering* abilities warped the
attention of posterity from his public guilt to his private
munificence!—The patron of learning immortalised the enslaver of his country." By 1785 John Pinkerton, indignant
about the first georgic's praise of the horrid Julius, insists
that Virgil could not be "a poet of real genius," for he lacks
honesty, is guilty of "fulsome flattery and adulation, unworthy of the soul of a slave," and deserves "execration" for
crowning a tyrant and making "superstitious offerings on
the altar of slavery."[10] The reservations of Dryden and the
annoyance of Spence have become sources of moral outrage that cast the highest doubt on the spiritual, literary,
and political worth of the greatest of court-poets.

T. W. Harrison has convincingly shown how Virgil and
his epic lost esteem and influence because of their association with Augustus: as seventeenth-century royalism waned,
so did admiration for that royalist poem.[11] In light of the
evidence so far presented, this could not be an unexpected
development. Cicero was berated for his early support of the
stripling tyrant Octavian; Velleius was heartily besmirched

10 Brown, *The History of the Rise and Progress of Poetry, Through
its several Species* (Newcastle, 1764), p. 255; Greene, "Essay on the
Fourth Book" of the *Aeneid*, in *Critical Essays* (London, 1770), p. 227,
and "The Influence of Government on the Mental Faculties," ibid.,
p. 176; Robert Heron [pseud. for John Pinkerton], "*Discussion of the
merits* of Virgil," in *Letters of Literature* (London), pp. 95-96.

11 "English Vergil: The *Aeneid* in the XVIII Century," *Philologica
Pragensia*, 10 (1967): 1-11, 80-92. This important essay, especially the
first part, deserves to be better known. The conventional view of Virgil
and Horace as consistently exalted models of imitation wants changing.
M. M. Kelsall's article is a useful step in that direction: "What God,
What Mortal? The *Aeneid* and the English Mock-Heroic," *Arion*, 8
(1969): 359-79. In the meanwhile, however, the older attitude prevails.
See R. D. Williams, "Changing Attitudes to Virgil: A Study in the
History of Taste from Dryden to Tennyson," which finds reservations
regarding Virgil's ethics in the romantic period but not earlier; in contrast, "the English Augustan Age [Dryden to about 1750] was the high
noon of admiration for Horace and Virgil" (*Virgil*, ed. D. R. Dudley,
Studies in Latin Literature and Its Influence [New York: Basic Books,
1969], p. 123).

for his fulsome adherence to the Augustan line. Virgil was painted with the same brush and, as several remarks quoted and Pope's epitaph make clear, so was Horace. Indeed, unless all the conventions of logic and association were to be abandoned, such would have to be the case, and such it was at least from the later seventeenth to the earlier nineteenth century. As Christopher Lake Moody put it in the *Monthly Review* for 1803, William Gifford's description of Horace was broadly accepted—he was the spoiled child (the "enfant gâté") of the court of Augustus.[12] Like Virgil, he repaid personal debts to his master through unwarranted compliments; like Virgil, he sacrificed his conscience for physical ease at the cost of his country's liberty; like Virgil, the commentators said, he supported the new government and its values. He was, in fact, sometimes regarded as even more compliant than his friend. Lewis Crusius agrees that the *Aeneid* celebrates "the finest parts of *Augustus's* life," but had Virgil intended that poem as "a meer Encomium of that Prince, he might, as *Horace* has done, have made his Panegyrick at several times, and on different occasions, with less expense of time and labour." A generation earlier, Dryden called Horace "a temporizing poet, a well-mannered Court slave, and a man who is . . . ever decent, because he is naturally servile."[13] Dryden's well-known strictures anticipated much of the politicized commentary to come, commentary that both influenced Pope and felt his influence, was securely linked to the rejection of Augustus, and had a wide chronological and political base. Here, for instance, is a typically indignant paragraph from Thomas Gordon's pro-Walpole Discourses on Tacitus (1728):

[12] Moody is reviewing Gifford's translation of Juvenal (1802), *Monthly Review*, second series, 40 (1803): 9. For the attribution, see Benjamin Christie Nangle, *The Monthly Review Second Series 1790-1815: Indexes of Contributors and Articles* (Oxford: Clarendon Press, 1955), p. 148.

[13] *Lives of the Roman Poets* (1726), 2 vols., 3rd ed. (London, 1753), 1:67; Dryden, "Discourse concerning . . . Satire," *Essays* (n. 4, above), 2:132.

The Renown of AUGUSTUS was also notably blazon'd by the Historians and Poets of his time; men of excellent wit, but egregious flatterers. According to them AUGUSTUS had all the accomplishments to be acquired by man. . . . After so many instances of his cruelty, revenge, selfishness, excessive superstition and defect in courage; after all the crying calamities and afflictions, all the oppression and vassalage, that his ambition had brought upon his Country and the globe, one would think that such praises must have pass'd for satyr and mockery. . . . Ambition, successful ambition is a credulous passion; or whether he believed such praises or no, he received them graciously, and caress'd the Authors. Hence so much favour to VIRGIL and HORACE, and to such other wits as knew how to be good Courtiers: and hence every admirer of those charming Poets, is an admirer of AUGUSTUS, who was so generous to them, and is the chief burthen of their Panegyricks. . . . When Truth was treason who would venture to speak it? and when Flattery bore a vogue and a price, there were enough found to court it, and take it. Hence the partiality or silence of Poets and Historians.[14]

In 1741 the unknown perpetrator of *The Art of Poetry* attacked the patriots in a satire that ironically tells rising and hungry bards how to prosper. " '*Tis boundless License* which secures *Success*." But, he cautions, with putative opposition outrage,

> That Bard, who follows *Horace* is undone:
> Detest his *Practice*, and his *Precepts* shun.
> Deck not, like him, AUGUSTUS in your Lays.
> We are too proud to hear a *Monarch*'s Praise.

Shortly thereafter, John Lord Hervey attacks Pope and uses as his theme the difference between the inner and written thoughts of poets. In the process, this eminent courtier reminds us that Horace was a miserable hypocrite who betrayed liberty and supported slavery. Indeed, he was "fond to Load

---

[14] *The Works of Tacitus*, 2 vols. (London, 1728-1731), 1:49-50.

Augustus' flatter'd Shrine," perfidiously applied his talents to the wrong side, abandoned "his Country's Cause," and "kiss'd the Feet that trampled on her Laws." Horace deserves his "dishonest Fame."[15]

The opposition author of *Plain Truth, or Downright Dunstable* (1740) wishes to share with us—and did with several readers in Tom's Coffee House—"Some Critical THOUGHTS concerning *Horace* and *Virgil*." Those authors were "*flattering, soothing, Tools*" who were "Fit to *praise Tyrants*, and *gull Fools*." They saved themselves with, in Horace's case, cowardly flight from the republican cause at Philippi, and in both cases by base praise of the enslaver. Even the mention of these poetic ogres is almost more than a good citizen can tolerate:

> *Away with 'em*, I can scarce bear 'em,
> And all their Friends, I do not fear 'em.
> In monstrous times, *such Weeds* thrive best,
> They *ornament a Tyrant's Nest.*
> They serve to *lull and blunt the Pain,* ⎤
> Of *vilest Crime*, still hide such Stain, ⎬
> In Luxury, they thrive amain. ⎦
> Of *Tyranny bear up the Train.*
> Their *Lyes and Flatt'ry*, is good Sense, ⎤
> Such Times, it ne'er can give Offence, ⎬
> *The Tyrant grants 'em a Licence.* ⎦
> More Youth and Men have sure been lost,
> By *Horace'* Book, you so much boast,
> Than any Author you can name,
> Or Strumpet of the *vilest Fame.*

The distinction of Horace and Virgil as poets only compounds the crime, since the best of talents turned to the "*worst use*" becomes the "*greatest abuse.*"[16]

[15] *Art of Poetry* (London), pp. 14, 2; [Hervey], *The Difference Between Verbal and Practical Virtue* (London, 1742), pp. 2-3.

[16] *Plain Truth* (London), pp. 13 (gull Fools), 15-16, 17. The British Library's copy (shelf mark 11630/1-22 c. 13) is dated, in a contemporary hand, "March 25, 1740," at Tom's Coffee House. Five readers have

This rage was not to burn out by the strength of its own fire. In 1748 Mark Akenside calls Augustus an "imperial Ruffian" unworthy of praise even by one "polluted Bard." A few years later James Grainger's review of Warton's *Essay on Pope* (1756) observes that there are few borrowings from Alcaeus in Horace: "as the hatred of tyranny" was Alcaeus' "characteristical excellence . . . could the courtier of Augustus imitate him in that?" Brockill Newburgh later complained that *"Horace* has acquitted himself as a good Poet and Panegyrist, but by no means . . . as so good a Commonwealth Man." His *Odes,* iii. 4, overpaid Augustus by "the Representation he has made of the brave Assertors of the Liberties of their Country, under the Semblance of Monsters, and Rebels to Heaven."[17] In 1759 Ralph Griffiths praised James Grainger's translation of Tibullus and joined him in distinguishing Tibullus' independence and patriotism from the court-poets' collaboration with Augustus and his imperial government. "Tibullus, never deviating from his political principles, does not once mention either that emperor or Maecenas," and in fact opposed Augustus' "projected" innovations. Thirty years later Lord Monboddo demonstrates Livy's greatness and "noble free spirit" by means of his honesty in describing Augustan Rome as com-

---

written their names on the title page. There were many houses so named: this one was at Deveraux Court. I am indebted to William Cameron for the identification. (The British Library's collections include several other poems, largely political, with Tom's imprimatur.) According to David Foxon, the author may be an unidentified "Dr. Kennedy" or, less likely, Dennis de Coetlogon. *English Verse 1701-1750,* 2 vols. (Cambridge: Cambridge Univ. Press, 1975), 1:589.

17 Akenside, *Ode* (London), p. 11. The poem was praised by James Grainger in the *Monthly Review,* 14 (1756): 550n, as an aside while reviewing Warton's *Essay* on Pope. The attribution is in Benjamin Christie Nangle, *The Monthly Review First Series 1749-1789: Indexes of Contributors and Articles* (Oxford: Clarendon Press, 1934), p. 98 (referred to hereafter as Nangle). For Grainger's remark on Horace, see *Monthly Review,* 15 (1756): 58; Newburgh, *Essays Poetical, Moral and Critical* (Dublin, 1769), p. 73.

pared with the misrepresenting flattery of Horace and Virgil. In that same year, Robert Potter had a ghostly, but adamant, Samuel Johnson applaud the rough Juvenal and denigrate the trivial Horace, "a turn-coat and debauchée."[18]

By about that time several major French authors had seconded the British motion to censure Horace. Voltaire labels Augustus "un monstre adroit & heureux" and adds that in praising him Virgil and Horace show "des âmes serviles." He is especially indignant regarding the nonsense of Augustan divinity "à la tête des *Géorgiques*" and the outright misrepresentation that begins the epistle to Augustus. Jean Dusaulx similarly urges that "Horace had learned to support the yoke of a master, and to lead the way for the deifying of tyrants." François-Jean, Marquis de Chastellux, warns that "we must not judge of the [bloody] Augustan age, by the works of contemporary poets." Even if Horace and Virgil were sincere (which he implies is not likely), their verse does not accurately mirror their times. Louis Racine was even blunter: Horace's and Virgil's celebrations and deifications of the enslaving Augustus were so outrageous they must have thought their emperor an imbecile to believe such stuff.[19]

[18] *Monthly Review*, 20 (1759): 62-63 (attribution in Nangle, p. 209); James Burnett, Lord Monboddo, *Of the Origin of Language*, 6 vols. (Edinburgh, 1773-1792), 5:26; [Robert Potter] *The Art of Criticism; As Exemplified in Dr. Johnson's Lives of the Most Eminent English Poets* (London, 1789), p. 207. Grainger's translation of Tibullus includes several anti-Augustan remarks. See *A Poetical Translation of the Elegies of Tibullus; and of the Poems of Sulpicia*, 2 vols. (London, 1759), 1:xxxv-xxxvi; 2:60-61, n. 29; 2:69-73n; 75, n. 12; 139-40, n. 3; 184-87, n. 13.

[19] Voltaire, *Questions sur l'encyclopédie*, 9 vols. (Geneva [?], 1770-1772), 2:351-52, 347 (georgics, epistle to Augustus); Dusaulx, "Discours Préliminaire," in *Satires de Juvénal* (Paris, 1770), as in the *Literary Magazine and British Review*, 7 (1791): 441; Chastellux, *An Essay on Public Happiness* (1772), 2 vols. (London, 1774), 2:251-52 (Chastellux is generally hostile to pagan Rome's version of civilization); Racine, *Refléxions sur la poésie* (1747) in *Oeuvres de Louis Racine*, ed. [C. Lebeau], 6 vols. (Paris, 1808) 2:516-17: "Comme les beaux esprits de

Like Virgil, Horace had his defenders—the mature Alexander Pope was not among them—and like Virgil, that defense sometimes did more harm than good. Richard Hurd's commentary on Horace's epistle to Augustus (ii. 1) is not distinguished by political acumen; he even accepts the "extravagances of adulation in the Augustan poets," since they were following senatorial and religious precedent already established under Julius' tyranny. Yet Hurd is amazed at the Romans' rapid decline from republican independence to "prostrate adoration of their first *Lord.*" They were "ripe for servitude." The historical circumstances justify apparently overdone flattery. "The adulation of Virgil, which has given so much offence, and of Horace, who kept pace with him, was, we see, but the authorized language of the times." As poets they complied with "the popular voice" and echoed it back to their prince, though they had too much sense and dignity to exaggerate such flattery.[20] Hurd's Augustan poets are thus reduced to sounding-boards, and are appreciably less noble than Dryden's or Warton's tainted and tortured benefactors who perhaps wrongly, but honestly, believed that the republic was dead and that calm for the nation was more important than their own impeccable morality.

Thomas Blackwell's discussion is both more complex and illuminating than Hurd's, for it makes a good but losing case for Horace and Virgil as court-poets apparently supporting the tyrant. Maecenas decided to "*subdue* and *new*

Rome ne seront pas accusés d'imbecillité, il falloit qu'ils crussent leurs empereurs bien imbécilles."

[20] *Q. Horatii Flacci Epistola ad Augustum. With an English Commentary and Notes. To which is added, A Discourse concerning Poetical Imitation* (London, 1751), pp. 34-35. Joseph Warton chastised Hurd for his silence regarding Horatian complicity with Augustus. See his edition of *The Works of Alexander Pope*, 9 vols. (London, 1797), 4:146-47, and chap. 6, sec. 1 at n. 16 in text, below.

model" the cruel Augustus,[21] and did so by employing Horace and Virgil to "give unsuspected Lessons of Moderation to their master" (2:355). Since "no Poet ever spoke more precisely the *Court-Language* than the *sly* and *soothing Horace,"* he was able to inculcate "the mildest maxims and weightiest precepts" under the guise of wild tales (2:455-56). Once Augustus learned moderation, he also learned the value of poetry for propaganda, and commissioned the *Georgics,* the *Aeneid,* and, among other examples, Horace's *Odes,* iv. 4, all of which serve Augustus' political needs. Both poets were really republicans manqués, who supported the throne to make the best of a bad job and reform the prince who had intruded himself upon the nation. But in making this argument for them, Blackwell is consistently apologetic and, at one point, even recreates his youthful hostility to the turn-toga Horace.

He recalls his early reaction to Horace's *Odes,* i. 2, in which Augustus is *deus, pater, princeps,* and *dux:* "in the heat of Youth [ca. 1721-1731?], I could not read this ODE without some Emotions of Indignation" (2:357). Upon mature consideration, however, Blackwell's stomach improves, and he rejects the possibility of Horatian flattery for selfish ends at the expense of honor and republican principles. The poet not only refused most favors, but "flattered for the PUBLIC GOOD—to reform" his absolute prince. Though Blackwell must admit that Horace "is defective" in the great moral end of "explaining and enforcing *the Duties we owe to our* COUNTRY," he again urges that Horace had no

21 *Memoirs of the Court of Augustus,* 2:349. Subsequent citations are given in the text. I have patched together this argument from several different places in the *Memoirs.* It is, however, perfectly consistent with Blackwell's beliefs and his exclamatory style. Blackwell's work, and its alternately harsh and sympathetic treatment of Augustus, Horace, and Virgil, later influenced William Boscawen. See his *Odes, Epodes, and Carmen Secularae of Horace* (London, 1793), pp. xxxiv-xxxvii, for an intelligent and generous evaluation of the court-poets' role in the Augustan world.

choice, since "tyranny and lawless Rule" had triumphed and only Maecenas' way of prudence and reform was open. In subsequent milder times, however, "we shall find him endeavouring, as a professed Patriot, to make ample amends," (3:65-66). Blackwell asserts, rather than shows, Horace's patriotic reformation and continues to relate Horace's poetry to "delicate" and "polite" court pleasures (3:467).

Virgil was also enrolled in the school of temporary expedience for the sake of permanent alteration of the beast into a beauty. When one considers the age, the kindness Virgil owed Augustus for *"personal favours,"* and the usual exaggeration of *"poetic phrase,"* the "Crookedness" (2:435) of his purpose in the *Aeneid* will "appear pardonable to a good-natured Man," especially since, like Horace's, Virgil's hidden politics soon emerged:

> Notwithstanding the high Compliments paid to *Augustus*, and even to *Julius Cesar*, Virgil's real Sentiments burst forth by Starts. The Strain of his Works discover the good Man and the Patriot. His Silence in regard to some illustrious Persons, particularly *Brutus* and *Cicero*, is solely owing to his Discretion: It was not proper for him *openly* to declare against *Augustus*; it was well enough that, when Prudence permitted, he let his Sentiments be known. The ascribing the Suppression of the great Names of *Cicero, Cassius, Brutus* to the Poet's Principle of *passive Obedience*, is a Dream of Mr. *Dryden*'s, dictated by his own favourite Creed. (3:346-47)

It was also the dream, or nightmare, of numerous other commentators on Virgil, Horace, and their relationship to the Augustan throne. Blackwell's effort to close the doors upon the court-poets' attackers lets them in at the windows. In defending the poets, he adds more fuel to the anti-Augustan fires he himself had in part hoped to kindle; he raises the very objections that their enemies raise; and he enhances those objections by recognizing their validity and by showing his own youthful indignation. He leaves the opponents unbloodied and unbowed by agreeing that these poets helped to enhance a pretty lie which often substituted for the ugly truth of the Augustan age, that they had the courage to speak only in safe times after the tyranny they buttressed had been solidified, and that in some cases personal favors led to flattery. Blackwell can only evoke mysterious unnamed and undiscussed passages written in mild times that do, after all, demonstrate the political virtue of Horace and Virgil. After such unconvincing arguments, and the post-Augustan decline of Rome, the reader's faith in the ability of the court-poets to save the nation may have been diminished. Regardless of how one responds to Blackwell's discussion of the poets, however, it is clear that he is defensive and raises arguments that question their moral integrity. It is also clear that for many readers those brilliant poets collaborated with tyranny.

Pope was certainly influenced by this harsh view of Horatian complicity. It was a muted part of his childhood inheritance and a vocal part of his adult opposition context. As I hope to show, his *Epistle to Augustus* (1737) uses these libertarian commonplaces to attack both Horace and his princely patron. The first *Dialogue* of the *Epilogue to the Satires* (1738), however, is even more overt, and suggests some of the "Juvenalian" poses and politics that motivated Pope's later satire. The poem begins with the remarks of a court devoté ironically labeled "Friend."

> Not twice a twelvemonth you appear in Print,
> And when it comes, the Court see nothing in't.[22]

[22] The Twickenham Edition of the Poems of Alexander Pope, vol. 4, *Alexander Pope: Imitations of Horace*, ed. John Butt, 2nd ed. (New Haven: Yale Univ. Press, 1963), p. 297. Subsequent references to this edition are cited in the text. Pope himself made the association of Juvenalian opposition to the court as being, lamentably, most appropriate for his situation. It was in Augustus' reign "that Horace was protected and caress'd; and in [Nero's and Domitian's] that Lucan was put to death, and Juvenal banish'd" (Pope to Arbuthnot, 26 July 1734, in *Correspondence of Alexander Pope*, ed. George Sherburn, 5 vols. [Oxford: Clarendon Press, 1956], 3:420).

In a note to this couplet Pope says: "These two lines are from Horace [*Sat.*, ii. 3. 1-4]; and the only lines that are so in the whole Poem; being meant to give a handle to that which follows in the character of an impertinent Censurer" (p. 297n). Pope dissociates himself from Horace's authority and uses him to offer a clue to the nature of his own adversarius. Junius Damasippus, the vaguely parallel Horatian character, has a dual history: in Cicero's *Letters* he is an agent in the purchase of works of art, and in Horace's satire he is a former art-dealer who is a convert to stoicism and thinks the whole world mad.[23] Renaissance and contemporary commentators blended the two and helped Pope to this now unused "handle."[24] The Friend, obviously an enemy, is trying to buy Pope's art and induce his own stoicism regarding court activities. Though Horace satirizes the stoic, he gives him a serious hearing and admits his basic point; Pope rejects stoicism and the easy view of universal madness, and disdains everything his interlocuter has said.

[23] For Cicero's reference to Damasippus, see *Ad Atticum*, xii. 29 and 33, and *Ad Familiares*, vii. 23. Pope is also adapting another remark of Damasippus—so far as George II's court sees, Pope is not writing poetry at all. Pope told Warburton that he "thinks he cou^d make something of the *Damasippus*, and intends to do it" (*Imitations of Horace*, p. 327n).

[24] See *Quinti Horatii Flacci Opera. Interpretatione & notis, illustravit Ludovicius Desprez* (London, 1722), pp. 446, n. 1, especially p. 448, n. 24; and *Oeuvres d'Horace*, ed. André Dacier, 10 vols., 3rd ed. (Paris, 1709), 7:194-97, especially 208: "Avant que de s'attacher à cette Secte [Stoics], il s'étoit ruïné à acheter & à revendre des Statuës, & toutes sortes d'Antiques." It is also possible that Pope remembered the Damasippus of Juvenal's eighth satire, lines 185-86; he apparently knew and commented upon George Stepney's manuscript translation and its edited version in Dryden's Juvenal of 1693. In that poem the newly impoverished Damasippus "Is forc'd to make the Stage his last retreat, / And pawns his Voice, the All he has, for Meat" (*George Stepney's Translation of the Eighth Satire of Juvenal*, ed. Thomas and Elizabeth Swedenberg, Publications of the William Andrews Clark Memorial Library [Berkeley and Los Angeles: Univ. of California Press, 1948], pp. 46-47). See also pp. 9-10 for evidence of Pope's knowledge of the manuscript and printed translations.

In the process he uses the conventional critical language that describes Horatian satire, shows how easily it can be adapted to modern political corruption, and actually portrays the Friend unconsciously adhering to the anti-Augustan tradition I have been describing. Moreover, he has the Friend employ only the most ambiguous part of Persius' description of Horace—his "sly insinuating Grace"—and ignore the affirmative lines immediately thereafter (as they appear in Dryden's translation of *Satires*, i. 231-34).[25] In the process Pope's Friend places Horace in the court, with the tyrannical Augustus, and against the "free" satirist's need to expose vice, wherever it might be. By implication, Pope associates himself with a "Juvenalian" Lucilius who "never fear'd the times; / But lash'd the City, and dissected Crimes" (2:748).[26] Horace, as now interpreted by a con-

[25] *The Poems of John Dryden*, ed. James Kinsley, 4 vols. (Oxford: Clarendon Press, 1958), 2:749. Subsequent citations are given in the text.

[26] The harsh, biting Lucilius was often associated with republican freedom. Dryden observes that Persius and Juvenal thought him more fit a model than Horace for their serious, antityrannic satire ("Discourse concerning . . . Satire," *Essays*, Watson, 2:136). Blackwell says that Lucilius "attacked Vice wherever he found it: no outward Shew or Substitution [sic], and much less could Eminence of Birth or Station secure the *base Priest*, th' *immoral Peer*, or purse-proud Plebeian from appearing in their proper colours" (*Memoirs of the Court of Augustus*, 3:50). Almost immediately thereafter Blackwell says that in spite of lip service to the contrary, Pope really was not Lucilian because really not virtuous. That severe satiric method is appreciably different from Horace's Augustan, imperial courtier. Yet even he inadvertently included "many *strong*, perhaps . . . *coarse* Expressions, hatched, to be sure, under the high liberty of the *Roman* State, and which had probably crept into his compositions from the Fountains whence he drew, *Lucilius'* Writings, or more licentious Authors of the *old Comedy*" (3:67). The relationship between harsh attacks on rich or highly placed rogues and "freedom" seems inevitable, and is considered in the next chapter. For further association of Lucilian and Juvenalian satire, see William Gifford, *The Satires of Decimus Junius Juvenalis* (London, 1802), p. xliii: "I suspect that there was something of political spleen in the excessive popularity of Lucilius under Augustus, and something of courtly complacency in the attempt of Horace to counteract it." Gifford then states that "Juvenal, like Persius, professes to follow Lucilius,"

temporary "Augustan," opposes the essential values of Alexander Pope. Though these lines are political hyperbole, they also reflect Pope's calm judgment of the ally of Virgil, "as slavish a writer as any of the gazetteers":

> But *Horace*, Sir, was delicate, was nice;
> *Bubo* observes, he lash'd no sort of *Vice*:
> *Horace* would say, *Sir* Billy *serv'd the Crown*,
> Blunt *could do Bus'ness*, H—ggins *knew the Town*,
> In *Sappho* touch the *Failing of the Sex*,
> In rev'rend Bishops note some *small Neglects*,
> And own, the *Spaniard* did a *waggish thing*,
> Who cropt our Ears, and sent them to the King.
> His sly, polite, insinuating stile
> Could please at Court, and make AUGUSTUS smile:
> An artful Manager, that crept between
> His Friend and Shame, and was a kind of *Screen*.
>
> (Lines 11-22)

One must, I think, modify John Butt's judgment that the *Epilogue* is among "the most Horatian of Pope's original work." This may be true in techniques like dialogue and colloquial expression; it is not true in tone and relationship with the moral authority of the court, especially since, in the last two lines quoted, Horace is likened to Walpole. Though this poem is labeled "Something like Horace," it is designed to be very much like the Juvenal described in the next chapter of this study. The satirist is the enemy of the corrupt court, not its friend; he cannot laugh at folly but must attack vice whatever the consequences; his indignation makes verse for which he may be banished or belittled by the court, and so he must make his own court in the country; he is a satirist for whom receipt of the court's praise

---

but, unlike Persius, has really understood his model's manner. Accordingly, in his magnificent language he deals with "eternal distinctions of moral good and evil, . . . the loveliness of virtue, and the deformity and horror of vice" (p. li; see also p. li, note). This should be compared with Pope's portrait of Horace, above.

would mean defeat. Thus the last allusion in the second
Dialogue dramatically inverts Dryden's translation of lines
170-71 of Juvenal's first satire, a sort of prologue to the other
fifteen. Juvenal says:

> Since none the Living-Villains dare implead,
> Arraign them in the Persons of the Dead.
>
> $(2:677)^{27}$

Pope says in his own line 251: "Are none, none living?
let me praise the Dead." Juvenal's beginning is Pope's end,
the "last poem of the kind printed by our author, with a
resolution to publish no more" (p. 327n), we hear in the
concluding note to the second part of the *Epilogue*. With the
exception of the final book and version of the *Dunciad*,
Pope obeyed his resolution, but in the meanwhile he had
contributed to the discrediting of Augustus and Horace as
exemplary political and satiric models for some of the best
writers of his age and the next. For Pope, the values of
Walpole, Horace, and Augustus are too close for moral or
satiric respectability. That satirist pleases and protects those
he should attack.

Both court and opposition, Hervey and Pope, agreed on
the lack of political virtue in the sycophantic Horace. We
recall that Pope associated Virgil with the *Gazetteer*, with
the administration's newspaper of blow and counterblow.
He must have associated Horace with the same and comparable organs. Then as now, politicians and their apologists
are remarkably supple, able to compartmentalize, say the
thing that is not and regard today's friend as tomorrow's
enemy, or vice versa. Augustus was bad, no doubt; Horace's

---

27 For Walpole and screens, see Maynard Mack, *The Garden and the
City: Retirement and Politics in the Later Poetry of Pope 1731-1743*
(Toronto: Univ. of Toronto Press, 1969), pp. 132, n. 10, 133, n. 14.
Among other sources, see also the *Craftsman*, nos. 117 (28 September
1728) and 419 (13 July 1734). Butt's remark is on p. vii of his edition
of the *Imitations of Horace*. Gilbert Wakefield also noticed Pope's echo
of Juvenal. See his *Observations on Pope* (London, 1796), p. 285.

support of him was bad, no doubt; but Horace was also a great satirist, as even the author of *Plain Truth* had to acknowledge. He vied with Juvenal as the chief classical exemplar of that genre, and clearly was safer—less angry and more congenial, a satirist of folly not vice, a satirist who was "in" and apparently had a price rather than one who was "out" and preferred to stay so. As a satirist he normally did not go beyond modest castigation (his morals in other instances were a different matter); he understood court behavior, was aware that respectable court favorites might be models for emulation, and certainly would not be so vulgar or wrongheaded as to attack all mankind rather than a few miscreants. He thus knew how to write proper satire—as Alexander Pope did not. I am suggesting that Pope reacted to the partisans as well as detractors of Horace—specifically, to the administration newspapers which, during the bitter political wrangling between about 1726 and 1742, used Horace as the model of a court satirist and often as the antithesis of opposition satire, especially Pope's.

This support took several forms. The most obvious were simple praise by Horace, or imitations or quotations from his poems adapted either to praise Walpole or George II, or attack their enemies.[28] The *London Journal* of 26 June 1725, for example, calls Horace a "darling *Antient*" and is delighted with his "excellent Epistle to AUGUSTUS." A more important prop appears in the same newspaper's enthusiastic response to Bubb Dodington's *Epistle to . . . Walpole* (1725), for here the administration begins to define its Horatianism. During the Augustan age, the monarch and his poets established a perfect symbiotic relationship: he encouraged and protected them and they softened and polished him and contributed "to confirm his new Empire, by endearing Him to the *Roman* People" (8 January 1726). Horace himself was "graced with a peculiar Manner, ex-

[28] For some of these, see the *London Journal*, 4 May 1726; the *Gazetteer*, 3 October 1735, 19 January and 22 March 1736, 6 April and 11 April 1738, 11 December 1740, and 14 February 1741.

quisitely adapted to the Politeness of a Court," and especially so in his epistles, where the statesman is "pleased, as he sees his worthiest Sentiments rising to his View in their full Lustre." The present-day statesman also must wish to further such poetry, and if Dodington is now too busy, "a new Field is opened to other Writers, who may pursue with Success" the same path. That is *"truly Horatian,"* the *Journal* repeats on 5 February, and indicates that such poetry shows how to attain "the Smiles of the Great Man." To be "Horatian," in this context, is to support the government and its ministers, to endear the monarch to the people, to receive praise and rewards for such services, and to teach others to follow a similar path.

The *Daily Gazetteer* seconded and expanded these views, for by 1735 the use of literary models and authorities had become more complex and heated. This government newspaper soon enrolled Horace on the side of stage-licensing. On 4 June 1737 it replies to *Common Sense* of 21 May, insisting that the comedic practice of Aristophanes was an argument for rather than against stage-licensing, since the growing nastiness stirred the Athenians to anger: "and finding, as *Horace* tells us, the Grievance *fit to be restrained by Law, they did restrain it by Law*," as is seen in the following quotation from Horace, *Ars Poetica*, lines 281-84. The modern licentious wits merely throw filth about and do not meet *"Horace's* Idea of a Poet." On 12 June the *Gazetteer* again quotes Horace (*AP*, 84; *Sat.*, i. 10. 40-42), who now indicates that "ever since the Old Comedy was put down by Publick Authority, and . . . with Shame," it never again attacked particular persons (see also 11 June). And on 16 July the same newspaper draws Horace even more deeply to its side by reiterating his support of death for the satirist who attacks *"another Man's good Name."* It quotes lines 151-55 of *Epistles*, ii. 1 (to Augustus) that Pope had already turned to his own use, and cites Horace's pleasure in the "good Effect [the Law of the xii Tables] had in that triumphant Republick. . . . The Dread of this

Cudgeling made the Poets take Care not to offend against good Manners and Discretion, in their Plays and other Poems." The final three words have moved both the administration and Horace into support of attacks on the freedom of the press as well as the stage. The opposition could hardly be blamed for fearing that one presaged the other. Horace has become an administration historical authority for the logic, wisdom, and prudence of restraint upon politically unpleasant literature, and a poetical authority for what the opposition is doing wrong.

By July of 1738 both parts of Pope's *Epilogue to the Satires* had appeared, and it was clear that there was no change in his or in comparable attacks upon the administration. Perhaps as a result, on 27 October 1738, the *Gazetteer* published one of its most savage and threatening replies, insisted that true satire was general not specific, rallied but did not attack, and supported and did not insult the state. It also accorded Horace a prominent place and made overt what was already present in earlier allusions to him: namely, that there was no similarity between Horatian and Popean satire. The author, "Curtius," reiterates the familiar view that opposition satirists should be "clubb'd or rather bastinadoed" as were those in ancient Rome; or perhaps they should be punished by being forced to *"lick off the Impression* of their Works" from the pages. Even Boileau argued that satirists "must not offend the *State* nor *Conscience*," both of which cry out against "Mr. *D'Anvers*, and a late Satyrist." Horace is the model of satire. He "rally'd best of any of the Ancients among the *Latins*; but he never took the Liberty to turn Persons of Consular Dignity into Ridicule: He was too much a Master of Reason, good Manners, and Discretion to offend against either, and much less to endeavour by fained and profligate Tales and Taints, to disturb the Peace and good Order of Society." Indeed, the opposition—always including "a late Satyrist"—has utterly broken from all satiric precedent ancient or modern in its "Insolence and Brutality." The *"Ridiculum* in *Horace"* is utterly unknown to those ig-

norant parrots, though there was ample precedent for it in
Voiture's and Walsh's letters. "But this, and every thing else
reasonable and commendable, is thrown away on such Libel-
lers and Lampooners as our Modern Raillers and Satyrists,
who can no more judge of such Things without Wit, than
they can add a Cubit to their Stature [*Matthew*, vi. 27], or
turn a Curve Line into a Right." The extravagant vulgarity
of the final insult is obviously un-Horatian, and obviously in
the spirit of what Curtius thinks Pope's satire represents and
deserves. Whether he is right or wrong is not as important
as the clear separation of Horace and Pope in satiric tone,
subject, and intention.

Less than three months later, on 9 January 1739, "M. P."
adds his voice to the *Gazetteer's* attack on Pope as a gro-
tesquely un-Horatian imitator, especially in the putative
imitations of Horace. In the "celebrated Epistle to *Augustus*, [Pope] endeavoured to erect his own *Poetical
Throne*, that he may reign the *sole Tyrant of Parnassus*."
True Horatian satire is neither so destructive nor, in other
examples cited in abundance, so obscene or so general in its
attacks "upon *Bodies* and *Societies* of Men in a *Lump*," including the shining lights of the law, church, court, city, and
government, nay, the entire nation. "And all this while
(which is the very Cream of the Jest) he pretends to imitate
Horace; and for raising the Price of his Copy, has been so
indiscreet as to print the Verses of that *fine, courtly Satyrist*,
with his own *Billingsgate*. But how ridiculous is the *Comparison*." Pope is yet more un-Horatian, for he "refuses to
acknowledge his Majesty to be his lawful King, and to give
the Government the slender Security of his Oath for his
good Behaviour."

Such disloyalty to genuine satire, good taste, the government, and monarch, is radically different from the style of
Horace the courtier. If he could have returned as a speaking
shade he no doubt would have given Pope a Roman scolding for even seeming—however ironically or well inten-
tioned—to be cast from his own mold. As good chance had

it, the *Gazetteer* received a copy of such verses, conveniently labeled "Q. HORATII FLACCI ad CURIONEM Epistola. *Or, An Epistle from Horace in Elizium to* CURIO *in England, faithfully translated into* English, *from* the Elizian *Copy. By* J. M. *of the Inner-Temple, Barrister.*" It appeared on 16 June 1739, and begins:

> Pert meddling Bard! must I arise,
> > From Bliss each Year, and fix my Name
> To *Gossips* Tales, and *Patriot* Lies,
> > To *St. John*'s Worth, and WALPOLE'S Shame?

The entire poem continues in the same spirit of the government's distinction between Horace and Pope: "If you quote more—I must protest, / And swear your Sense is none of mine," Horace insists. He hopes to be praised by the ruler Pope and his friends attacked, for "If on my verse OCTAVIUS smile, / Who ever blames, I ask no more." Two other stanzas make dramatically clear the change in one aspect of Horace's reputation and the difference between the administration and opposition satirist:

> Own'd by MAECENAS Good and Just,
> > How diff'rent now his Poet's Doom?
> *Britain* with Scorn now treats my Dust,
> > Tho' deem'd an honest Bard at *Rome.*

> 'Twou'd blast the Wreath that *Phoebus* gave,
> > At my fair Fame and Honour strike;
> Cou'd it be wrote upon thy Grave,
> > That P—— and HORACE thought alike.[29]

---

[29] This poem also appears in *A Miscellaneous Collection of Original Poems* . . . and earlier prose pieces in defense of the Walpole administration (London, 1740), pp. 52-56. The author is T[homas] N[ewcomb]. The same volume, pp. 49-51, includes "*An Ode of similies, on some late imitations of* Horace: *The* Latin *printed on one side, and the* English *on the other.*" Newcomb again emphasizes the difference between Pope and Horace.

> Those who deserv'd the ax and rods,
> > In thy own lov'd *Octavius'* days,

Horace and J. M. surely had readers willing to hear more of the same, and so on 6 July the *Gazetteer* played a variation on the Elizium theme, berating Pope for the harshness and breadth of his satire, for foolishly thinking himself equal to the best poets of antiquity, and "rashly, I wish none had thought *ridiculously*, assum'd the Style and Authority of *Horace*; and in that superior Light, look'd down on your Brethren as Creatures whose Character and Fame depended wholly on your Imperial *Fiat*." If Pope had bothered to think that ridiculous irony may temporarily entertain, but "Virtue and Beneficence alone *continue to please*," his reputation—and sales—might have been better, and he "would have left some of *Horace*'s Epistles without Imitation."

By the mid to late 1730s, then, for those politically involved there were two important images of Horace: he was for the opposition and many in the court party the friend of Augustus and thus the active enemy of liberty; for the smaller group charged with answering opposition tirades, he was the exemplar of proper support for a good government, reasoned discourse, polite satire that avoided names, and the enemy of "patriotic" excess. As we have seen, Pope used both views to satiric, if not personal, advantage in the first *Dialogue* of the *Epilogue to the Satires*, where his "Friend," a loyal court apologist, provides the vision of a compliant house-satirist. Those lines—not to mention the *Gazetteer*'s ghostly epistle—align Horace with the court and Walpole, and should make it difficult to support the hy-

---

Make pious hero's, saints, and gods,
In *British* verse, and *Tw——am* lays.

(P. 51)

Lady Mary and Lord Hervey had already noticed Pope's typographical and literary methods. In 1733 they complained that in Pope's *Fortescue* "on one side we see how *Horace* thought; / And on the other, how he never wrote" (*Verses Address'd to the Imitator of the First Satire of the Second Book of Horace* [London, 1733], p. 3).

147

pothesis that Pope and his friends wished to reproduce an image of the Horatian-Augustan civilized enclave.

Of course it was not always that way, and it is fair to say that Horace did not indelibly become the collaborator until about the middle of the 1730s. As late as 1735 Pope tells the readers of *The First Satire of the Second Book of Horace Imitated* that *"An Answer from Horace was both more full, and of more Dignity, than any I cou'd have made in my own person."*[30] Even well into the 1730s the opposition occasionally tried to portray Horace as a snippy, independent railer, and thus still a paradigm for their own methods. Such attempts were likely to be met by the withering blasts of the *Gazetteer* of 27 October 1738, discussed above, a reaction to "Mr. *D'Anvers* and his Fellow Labourers."

D'Anvers' affection for Horace faded after a short while.

---

[30] *Imitations of Horace*, p. 3. The Advertisement to the poem (1733) was added in 1735. Horace and Pope were not always considered as enemies, and Horace, of course, was not always rejected as the fawning sycophant. What I have called compartmentalization—the willing suspension of moral judgment in the face of aesthetic pleasure—was consistently present. For one amiable discourse between the two very different satirists, see D. M., *Ancient Rome and Modern Britain Compared. A Dialogue, In Westminister Abbey, Between Horace and Mr. Pope* (London, 1793). Though Horace receives some criticism, he and Pope have a civilized, if tiresome, discussion in a place uncongenial to each man. Pope and Horace would have been opposed on several nonpolitical matters as well. As one instance of the reaction to Horace's sexual preferences, see *Advice. A Satire* (London, 1746), in which a poet and his friend, the former a reincarnation of Pope, discuss the times and the proper reaction to them.

> Let *Ch——rd——n* with a chaplet round his head,
> The taste of *Maro* and *Anacreon* plead;
> "Sir, *Flaccus* knew to live as well as write,
> And kept, like me, two boys array'd in white.
> Worthy to feel that appetence of fame
> That rivals *Horace* only in his shame!" (P. 9)

"Appetence" has lost its earlier, and here appropriate, meaning of "Carnal desire; sensual desire" (Johnson's *Dictionary*, 1755).

The *Craftsman*, nos. 122 and 182 (2 November 1728, 27 December 1729), for example, are warmly pro-Horatian. In the former he is "an honest brave Man" for continuing to write satire, and in the latter he is Caleb's "old Friend" who, in the Damasippus (*Sat.*, ii. 3), vents "his *own Reflections* on the Vices and Follies of those Times." As long as a remotely reasonable case could be made for Horace as an underground Bolingbroke or intermittently in opposition, he could be used as an authority. But even in the opening years of the *Craftsman*'s campaign Horace's association with the court created an uncomfortable tension, one that could be resolved only by the divorce of that poet from most opposition rhetoric and authority. Numbers 7 and 10 (26 December 1726, 6 January 1727) already equate Horace with Walpole; number 143 (29 March 1729) attacks those instruments of state who serve bad ends and prostitute themselves "for a *Place*, a *Pension*, or a *Bribe*"; numbers 105 and 117 (6 July, 28 September 1728), among others, attack Walpole as a screener of the vicious, a term that Pope, we saw, adapted for Horace himself. By 1738 the administration had, as it were, stolen Horace from the opposition in any case, for he was the archetypal supportive poet. Virgil's exalted pro-Augustan poems were less valuable because less topical and thus less adaptable than Horace's, though he too suffered gravely from the cluster, with varying emphases, of Augustus-George II-Walpole-Tyranny or, more simply, Augustus-Tyranny. But Horace was a satirist, and thus firmly committed to "attack"—an attack nevertheless affirming that Augustus is on his throne and all's right with the world. Nothing could be further from the spirit of Pope's later poetry; but Pope's spirit is like that of the indignant, free, protesting, risky satire that many readers, commentators, and poets between about 1600 and 1800 thought characterized much British satire in general, and Juvenal in particular.

CHAPTER 5

"Juvenal alone never prostitutes his muse": The Juvenalian Alternative

THE EIGHTEENTH-CENTURY DEBATE REGARDING THE MERITS of the classical satirists normally reduced itself to a contest between the partisans of Horace and Juvenal. Only Casaubon among the major critics made a sustained case for Persius' superiority, while most others were content to let him hold the coats as the courtier insinuated and the rhetor declaimed their different ways to the same laurel.[1] Modern students have decided that Horace won during the later years of the seventeenth and the early years of the eighteenth century, and that Juvenal was revived, rehabilitated, or otherwise brought back into fashion some time after mid-century.[2]

[1] The best contemporary account of these several seventeenth-century debates is in Dryden's "Discourse concerning the Original and Progress of Satire," prefatory to his translation of Juvenal and Persius in 1693. Isaac Casaubon's *De Satyrica Graecorum poesi et Romanorum satira* (1605), and his Prolegomena to his edition of Persius (1605), argue for Persius' superiority. Dryden's "Discourse" and its backgrounds have recently been well discussed by William Frost in *The Works of John Dryden: Poems 1693-1696*, vol. 4, ed. A. B. Chambers, William Frost, and Vinton A. Dearing (Berkeley and Los Angeles: Univ. of California Press, 1974), pp. 514-27. For further discussion of the arguments and their progress, see William Frost "Dryden and 'Satire,'" *SEL*, 11 (1971):401-16, and chapters 2 and 3 of P. K. Elkin, *The Augustan Defence of Satire* (Oxford: Clarendon Press, 1973), pp. 11-43.

[2] For some of these, see W. B. Carnochan, *Lemuel Gulliver's Mirror for Man* (Berkeley and Los Angeles: Univ. of California Press, 1968), pp. 18-19, 29-30; Carnochan, "Satire, Sublimity, and Sentiment: Theory and Practice in Post-Augustan Satire," *PMLA*, 85 (1970): 260. For the view of later eighteenth-century Juvenalian popularity, see R. C. Whitford, "Juvenal in England 1750-1802," *PQ*, 7 (1928): 9-16. More recently Elkin has claimed that Horatian satire was the sort that men of the seventeenth and eighteenth century "could confidently approve and which they would have liked to live by" (*The Augustan Defence of*

This is not the place to offer a full or even ample history of the contemporary reputations of those two great satirists; but some reconsideration is relevant for my present purpose of tracing the literary implications of the rejection of Augustus in "Augustan" Britain.

Short of tallying the votes of learned shades from 1660-1800, the quarrel must remain at the level of conflicting hypotheses. This is probably as it should be, since such conflict mirrors the ambivalence of the eighteenth century itself. But on balance, I believe, more readers of satire between 1660 and 1800 preferred Juvenal to Horace, though they enjoyed Horace and praised his extensive nonsatiric poetry as well. Another large group regarded the debate as insoluble because the poets were working within different and incomparable species. A third group considered Horace superior.[3] After reading numerous contemporary evaluations, however, I am unwilling to posit convenient Horatian or Juvenalian eras. I am willing to say that the Renaissance view of rough, severe, Juvenalian-Persian satire was alive and influential until at least the later seventeenth century (witness the repetitive poems on the death of Oldham);[4] that the full implications of Casaubon's (1605) derivation of

Satire, p. 156; see also pp. 146 and 152, among other places). According to Elkin, however, in a reversal of the conventional notion, not until "towards the end of the eighteenth century" did most critics commit "themselves completely to a preference for Horace" (p. 160). Such a commitment is doubtful.

[3] Several of the pro-Juvenalians are cited in this chapter. John Dennis offers a classic statement of the generic difference between the two satirists in *"To Matthew Prior, Esq; Upon the Roman Satirists"* (1721), in *The Critical Works of John Dennis*, ed. Edward Niles Hooker, 2 vols. (Baltimore: The Johns Hopkins Press, 1939-1943), 2:218-20. Thomas Blackwell urges Horace's praise in *Memoirs of the Court of Augustus*, 3 vols. (Edinburgh and London, 1753-1763), 3: 63-74.

[4] For some of these, see the prefatory poems by Dryden, Thomas D'Urfey, Thomas Andrews, Thomas Wood, and Robert Gould, in *The Works of Mr. John Oldham, Together with his Remains*, 7th ed. (London, 1710).

satire from *satura lanx* (a full charger) helped to lessen the sting of satire and raise Horace to a genuinely competitive, though not superior, position; that in the first 30 years or so of the eighteenth century many, but not most, readers and writers found Horace preferable to Juvenal; and that by about mid-century the older and always respected Juvenalian mode reasserted itself. Any modification this "progress" may need is in degree, not in essence: it is possible, for example, that Horace was slightly more popular slightly earlier and slightly longer than I suggested. But on the whole, the dominant cast of and taste for English satire during the Restoration and eighteenth century was "Juvenalian" and was so perceived by critics at home and abroad.

In a posthumous work of 1673, for example, Barten Holyday states that "*Horace* had excelled had not *Juvenal* written"; in 1693 Dryden argues that Juvenal was the better satirist; in 1707 Tom Brown describes English satire of his and the preceding generation as overwhelmingly Juvenalian (that is, harsh, exalted in tone); in 1711 Joseph Trapp says that "the *Horatian* Satire is but little affected among us"; in 1721 John Dennis observes that the generality of readers prefer Juvenal to Horace; in 1748 Montesquieu insists that in England "satirical writings are sharp and severe, and we find amongst them many Juvenals without discovering one Horace"; in 1755 Thomas Blackwell complains that, like Juvenal and Persius, "the greater part of the modern Satyrists seldom afford us a smile"; in 1778 Vicesimus Knox claims that the English "have copied the manner of Juvenal rather than of Horace"; in 1782 Joseph Warton can only cite Dorset as a properly Horatian satirist in "refutation" of Montesquieu; and in 1808 Thomas Denman says that Juvenal's traits "are peculiarly consonant to the habits of thinking which have long prevailed in England."[5]

---

[5] Holyday, *Decimus Junius Juvenalis, and Aulus Persius Flaccus Translated* (Oxford) sig. a1v; Dryden, "Discourse concerning . . . Satire," in *John Dryden: Of Dramatic Poesy and other Critical Essays*, ed. George Watson, 2 vols. (New York: Dutton, 1962), 2:129-35; Brown,

Since Juvenal was both pagan and sublunary, he was also subject to certain weaknesses: he was sometimes excessive in declamation and rhetorical posturing; he was often harsh, even vulgar; he was too ugly by far in describing women; he may not have picked his victims carefully enough in flailing at so many around him.[6] One bad trait he did not have was the political sycophancy, collaboration, and support of tyranny commonly attributed to Horace. Instead, he was characterized as the satirist who risked all to protest imperial despotism and decadence and to proclaim the values of the republic that Augustus and his nest of singing birds helped to destroy. It was altogether in the Juvenalian tradition for Johnson's indignant Thales to damn "the laureate tribe" who "in servile verse relate" the establishment's virtues.[7]

"A Short Essay on *English* Satire," in *The Works of Mr. Thomas Brown*, 4 vols., 5th ed. (London, 1720), 1:28-32; Trapp, *Praelectiones Poeticae* (1711-1719), trans. William Bowyer and William Clarke as *Lectures on Poetry* (London, 1742), p. 236; Dennis, "*To Matthew Prior*," *Critical Works*, 2:218; Montesquieu, *The Spirit of the Laws*, trans. Thomas Nugent, 2 vols., 5th ed. (London, 1773), 1:467; Blackwell, *Memoirs of the Court of Augustus*, 3:64; Knox, "On Satire and Satirists," in *Essays Moral and Literary*, 2 vols. (London, 1778), 2:159; Warton, *An Essay on the Genius and Writings of Pope*, 2 vols., 5th ed. (London, 1806), 2:48-49; Denman, *Monthly Review*, second series, 55 (1808): 247. The attribution is in Benjamin Christie Nangle, *The Monthly Review Second Series 1790-1815: Indexes of Contributors and Articles* (Oxford: Clarendon Press, 1955), p. 148 (referred to hereafter as Nangle, *Second Series*).

[6] These complaints appear in several places and are exemplified in Gibbon's largely positive discussion. See his Examination of Juvenal's satires, in "Extraits de mon journal," *Miscellaneous Works*, ed. John Lord Sheffield, 2 vols. (London, 1796), 2:95-119. The 1796 edition, unlike the expanded one of 1814, includes both French and English versions.

[7] The Yale Edition of the Works of Samuel Johnson, vol. 6, *Samuel Johnson: Poems*, ed. E. L. McAdam, Jr., with George Milne (New Haven: Yale Univ. Press, 1964), p. 57, line 198. Subsequent quotations are from this edition.

I: JUVENAL AS OPPOSITION SATIRIST

The image of Juvenal as enemy of tyrants begins at least
as early as 1616 with Nicolas Rigault's—Rigaltius—essay
on Juvenal and Roman satire, a widely read seventeenth-
century commentary and one of Dryden's sources for his
"Discourse" (2:97). Rigault is conventional in many respects: for instance, in his distinction between satiric styles
and the ages appropriate for them.[8] However, he does appear to introduce the image of Juvenal as a libertarian, republican poet whose outrage is the product of a true antique
Roman, the "liberrimi spiritus poeta" who sees his nation's
greatness in decay, hopes to punish those responsible, and
holds up the tattered flags of bygone Roman virtue as the
antidote to imperial poison.[9] Hence the end of Juvenal's
fourth satire, which deals with the terrible reign of Domitian, shows the satirist using the tradition of Corellius Rufus
whose "free and forthright words" encouraged brave men
to curse "their terrible bondage."[10] The fifth satire and its
praise of Thrasea and Helvidius drinking to the birthdays
of Cassius and the Bruti again allude to the republic, "for
certainly anyone born free and noble of spirit will be aware
that those two last verses refer to an intense desire to regain

[8] See Howard D. Weinbrot, review of *Lemuel Gulliver's Mirror for Man*, by W. B. Carnochan, *ECS*, 4 (1970): 111.

[9] All references to Rigault are from *D. Junii Juvenalis et A. Persii Flacci satyrae, interpretatione ac notis Ludovicus Prateus* (London, 1694); sig. b2ʳ for this quotation. I now wish to disown my earlier agree-ment with G. G. Ramsay: "Juvenal was no politician; he never casts an eye on the political conditions of his day" (*Juvenal and Persius*, Loeb Classical Library [Cambridge, Mass.: Harvard Univ. Press, 1961], p. xxxvii). See Howard D. Weinbrot, *The Formal Strain: Studies in Augustan Imitation and Satire* (Chicago: Univ. of Chicago Press, 1969), p. 182, n. 27. Whatever the Platonic Juvenal might be, the Restoration and eighteenth century thought of him as a political activist in the cause of "freedom."

[10] Sig. b2ᵛ: "Nempe his vocibus erectis & liberis diram servitutem fortissimi viri exsecrabantur."

liberty."[11] The fourteenth satire laments that one can find a Catiline anywhere, but a Lucius Junius or Marcus Brutus nowhere. Rigault knows that for Juvenal most of the Caesars were "so cruel and tyrannical" that in comparison even the hated King Tarquin the Proud could be considered good. Satires Three and Thirteen also include attacks upon absolute kings: in the one Juvenal degrades his own age by showing that it is more corrupt than that of the royal era, and in the other he mockingly complains that even the shades below were happier in the underworld, without kings ruling them.[12]

Juvenal was not limited to obscurely political attacks; he generally gives shocking examples of varied evils and so rebukes them that all must curse and consign them to darkness. Indeed, like the early Church Fathers who used gross language to awake their readers to the horrors of pagan theology, Juvenal vividly exposed the many vices of Rome. Hence "from that time on, the stirred-up smut assailed the nostrils and the brain; and, in consequence, that sleep-like apathy, which had been crushing out the spirits of the Romans, was shattered and dissolved."[13] Rigault includes political vice in this smut and praises Juvenal for satirizing it. "He kept on writing in an age corrupted by the vices of the Caesars, an age when laws were vanishing along with the throttled voice of magistrates, an age when that one time

11 Ibid.: "Profecto enim quisquis erit natus ingenuus & liber, intelliget duobus postremis versibus ingens [regarding Thrasea and Helvidius] retinendae libertatis desiderium significari."

12 Ibid.: "At Caesarum, si paucos excipias, adeo saeva fuit & importuna dominatio, ut prae illis etiam Tarquinius bonus haberi potuerit." Sig. b3^r: Et suorum temporum saevitiam regiorum comparatione exaggerat in tertia. . . . Quin & decima tertia umbras & maneis ex quo sub regibus degere coeperunt, infeliciores fuisse ait, & continuo paratas ijs poenas."

13 Sig. b5^v: "ut inde excitata spurcities nares & cerebrum feriret; ac per hoc somniculosus ille marcor qui Romanorum animos oppresserat, vehementi indignatione, tamquam sternutamento discuteretur."

Roman courage grew feeble in an almost death-like sleep."[14] Juvenal, he says shortly thereafter, was "a kind of compendium of political principles" whose bias is clear: he was "a magistrate of the old disciplinary code and the most weighty censor of the whole of human life and one who pried deeply into the very secrets of traditions with supreme authority." He attacks many vices "in all his satires," including "the unjust sway of tyrant power."[15] Rigault's Juvenal is a satirist whose occasional excesses are required by the age and justified by his energetic morality and political virtue.

Several other commentators joined Rigault in so characterizing Juvenal. Schrevelius, for example, glosses ii. 28— "if Sylla's three disciples rail against proscription"—in this way: "the triumvirs Augustus, Lepidus, Antonius; who, united by a bloody compact when they invaded the republic, imitated Sylla by ordering senators and knights to be proscribed."[16] Prateus, whose notes, like Schrevelius', were carefully read by Samuel Johnson, is even stronger in his judgment: "The triumvirate simultaneously suppressed liberty and the republic, as also Sylla did, or rather they dared to be infected by the despotic rule of Sylla."[17] Schre-

---

[14] Ibid.: "scribebat seculo Caesarum flagitiis contaminatissimo, legibus una cum elisa magistratuum voce evanidis, Romana illa quondam virtute sopore paene letali marcescente."

[15] Sig. b7ʳ: "Dicamus igitur hosce duos auctores [Juvenal and Marius Maximus] ut civilium doctrinarum compendia quaedam, illius aevi delicatis maxime placuisse: . . . Juvenalem vero ut magistrum veteris disciplinae ac totius vitae humanae censorem gravissimum, in arcana ipsa morum summo cum imperio penetrantem. . . . nam, ut ea mittamus quae sunt publica & ob oculos omnium posita, puta impietatem, fastum, avaritiam, libidinem, iniqua tyrannicae potestatis imperia, quae totis satiris persequitur."

[16] Cornelius Schrevelius, *D. Junii Juvenalis, et Auli Persii Flacci satyrae* (Leiden, 1671), p. 32n: "Augustus, Lepidus, Antonius Triumviri; qui per cruentum foedus juncti, cum remp. in vasissent, Syllam imitati, Senatum, & equestrem ordinem proscripsere."

[17] Ludovicus Prateus, *D. Junii Juvenalis, et A. Persii Flacci satirae . . . in usum serenissimi delphini* (London, 1736), p. 23n.: "Triumviri libertatem & Rempublicam pariter ac Sylla fecerat, opprimentes, an Syllae

velius addressed himself as well to viii. 242-44, and stated
that Cicero's title "father of the country" was earned in the
dangerous defense of liberty, whereas Augustus received his
through flattery.[18]

The spirit of these and comparable glosses was readily
transferable to seventeenth-century English (and French)
translators. Barten Holyday believes that Juvenal expresses
"just indignation . . . against the impotent disingenuities of
Flaccus, who for outward respects would flatter vile
Princes."[19] His Argument to Satire Two proclaims that
"*The Emp'rour then scapes not his quill; | Nor any Great-
ness that dares ill*" (p. 19). Like his predecessors who discussed ii. 28, he blames the Augustan triumvirate for imitating Sylla (p. 24 and p. 275, n. 11), notes that in Satire Five
Juvenal praises those stoics who celebrate the birthdays of
the two Bruti, "both accounted Patriots of their Country"
(p. 81; see also p. 84, n. 6), and clarifies Juvenal's eighth
satire and its fulminations against tyrants and those consuls
in old Rome who aided them (p. 167, n. 28). Holyday also
insists that these several passages show that Juvenal is "a
Lover of the Liberty of . . . the *Roman Commonwealth*" and
a hater of the intruding Caesars, who "by force and fraud
mastered their own Countrey" (p. 275, n. 11). Robert Stapylton (1647) gives comparable glosses and says that Thrasea

---

tyrannidem infectari ausint?" For Johnson's knowledge of these texts,
see Edward A. and Lillian D. Bloom, "Johnson's *London* and its Juvenalian Texts," *HLQ*, 34 (1970): 1-23.

18 Schrevelius, p. 293: "Non per adulationem, ut Augustum. Hoc nam
differt ab Augusto Cicero, quia alia armatus, alia pacatus defenderit
libertatem & civitatem." For further comments on this passage in
Juvenal, see sec. II, below, at notes 37-39.

19 Holyday, *Juvenalis and . . . Persius* (n. 5, above), p. 11. Subsequent
quotations are cited in the text. For a French adaptation of the spirit
of these remarks, see the de la Valterie translation, *Les Satyres de
Juvénal et de Perse*, 2 vols. (Paris, 1681), 2:196. Juvenal surpasses Horace in the quality most necessary for a satirist: "un ame libre, élevée
au dessus de la bassesse des opinions communes, qui ne sçait ce que c'est
que la contrainte, la servitude, la complaisance, & la flaterie."

and Helvidius (praised in v. 42), "would as gladly have ad-
ventured their lives to have freed *Rome* from the tyranny
of *Nero*, as *D. Junius Brutus* ventured his, to free *Rome* of
Tarquin: or *M. Brutus* and *Cassius* theirs for delivering
Rome from the incroachment of *J. Caesar.*"[20]
   Juvenal was thus adaptable for political purposes, and
was so in tone and convention in several satires of the
Restoration period. "A Satire in Answer to a Friend"
(1682?), for example, rails against court politics and the
general depravity of the age, and "A Loyal Satire against
Whiggism" (1682) borrows Juvenal's flight from the corrupt
city where "universal leprosy taints all."[21] By 1683 Thomas
Wood had imitated Juvenal's first satire and used it as a
stick to beat the Whiggish "Faction."[22] The last three satirists show Juvenalian poems and devices in the service of the
court. Such an association could not last long, for as Thomas
Shadwell observed in his imitation of the tenth satire
(1687) "The word [sic] *Reges* and *Tyranni* were become
odious to the *Romans* ever since the time of the *Tarquins*:

[20] *Juvenal's Sixteen Satyrs, or, a Survey of the Manners and Actions
of Mankind* (London, 1673), pp. 23, 139, 225 for the glosses comparable
to Holyday's; p. 66, note m for the quotation. A contemporary hand in
my own copy has substituted "rivalled" for "repealed" in the last sentence above. Stapylton's translation appeared in 1647 and was reprinted
in 1673, at about the time of Holyday's, also of early- to mid-seventeenth-century inspiration.

[21] *Poems on Affairs of State: Augustan Satirical Verse, 1660-1714.
Volume 3: 1682-1685*, ed. Howard H. Schless (New Haven: Yale Univ.
Press, 1968), pp. 28-33, 358. The latter quotation is from the editor's
headnote.

[22] *Juvenalis Redivivus. Or The First Satyr of Juvenal taught to speak
plain English. A Poem* (London), sig. A3ᵛ. Wood follows Rapin in
thinking Juvenal too severe and "scolding," not sufficiently merry and
"sporting," and thus in need of his own softening (sig. A3ʳ). It is worth
noting that Juvenal was apparently respectable enough for Bossuet to
teach to the royal family. See *Oeuvres inédites de J. B. Bossuet. . . . Le
Cours royal complet sur Juvénal*, ed. Auguste-Louis Ménard, 2 vols.
(Paris, 1881), vol. 1.

And *Juvenal* here declares himself a *Republican*."[23] Even the so-called Horatian Charles Sackville, Earl of Dorset, is harshly satiric in his opposition to James II and the aberration of his court as portrayed in "A Faithful Catalogue of Our Most Eminent Ninnies" (1688): "Oh, sacred James! may thy dread noddle be / As free from danger as from wit 'tis free!"[24]

Some years later the Third Earl of Shaftesbury joined his own vision of Juvenal to that of the already emergent one —not so much the scourge of faction but of tyranny. In *Sensus Communis* (1709) he discusses Juvenal, viii. 73, which he apparently reads as "the communal sense is rare in those high places" at Nero's court.[25] Shaftesbury hopes to change the view that Juvenal is being especially satirical in criticizing the court (1:69), for the commentators have taught him that by *sensus communis* Juvenal means a "sense of public weal, and of the common interest; love of the community as society . . . a just sense of the common rights of mankind, and the natural equality there is among those of the same species" (1:70). Under those circumstances it was not extraordinary "to question whether this was properly the spirit of a court," since there was no "community

[23] *The Tenth Satyr of Juvenal, English and Latin* (London), p. 45, n. 60. The note should annotate lines 112-13 of Juvenal's poem: "ad generum Cereris sine caede ac vulnere pauci / descendunt reges et sicca morte tyranni." For another indication of Juvenal as opposed to absolutism, see J. H., *The Tenth Satyr of Juvenal Done into English Verse* (London [1693]), pp. 20-21 (the latter misnumbered p. 9).

[24] *Poems on Affairs of State: Augustan Satirical Verse, 1660-1714. Volume 4 1685-1688*, ed. Galbraith M. Crump (New Haven: Yale Univ. Press, 1968), p. 193.

[25] Anthony Ashley Cooper, *Characteristics of Men, Manners, Opinions, Times* (1711), ed. John M. Robertson, 2 vols. in 1 (rpt. Indianapolis: Bobbs-Merrill, 1964), 1:69: "rarus enim ferme sensus communis in illa / fortuna. . . ." Subsequent citations are given in the text. The quotations regarding France, Horace and Augustus are from *Advice to an Author* (1710) in the *Characteristics*. Shaftesbury's use of Juvenal as an enemy of the court was quoted in the *Gazetteer*, 1 January 1736.

among . . . courtiers," and no "public between an absolute
prince and his slave subjects" (1:70-71). Juvenal thinks that
a court education is unlikely to induce affection for one's
country. Indeed, the overindulged and licentious young
princes are taught "that thorough contempt and disregard
of mankind, which mankind in a manner deserves, where
arbitrary power is permitted and a tyranny adored" (1:71-
72; he then quotes Juvenal, viii. 73-74).

Shaftesbury's respect for Juvenal's politics is consistent
with his own praise of England's revolution. She now has "a
happy balance of power . . . settled between our prince and
people" and can resist France, that modern incarnation of
Rome, which threatens the world with universal monarchy
(1:141). Juvenal is the poet of opposition to court and tyranny, of support for constitutional checks, of the man of wit
outside the establishment because his virtue is too great for
him to be in it. Shaftesbury also admires Horace—"the best
genius and most gentleman-like of Roman poets" (1:211);
but he knows that Horace was inextricably bound to the
court which solidified the absolutism that Nero was to practice so badly, and that he and Virgil helped Augustus'
"usurped dominion" appear enchanting in spite of its chains
(1:144).

The contrast between Horace as tutor and Juvenal as
enemy to an arbitrary court is implicit in the *Characteristics*, though Shaftesbury himself does not draw the infer-
ence. Others had already done so, and in the process elevated Juvenal above Horace precisely because of his resistance to absolutism. To be sure, Juvenal's faults were never
forgotten; but these venial sins were forgiven through the
happy penance of demonstrable commonwealth virtues. The
combined depot and embarkation point for such views was
Dryden's "Discourse concerning . . . Satire" (1693), the long
and influential preface to his translation of Juvenal and
Persius, which is indebted to Rigault—among others—and
his vision of a politically motivated satirist.[26]

[26] All quotations are from volume 2, *Of Dramatic Poesy and other
Critical Essays*, ed. Watson (n. 5, above).

Dryden offers high praise for Horace, whose instruction,
subtlety, and general poetic skills are superior to Juvenal's;
but Juvenal affords more pleasure, thus "we cannot deny
that Juvenal was the greater poet . . . in satire" (2:131) and
should "ride first in triumph" (2:141) in the contest with
Horace and Persius. Horace attacks folly, Juvenal attacks
vice; Horace's style is the comic, low, and "generally grovel-
ling," Juvenal's is lofty and sublime (2:129-30;144); Horace's
"wit is faint; and his salt . . . almost insipid," Juvenal is of
a more "vigorous and masculine wit" and is "much more elevated . . . and more noble" (2:130). The time and temperament of each is reason for these differences—and Juvenal's
superiority. Horace, "as he was a courtier, complied with
the interest of his master," an interest that demanded attacking neither the foibles of Augustus nor his friends. He
was "a mild admonisher, a Court satirist" fit for Augustus'
relatively gentle reign, "and more fit" because he himself
"was dipped in the same actions" as Augustus and hence
could not portray their ugliness. As a result, Horace's subjects "are of a lower nature" than Juvenal's (2:134-35).

That lowness is both a qualitative and a political judgment. Horace acknowledges as master a prince who violently
usurped the freedom of Rome; he thus accommodates his
style to the groveling mode. Juvenal fights the imperial settlement that Horace helped to propagate. Dryden's final
judgment is clear as he explains what he means by "Juvenal
was the greater . . . in satire."

> His thoughts are sharper; his indignation against vice is
> more vehement; his spirit has more of the commonwealth
> genius; he treats tyranny, and all the vices attending it,
> as they deserve, with the utmost rigour: and consequently
> a noble soul is better pleased with a zealous vindicator of
> Roman liberty than with a temporizing poet, a well-man-
> nered Court slave, and a man who is often afraid of laugh-
> ing in the right place; who is ever decent, because he is
> naturally servile. . . . [For Juvenal] oppression was to be
> scourged instead of avarice: . . . the Roman liberty was to

be asserted. There was more need of a Brutus in Domitian's days, to redeem or mend, than of a Horace, if he had
been living, to laugh at a fly-catcher. This reflection at the
same time excuses Horace, but exalts Juvenal. (2:131-32)

Dryden's censures and judgments were so well known that
in 1721 John Dennis tells Matthew Prior that the generality
of readers prefer Juvenal to Horace because Dryden does.
Many of those readers agreed with Dryden's character of a
political Juvenal. Tom Brown, for instance, will not in-
volve himself in the evaluation of Horace and Juvenal since
Dryden's able hand was before him. But he does characterize Juvenal as the opposition lasher of tyrants and the base
Roman Empire. He hoped only "to reform a luxurious,
bloody Court, a cowardly Senate, and despicable Populace."
Shortly thereafter, the author of *Mirth in Ridicule* also refuses a lengthy comparison and contrast between the two
satirists, since many of the best writers of England and
France had already done that job. But he does insist that
Horace was far too polite and laughing in his desire to
please great men who, like himself, "had lately lost the
Liberties they were born to." He tickled rather than cut
vice deeply. "*Juvenal* with a more generous Freedom de-
claim'd against Vice, like a free-born *Roman*, as if he had
breath'd an Air of Liberty under the Power of the ancient
Consuls, and had not seen both himself, and the Imperial
Majesty of *Rome*, subjected to the Humours of a tyrant." Joseph Trapp's lecture on satire favors Juvenal over
Horace on many of the same standards that Dryden used.
Juvenal is the fiery, tragic, exalted, biting satirist, whose
"Smiles are very different from those of *Horace*; they
are not the genteel ones of a Courtier, but mix'd with
Gall and ill Nature" against the vicious reprobates he
attacks. A few years later Lewis Crusius also evaluates
the chief Roman satirists, embodies the accepted wisdom,
and is confident that Juvenal, in whom "satire seems to
have arrived to its highest perfection," will "appear a true

generous spirited *Roman*, a friend to liberty and virtue."[27] Though Crusius gives full credit to Horace and some to Persius, he believes that the more exalted Juvenal "has undoubtedly improved on both" (2:80), and that if Horace were "a worse courtier, he would have been more severe" (2:89)—that is, better. The anonymous compiler of the *Biographia Classica* (1740) quotes much of Dryden's decisive passage on Juvenal's superiority and agrees that Juvenal, like a Brutus, had to assert the *"Roman* Liberty." The student who read a Dublin edition of the following year annotated his copy in many of Dryden's most political sections. He records that *"Dryden did not admire Horace's Satires,"* and later underscores key descriptions of Juvenal's satire and Horace's character: Juvenal's "Indignation against *Vices* [was] *more vehement"* than that of Horace, who was "a well-manner'd *Court-Slave"*; and he places a line in the margin here and where Dryden labels Horace the "naturally servile" and *"Temporizing* Poet." Corbyn Morris prefers Juvenal to Horace because the severe attack of true satire shows "a generous free Indignation, without any sneaking Fear or Tenderness; It being a sort of partaking in the Guilt to keep any Terms with Vices." Such partaking in guilt, we may infer, is well exemplified in Horace's relationship with Augustus. In 1745 we again hear a traditional evaluation of the two satirists based to some degree, I suggest, on political purity. Horace, John Brown says in celebration of Pope's death, "Politely sly, cajol'd the foes of sense"; but Juvenal's "mighty numbers aw'd corrupted *Rome* / And swept audacious greatness to its doom." Indeed, satire must raise its voice "When private Faith and publick Trust are sold, / And traitors barter liberty for gold."[28]

[27] Dennis, *Critical Works*, 2:218; Brown, *Works*, 1:30; *Mirth* (London, 1708), pp. 3-4; Trapp, *Lectures*, p. 228; Crusius, *Lives of the Roman Poets* (1726), 2 vols., 3rd ed. (London, 1753), 2:78, 80. Subsequent quotations from Crusius are cited in the text.

[28] *Biographia Classica*, 2 vols. (London), 1:303. These volumes are especially interesting, since they were "chiefly design'd for the Use and

Juvenal's pro-republican, anti-imperial character was established early in the seventeenth century, transported to later seventeenth-century England, and solidified as one part of his positive satiric reputation. This familiar concept and the comparison with Horace's unpleasant collaborative behavior influenced Gibbon in 1763 and, across the Channel in France, Jean Dusaulx in 1770 and beyond.

Gibbon's remarks are especially instructive, since he admired Horace, had a clear perception of Juvenal's weaknesses, and, until his stay in Lausanne in 1763, had never read Juvenal. Between 17 August and 17 September of that year, however, he becomes so thoroughly acquainted with Juvenal that he will "in future . . . be one of my favourite authors."[29] Gibbon has reservations about some of Juvenal's exaggerations, "malignity of heart" (2:99), occasional lapses of reasoning, and excess of declamation, but he regards these as small blemishes on a great poet's art, its noble indignation against vice, and transcendent style. "Managed by him, the Roman language loses all its roughness" (2:117-18). The greatest area of Gibbon's praise, however, relates to Juvenal's refusal to surrender republican ideals for imperial realities. On 24 August he praises "the council of Domitian" in the fourth satire as "perhaps, the most striking passage of satire to be met with in any ancient author." The subject is "perfectly suited" to Juvenal's genius, well employs his "seriousness of indignation, and energy of expression," and

---

Instruction of *younger* Scholars" (1:iv) and thus serve as a compendium of received knowledge. There was a second London edition in 1750. The Dublin 1741 edition's relevant MS notes are on pp. 193 and 274 (British Library shelf mark 10605 aaa.2). The same information was expropriated for Edward Harwood's *Biographia Classica* (1778). Morris, *Essay Towards Fixing the true Standards of Wit, Humour, Raillery, Satire, and Ridicule* (London, 1714), pp. 50-51; Brown, *Essay on Satire: Occasion'd by the Death of Mr. Pope* (London, 1745), pp. 25, 26, 21.

29 Sheffield, *Miscellaneous Works*, 2:116. Subsequent citations, all from this 1796 edition, are given in the text. The entire passage, from the "Extraits de mon Journal," is pertinent to the study of Juvenal.

demonstrates his justifiable "detestation for the tyrant and contempt for the Romans" (2:96). On 6 September he states that Satire Thirteen shows Juvenal "an old Roman, who hearkened to Cato rather than Chrysippus" (2:111).

Gibbon's most sustained expression of Juvenal as a political creature comes on 31 August in his discussion of the eighth satire, the poem in which Cicero's preservation of the republic is preferred to Octavian's creation of the empire:

> Juvenal speaks, from one end of it to the other, the language of an ancient Roman. We perceive throughout, not only the dignity of a true censor, who arraigns vice, exposes folly, and appals guilt, but the soul of a republican, reluctantly bending under the new constitution, the sworn enemy of tyranny, and the friend of a mild and equitable monarchy, rather through necessity than inclination. This love of liberty, and loftiness of mind, distinguishes Juvenal from all the poets who lived after the establishment of the monarchy. Virgil, Horace, Ovid, Lucan, Martial, Statius, Valerius Flaccus, all sing the ruin of their country, and the triumph of its oppressors. . . . Juvenal alone never prostitutes his muse. . . . he never loses an opportunity of arraigning the folly and tyranny of those masters of the world and their deputies. He does more; he teaches how the evils inflicted by them may be cured [through revolution]. (2:103-4)

By refusing to sing his country's ruin Juvenal establishes himself as the darling of those for whom politics, history, and literary evaluation were intimately connected.

As the years passed, such praise of Juvenal and contrast with Horace became even more entrenched in literate Britain's inheritance from the classics. These methods and judgments were also to become part of France's inheritance, to revisit Britain as a Gallic plant, and to put down deeper roots in congenial British soil. I am speaking of Jean Dusaulx's important edition and discussion of Juvenal, announced in 1757, published in 1770, and reissued with an expanded discourse on the Latin satirists in 1782, 1789, and 1803.[30] His edition of 1770 earned an invitation to membership in the Académie des Inscriptions et Belles-Lettres (1776); he subsequently was politically active on behalf of the French Republic, found himself resisting its direction,

[30] The first volume of the fourth edition (Paris, 1803), includes a long "éloge historique de DUSAULX, par M. *Villeterque*," which supplies relevant biographical information. R. C. Whitford notes that Dusaulx's Juvenal "was well known in England during the half-century" ("Juvenal in England 1750-1802" [n. 2, above], p. 12, n. 16). Since the first edition appeared in 1770, Whitford overstates, but his general point is correct. As a fourth edition in 1803 suggests, Dusaulx was also read in France, in spite of the new, Napoleonic dispensation. For some of this fame, see Dr. Charles Burney's review of the relevant volume of *Lycée ou cours de littérature ancienne et moderne* by La Harpe, in *Monthly Review*, second series, 34 (1801): 8-9. For the attribution, see Nangle, *Second Series*, p. 234. La Harpe himself parallels Horace and Juvenal and offers a respectful and reasoned, if sometimes hysterical, "refutation" of Dusaulx. See also Michel de Cubières-Palmézeaux, "Lettre à M. de Ximinès, sur l'influence de Boileau en littérature" (Paris, 1787), and Pierre Claude François Daunous' reply, "Observations sur la lettre précédente," each in *Boileau jugé par ses amis et par ses ennemis* (Paris, 1802), pp. 80, 166-67. Dusaulx would, of course, have been known to all the readers of the Boileau controversy of 1786-1787, and to subsequent readers and translators of Juvenal in eighteenth- and nineteenth-century France. See, for example, L. V. Raoul, *Satires de Juvénal, traduites en vers français*, 2 vols. (Paris, 1818), 1:1-6. Jean Marmier discusses Dusaulx briefly—apparently as a minority point of view and revolutionary hangover (*La Survie d'Horace à l'époque romantique* [Paris: Marcel Didier, 1965], pp. 40-41, 82). Dusaulx's distinction was enhanced through his long essay "Sur les satiriques Latins. Premier Mémoire. . . . Horace," read to the Académie des Inscriptions et Belles-Lettres," April 1777. See the Académie's *Mémoires de Littérature* 43 (1776-1779): 157-95. For further, frequently hostile, early nineteenth-century French political evaluation of Horace, see Eusèbe Salverte [Anne-Joseph Eusèbe Baconniere], *Horace et l'empereur Auguste* (Paris, 1823), passim. For yet more French nineteenth-century discussion of Augustus, his poets, and historians, see A. E. Egger, *Examen critique des historiens anciens de la vie et du règne d'Auguste* (Paris, 1844), especially chap. 2.

and was jailed from 1792 to 1794. Long before that, however, his 1770 text and its "Discours Préliminaire" (a more
compact and intense version of the later materials) were
welcomed in Britain. At least three English publications
turned to and printed the same passage—the praise of Juvenal the republican, and the blame of Horace the collaborator. William Rose, in the *Monthly Review*, calls
Dusaulx's the best of the French translations, commends the
"detestation of vice and tyranny" in the "Discours," and
says that no writer has so well and so briefly characterized
the two satirists "with so much truth and justice." *The
Literary Magazine* for December 1791 reprints the relevant
section without attribution or comment, merely calling it
"A Parallel between Horace and Juvenal. Translated from
the French." In 1802 William Gifford, ignorant of this
effort, translates much of the same passage for his preface
to Juvenal. Gifford thinks that Dusaulx is too hard on
Horace and that he is wrong in thinking there was any
liberty left for Augustus to destroy; he also commends
Dusaulx's force and conclusions, and insists that "this de-
clamatory applause" of Juvenal is generally deserved.[31]

Dusaulx is aware that his own countrymen normally prefer Horace to Juvenal, even though neighboring nations
are taken by Juvenal, elevate him above Horace, and follow
Scaliger and others in naming him the prince of satirists.[32]
Though Dusaulx admires Horace as a poet, it is clear that
he disapproves of his personal and political morality, for

[31] Rose, *Monthly*, 42 (1770): 548; attribution in Nangle, *The Monthly
Review First Series 1749-1789: Indexes of Contributors and Articles* (Ox-
ford: Clarendon Press, 1934), p. 105 (referred to hereafter as Nangle);
The Literary Magazine and British Review, 7 (1791): 440-43; Gifford,
The Satires of Decimus Junius Juvenalis (London, 1802), p. liv.

[32] Paraphrased from *Satires de Juvénal traduites par M. Dusaulx*
(Paris, 1770), p. ii. English quotations are from the section translated
in the *Literary Magazine*; sections not there are paraphrased from
Dusaulx's own 1770 "Discours Préliminaire," and are cited in roman
numerals.

he helped "the cruel, but political Augustus, [who] strewed with flowers the path he was silently opening to despotism" (p. 440). Horace adapted himself to the needs and pleasures of the moment rather than posterity, to self-interest rather than national interest, and to the court rather than Rome. The case is altered for Juvenal, who addressed himself to the correction not of taste but of tyranny, and "did not cease to exclaim against usurped power, and to recall to the Romans the glorious ages of their independence" (p. 441). His own age was so hopelessly corrupt that no one dared to mention liberty—except Juvenal, who despised Horace's feeble ridicule and struck out at anyone of any rank who deviated from virtue. Unlike the supple Horace, he was "an incorruptible censor" who spoke only of "vice and virtue, slavery and liberty, folly and wisdom . . . he staked his life on what was true" and dismissed "all those politic consider-ations" which concern "those whose morality consists in ex-teriors." Juvenal "was too generous to flatter tyrants, or to beg the suffrage of their slaves. Panegyrics are generally given for returns; such a traffic he despised" (p. 442). Dusaulx concludes that Horace wrote as a skillful courtier, Juvenal as a zealous citizen (p. xv). Late seventeenth- and early eighteenth-century English critics often cited Rapin's strictures on Juvenal for being too harsh, inadequately genteel, and lacking the polish of an Augustan court; that judgment is reversed, and Dusaulx replaces Rapin as the touchstone of sophisticated French reaction to Juvenal, a reaction that reinforces the established one in Britain and becomes standard in philosophe circles. Just one year after Dusaulx's version appeared, Henri Ophellot de la Pause told readers of his Suetonius that however fine a poet Horace might have been, "peut-être desireroit-on que cet écrivain immortel eût une plume plus chaste avec un esprit plus républicain, & qu'il n'eût jamais fait de satyres." As for Juvenal—"le premier des Poètes pour ceux qui aiment l'emphase [high-toned rhetoric] & la satyre"—he has "beau-

coup tonné contre le despotisme," a fault into which too
few persons have the courage to fall.[33]

Two further examples indicate the breadth and depth of
the view that Juvenal was superior to Horace as a satirist
because superior in political morality: some remarks by
and critical response to the three major translations of
Juvenal between 1789 and 1807, and the almost 200 years
of international comments upon and interpretations of a
particularly delicate anti-Augustan passage in Juvenal.

II: The Continuing Tradition

In the *Monthly Review*, Christopher Lake Moody praises
Martin Madan's Juvenal (1789) and Juvenal and Persius
themselves for their "serious," "manly," "spirited," and
"genuine expressions of virtuous indignation." These satirists were not content with Horatian frivolity and, instead,
"aspire to the honour of pulling wickedness from its very
throne, levelling their darts both at Patrician and Imperial
profligacy."[34] Some years later, Moody also reviews William

[33] Rapin's remarks appear in *Reflections on Aristotle's Treatise of
Poesie*, trans. [Thomas Rymer] (London, 1674), pp. 138-39, sec. 28. It
was almost certainly known to Dryden (*Essays*, 2:239n), reappeared in
Sir Thomas Pope Blount's *De re poetica* (London, 1694), p. 117, in
"Characters and Censures," and in *Biographia Classica*, 1:303-14, among
other places. For Ophellot de la Pause [J. B. C. Isoard Delisle], see
Histoire des douze Césars de Suétone, 4 vols. (Paris, 1771), 4:61-63. At
another place Ophellot, behind the English mask of "Sidney" lecturing
Cromwell, makes this hostile remark: "Virgile & Horace étoient de
beaux génies sans doutes, mais ils n'étoient pas philosophes"—that is,
men of peace who attacked tyranny and bad government (1:343).

[34] *Monthly*, 81 (1789): 481; attribution in Nangle, p. 152. The *Critical
Review* also reviewed each of these translations: Madan, 69 (1790):
22-29; Gifford, second series, 36 (1802): 10-17, 188-92, 316-27; Hodgson,
third series, 14 (1808): 225-41. The *Critical's* reviewers all honor
Juvenal, generally avoid political remarks and praise or blame of the
translators for theirs, and largely consider the quality of the translation
itself. The attack on Gifford is so harsh that a reader of the University
of Chicago's copy (1802), pp. 188, 327, twice records his guess that "Dr.
Wolcot" is the writer.

Gifford's translation of Juvenal (1802), notes his debt to Dusaulx, and says that everyone agrees with Gifford in considering Horace the spoiled child in Augustus' court. Horace reluctantly helped in Augustus' efforts to seek "universal depravation" through the arts (pp. xliv-xlv).[35] For Juvenal, however, no apology need be made—he was, Gifford says, "a republican, who looked upon Trajan as an usurper, no less than Domitian" (p. xxvi, note). The British translator joins Dusaulx in believing that Juvenal recognized "no sovereign but the senate" and "generously celebrated the ancient assertors of liberty" rather than contemporaries whom he might endanger (p. lv).

Francis Hodgson's translation came just five years later and, like the translations by his recent predecessors, received favorable review in the *Monthly*. Thomas Denman argues that Juvenal's "high-toned morality, his noble contempt for meanness, and his irresistible indignation against vice, place him in the first rank of writers formed for the improvement and correction of man." Indeed, his distinguishing traits of character are peculiarly English.[36] These traits

[35] *Monthly*, 40 (1803): 8-9; attribution in Nangle, *Second Series*, p. 148. The quotations are from Gifford's own *Satires of . . . Juvenalis* and are cited in the text. Many of Gifford's notes—like Owen's, Madan's, and Hodgson's—include discussion of Juvenal the republican. See, for instance, p. 290, *Satires*, viii. 303, and p. 300, *Satires*, viii. 373.

[36] *Monthly*, second series, 55 (1808): 246-47; attribution in Nangle, *Second Series*, p. 148 (some notes are by Moody). Denman knew Hodgson and was a subscriber to his translation. The quotations from Hodgson, cited in roman numbers, are from *The Satires of Juvenal* (London, 1807). The line "And branded Vice, however high her name" is probably a conscious echo of Pope's imitation of Horace, *Satires*, ii. 1 (*Fortescue*), line 106, and of the indignant opposition tone of that section. "Call'd back the glories of the past in vain" may echo Johnson's *London*, line 26. Each satirist resists oppression. Juvenal was also thus characterized by Henry Richard Vassal Fox, Lord Holland. See his "Secession," an imitation of Juvenal's third satire, in *Imitations* (London, 1799 [?]). The speaker laments: "Born to my Rights, while England yet was FREE, / This busy City has no charms for me!" (p. 5). Lord Holland later said that if "I infused little of the poetry, I forced at least much

included Juvenal's political sympathies and the risks he took in proclaiming them. Denman quotes much of Hodgson's prefatory poem on the progress of satire, thus giving it yet wider circulation. We see that Horace "taught the struggling soul that captive gait, / That vain urbanity which wins the Great." Juvenal's force is anything but captive, even though he appears after "sly Octavius seiz'd th' imperial reins, / And hid in flow'rs the despot's iron chains" (p. xxxvii), and even though the tyrants who feared him deluged Rome "in her children's blood."

> The poet's courage with the danger grew,
> And fiercely at the eagle's nest he flew;
> With daring soul tyrannic pow'r defied,
> Spoke the plain truth, and spoke it, though he died.
> His noble rage despis'd all humbler game,
> And branded Vice, however high her name;
> To slavish use no weak respect he paid,
> But still rever'd the Senate's empty shade;
> Call'd back the glories of the past in vain,
> And breath'd his strong, republican disdain.
>
> (Pp. 250-51; Hodgson, p. xxxviii)

The lines that Denman omits are equally insistent on Juvenal's political virtue, consequent glory, and superiority to his delicate and philosophical satiric ancestors.

> While blaze the fires of Liberty, enshrin'd
> In their pure seat, the patriotic mind;
> And while, exalted by such holy fires,
> Far o'er the courtly slave that mind aspires—
>
> .   .   .   .

---

of the bitterness of the original" (*Memoirs of the Whig Party During My Time,* 2 vols. ed. Henry Edward Lord Holland [London, 1852], 1:134). Juvenal and Hodgson did not receive a uniformly good press. The first owner of my own copy of Hodgson—William Lamb—notes the *Edinburgh Review,* 12 (1808): 50-62 on the title page. That journal largely disapproves of the author and his translator.

So long th' Aquinian shall transcend in praise
Flaccus' light wit, and Persius' rugged lays;
So long shall Vice beneath his lashes groan,
And future times be punish'd in his own;
Apply th' anticipating scourge, and dread
The thunder launch'd at a forefather's head.

(Pp. xxxviii-xxxix)

Denman, of course, approves of these passages and the ones in Juvenal that support them and, in general, confirms the paradoxical view of Horace's imperial debility and Juvenal's republican vigor.

Juvenal as proper political mentor thus gains approbation from the earlier seventeenth through the earlier nineteenth centuries: from Rigault to Hodgson one could agree that so long as indignation against tyranny was superior to collaboration, "So long th' Aquinian shall transcend in praise." This view may be seen in microcosm in the responses to lines 240-44 of Juvenal's eighth satire, which praise the "new man" Cicero for his defense of the republic against Catiline, and insist that he deserves more honor for such an action than the aristocratic Octavian deserves for his victories at Actium and Philippi. Here is the Loeb text's neutral translation: "Thus within the walls his toga won for him as much name and honour as Octavius gained by battle [in] Leucas; as much as Octavius won by his sword wet from constant killing on the plains of Thessaly; but then Rome was yet free when she styled Cicero the Parent and Father of his country!"[37]

Almost all who comment on these lines say or imply that the praise of Cicero was genuine, the praise of Octavian flattery. Similarly, all the translators, including those who are relatively literal, urge the presence of "*Octavius's* bloody Sword" (Holyday [1673], p. 157), the "discolour'd" field of Philippi (Stepney-Dryden), his "Sword stain'd with continual Slaughter" (Sheridan), or his "continual slaughters"

---

[37] Ramsay (n. 9, above), pp. 177-79.

(Madan).[38] One thus need not have immediate political interests to find the contrast between Augustus' destruction and Cicero's protection of the republic.

But if one were so motivated, or if one were simply feeling melodramatic, the passage allowed for heated interpretations. Hence, in 1695 Père Tarteron's prose version bravely proclaims: "Auguste doit sa gloire au sang de mille & mille citoyens immolez à sa ambition, qui mit Rome dans les fers: mais Rome encore libre a honoré Cicéron du beau nom de Père de la patrie." By 1763 Edward Burnaby Greene's imitation makes Tarteron seem muted. Though Greene mentions neither orator nor triumvir, he grasps the point of Juvenal's lines. If one is benevolent, virtuous, religious, and truly patriotic, not courtly and sycophantic, then "Ev'n monarch's selves shall crown thy mighty race." That is the archetype of the republican Cicero; here is the imperial Octavian:

> But if thy hands, in slaughter's streams imbru'd,
> Incessant riot in a loose of blood;
> If, proudly trampling on another's rights,
> Ambition fires thee, or if lust incites;
> If still thou revell'st in th' oppressive joys,
> Till the arm wearies, and the bosom cloys;
> Curse on thy birth,—no traces I descry,
> But of a haughty murd'rer rear'd on high;
> Insulted lineage stares thee in the face,
> Thy nation's monster, and thy friend's disgrace.

Dusaulx predictably shows his hostility in this comment: Juvenal describes "la tranquilité de son regne, si fécond en flatteurs, qu' à l'extinction de tous les vrais citoyens, qui avoient péri, soit dans les champs de Philippes, soit à la bataille d'Actium, ou pendant le cours des proscriptions."

---

[38] For Stepney, see Dryden's *Satires of Decimus Junius Juvenalis* (London, 1693), p. 164; [Sheridan], *The Satires of Juvenal* (London, 1739), p. 241 (2nd ed., 1745); Madan, *A New and Literal Translation of Juvenal and Persius*, 2 vols. (London, 1789), 1:411.

Edward Owen was but slightly less indignant when, in 1785, he depicted Cicero's successful "patriot cares" and "Octavian's false renown" for his victories "drench'd with blood of thousands basely slain." As a result of those victories, his translation suggests, "slavery . . . prevail'd" and Rome's "free voice" was stifled.[39]

William Gifford's translation appeared in 1802, but its tone and, in this instance, intention are the same as those of his predecessors. The text itself is a reasonably close but colored version, for his Augustus (not Octavian) gained less than the highest honor through his "flood / Of patriot gore, and sword still drench'd with blood" (p. 300). What was implicit in Juvenal has been made explicit in Tarteron's "citoyens," Greene's "oppressive joys," Owen's "slavery . . . prevail'd" and Gifford's "patriot gore." Gifford's long note on the passage sums up two centuries of multilingual commentary; it stresses Juvenal's "trait of the stern republican," his criticism of Rome's slavery under the emperors, his "manly and independent spirit," the price—banishment— he paid for this "indignation at the fallen state of his country," and the essential point of the lines themselves:

> The *toga* of Cicero, and the *sword* of Augustus, are strikingly contrasted. It must be admitted, that this emperor was, at one period of his life, too lavish of human blood; but his clemency was more fatal, perhaps, to our author's cause, than his cruelty. Juvenal, however, was no compromiser; he hated Augustus. (P. 300n)

39 Tarteron, *Les Satyrs de Perse et de Juvénal* (Paris), p. 369; Greene, *The Satires of Juvenal Paraphrastically Imitated, And adapted to the Times* (London), pp. 116-17; Dusaulx, *Satires de Juvénal*, p. xxix, n. 8 (see also pp. vij and xxx, n. 12); Owen, *The Satires of Juvenal*, 2 vols. (London), 1:186. According to Owen, "It seems but worthy of the spirit of freedom, which Juvenal generally breathes, to suppose that he means a reflection upon the cool cruelty of Octavian after . . . Philippi" (1:186, n. 242). Owen's notes express much awareness of Juvenal's political satire.

III: JUVENAL AND WALPOLE

We have gone from 1616 to 1807 and have seen Juvenal emerge first as generically political in the simple sense of being for free and against tyrannic government. During part of the Restoration period he is briefly enrolled on the side of the Cavaliers as a scourge of disloyal Whigs; he is soon moved out of that courtly company and into the "republican" enclaves of opposition to imperial abuse of absolute power. Consequently, he is elevated above Horace precisely because of that opposition status as the romanticized defender of the glories of yesterday's virtue in the heart, home, and state. Once we recall the many poets and men of letters in the opposition to Sir Robert Walpole and their rhetoric of protest against tyranny, it is not surprising that Juvenal, even in the mutilated mask of Horace, should be attractive.

Seventeen thirty-eight through 1740 are vintage years for such practically employed Juvenalian tones and adaptations, especially so since they show Pope irrevocably committed to the opposition, no longer holding out hope for reconciliation with the first minister, and no longer needing even the flimsy and intentionally deceptive façade of court satirist that the *Epistle to Augustus* (1737) provided. As we have seen, the first *Dialogue* of the *Epilogue to the Satires* (1738) establishes Pope's ultimate anti-Augustan, pro-Juvenalian stance. Almost simultaneously the transference of Juvenal from covert to overt opposition eminence was made in Johnson's *London*, his imitation of Juvenal's third satire. That poem offered a natural parallel for opposition purposes: Walpole's London was so corrupt that it could be described only in terms of Domitian's and Nero's Rome; Walpole and his client George II are linked with absolutism and usurpation; the decay of England is foreshadowed through the decay of Rome. Similarly, in each the true citizen and values that made national greatness are lost in

175

favor of corrupting foreigners, and the parliament is debased and acts at the command of its tyrannical head. Johnson punctuates his poem with the appropriate and familiar emotional counters—praise of Elizabeth, Alfred, and previous English greatness; attacks on pensioned court-flunkies; moans about the licensed stage and its neutered foreign warblers; the court's and *Gazetteer*'s dullness; and, of course, the consequent persecution of surly but real native virtue and talent. Johnson also includes the implications of revolution that Gibbon was to find 26 years later in the eighth satire: "Quick let us rise, the happy seats explore, / And bear oppression's insolence no more" (lines 174-75).[40]

All this is clear enough. Juvenal has, as it were, come out of the closet of theoretical, occasional, or simply allusive attack. Not tone and conventions but a complete satire has been pressed into service. What has not been clear, however, is the way in which Johnson's Juvenalian satire may have adapted an aspect of classical Augustan history for its own anti-Augustan (king and princeps) purposes. Specifically, the Orgilio passage in which a rich and corrupt minister sees his house burnt down by "heaven's just bolts," but also sees his pensioned band replace everything he had in excess (lines 194-209), has no warrant in the London of 1737-1738. It is a serious mistake unless it has a relevant political link. Since Johnson easily could have omitted it, as he did other passages, he may have wished us to see the parallel with Augustus Caesar's own palace that was burnt to the ground and restored by Roman citizens. Suetonius places the fire within a context of the people's affection for their master:

40 The verb "Rise," in definition 14 of Johnson's *Dictionary* (1755) is "To break into military commotions; to make insurrections." We know that line 37 of Pope's Prologue to Addison's *Cato* (1713) had to be changed from "Britons, arise" to "Britons attend," to soothe Addison's fears of seeming seditious (The Twickenham Edition of the Poems of Alexander Pope, vol. 6, *Alexander Pope: Minor Poems*, ed. Norman Ault and John Butt [New Haven: Yale Univ. Press, 1954], p. 98).

The Veteranes, the Decuries [a body of ten men in the army], the Tribes, and even Persons of every Rank, made a voluntary contribution, according to their Ability, to the Rebuilding his House on Palatine Mount, which was consum'd by Fire. But he accepted only a small Portion out of the Heaps which were advanc'd him, not suffering any Man to go beyond a *Denarius.*

According to Dio Cassius, after the fire "tho' several persons made him great offers to repair the Damage, he contented himself with taking a piece of Gold of every Corporation, and a Drachma of every Private Man.... When Augustus had rebuilt the Palace, he made it all publick."[41]

These are positive views of Augustus, but considering the wide hostility to him, especially among the opposition of the moment, a patriot author and reader might have responded like this: The agent of the modern Augustus is all too like the Roman tyrant who received "voluntary contributions" from the army dependent upon him for donatives and advancement, and who tested great men by seeing whether they would respond with undemanded gifts; in effect he taxed the common people in order to rebuild his own palace, which he allowed them to visit partly out of obligation, partly out of prudent politics, and, one suspects, under strict supervision and probably when he was not in residence. His acceptance of "a small Portion" of the offered "Heaps" nonetheless must have equalled or exceeded the

41 *The Lives of the XII. Caesars, or the First Twelve Roman Emperors,* trans. [Jabez Hughes], 2 vols. (London, 1717), 1:109: Augustus 57; *The History of Dion Cassius Abridg'd by Xiphilin,* trans. Francis Manning, 2 vols. (London, 1704), 1:171-72: lv. 12. 5. The episode was also recounted in Laurence Echard's *The Roman History,* 2 vols. (London, 1695-1698), 2:40, and Thomas Hearne's *Ductor Historicus,* 2 vols., 2nd ed. (London, 1705-1704 [sic]), 2:3. Each modern version sounds indebted more to Dio Cassius than Suetonius; Hearne is also using Echard as a source. For a discussion of Johnson's apparently inept imitation of the fire-scene, see Thomas E. Maresca, *Pope's Horatian Poems* (Columbus: Ohio State Univ. Press, 1966), pp. 197-98.

real loss, since "Persons of every rank" in the city, the army, and even the country (there were rustic "Tribes") contributed. Such an Augustan act, Johnson may have wished to remind us behind the Juvenalian parallel, is what one can expect from King George II and his prime minister. If this conjecture is accurate, Johnson's Orgilio scene is not the excrescence we have thought it, but is yet another way for the modern Juvenal to proclaim himself an enemy of the corrupt court, of whichever Augustus at whatever time.

Both Pope's and Johnson's poems were popular, so much so that Pope's earned him a real threat, and Johnson's a fancied one, from the government.[42] Such success in galling the administration's flanks did not go unnoticed. Just one year later, they were joined by Paul Whitehead's *The State of Rome, under Nero and Domitian . . . By Messrs. Juvenal and Persius.* A successful imitation depends, in part, on the reader's connecting the situation imitated with the situation portrayed, as Whitehead reminds us by saying *"Alter & Idem"* on the title page and by providing an occasional reference, within, to the Roman original.[43] White-

[42] The *Gazetteer*'s threat was on 27 October 1738, quoted in part in chap. 4, p. 144, above. James L. Clifford joins Boswell—against Hawkins—in questioning both Johnson's flight and the reason for it. Clifford, however, is more tentative than Boswell (*Young Sam Johnson* [New York: McGraw-Hill, 1955], p. 215).

[43] Whitehead, 2nd ed. (London, 1739); but the attribution to Whitehead is not certain. See David Foxon, *English Verse, 1701-1750*, 2 vols. (Cambridge: Cambridge Univ. Press, 1975), 1:755. I am indebted to Foxon for the attribution of *The First Satire of Juvenal Imitated* to Thomas Gilbert: 1:393. Page references to Whitehead are given in the text. Whitehead's earlier *The State Dunces. Inscribed to Mr. Pope* (London, 1733), is equally vigorous in opposition, and at one point flirts with encouragement to assassination. He addresses Pope, urges him to preserve Roman hatred "of tyrannic Rage" (p. 3), and then evokes the "other" Brutus at the last moment:

> How blest, while we a *British Brutus* see,
> And all the *Roman* stand confest in Thee!
> Equal thy Worth, but equal were thy Doom,
> To save *Britannia* as he rescu'd *Rome*;
> He from a *Tarquin* snatch'd the destin'd Prey,
> *Britannia* still laments a W——'s Sway. (P. 4)

head is adapting not only Juvenal (especially the third and fourth satires) and Persius, but also Pope—his language, exalted antiministerial tone, colloquial dialogue form, and a particular bête noir. He will "once more" drag *Arbuthnot*'s Sporus "on the Stage" and proclaim him a strutting *"Male-female* Thing," and a loathsome pathic who, unfortunately, has influence with the monarch (p. 9). Satire thus shall "spread thy Wings, and fearless fly / To seize thy Prey, tho' lurking ne'er so high" (p. 5; compare *Fortescue*, line 106f., and the second *Dialogue*, line 15). Satire must indeed behave that way "When *Roman* Liberty's so far bereft / The Honest Heart—that scarce the Name is left" (p. 6). With Calliope's help, Nero, a "Booby . . . King" (p. 13) from the past, emerges as the apparent object of satire. The tale of the huge turbot from Juvenal's fourth satire follows, and includes the figure of the great senator Catullus, a decrepit lover, who is consistently visited by those sycophants from "a depending, gaping, servile Court" (p. 14). This powerful Walpolean figure is one "who grants all Honours" or "ruins with a Frown," who leads "his Emp'ror in a String" and controls the proud *"Roman* Nobles" (p. 14).

Alter & Idem indeed, and *alter & idem* as concerns Johnson's *London*, for parts of *The State of Rome* imitate Juvenal's third satire and thus echo both predecessors, though Juvenal is paramount:

> Here let *Arturius* live, and such as He,
> Such Manners will with such a Land agree;
> Chiefs who, in Senates, have the golden Knack
> Of turning Truth to Lies, and White to Black.
> Who build vast Halls to lodge their *wedded Whore*,
> And by Excise and Taxes starve the Poor.[44] (P. 9)

Whitehead's *Manners* (London, 1739), is avidly Popean in sympathies, echoes, and politics, and evoked a response from the *Gazetteer* on 15 February 1739.

44 Compare Johnson's *London*, lines 50-52, 57-58. Whitehead's verses, however, could have been so written without benefit of Johnson's.

Pope, Johnson, and Juvenal are all part of Whitehead's allusive context, and all part of the resistance to a modern, recycled Augustanism.

Not long thereafter, Thomas Gilbert's *First Satire of Juvenal Imitated* (London, 1740) added its own shrill voice to the opposition's Roman chorus. Though he hopes to *"leave Sir* Robert—*to his Country's Laws"* (p. 5), he knows that the hopelessly corrupted senate is likely to enslave him and other patriots, especially since the conscienceless *"Sylla"* uses "A Standing Army, and a Royal Dow'r" to control the wicked and intimidate the good (p. 10). The Juvenalian satirist has resigned himself to defeat and symbolic protest in this world; but the printed page allows him to triumph in the future, and he does so with the aid and precedent of Pope, who parallels the lashing, republican Lucilius, who is borrowed from Juvenal's original printed at the foot of the page. A fool or secret villain "Dreads more his Censure than the penal Law" and will reform. The incorrigible shall be duly punished by the daring satirist.

> Tho' *Walpole's* Virtues claim Applause from Peers,
> From Courtiers, Senates, Bishops, *Gazetteers.*
> The Muse secure may point each venom'd Line
> With *Empson, Dudley,* or a *Cataline* [sic],
> Brand their foul Names to each succeeding Age,
> And make the Living dread the future Page. (P. 20)

One need not have been directly involved in contemporary politics, or even have preferred Juvenal to Horace, to have supported the opposition's Juvenalian posturing. Thomas Sheridan (1687-1738), Swift's sometime friend, was willing to *"allow to each* [satirist] *his several Merit"* and thus avoid the commonplace and often ill-natured comparisons between them. Nevertheless, the Preface to his translation of Juvenal describes him as an enemy *"of a debauched and corrupt Court, of a starving, sharking, and depending Nobility, of a slavish, beggarly, and mercenary*

Set of Commons." Such an attitude, together with other traits, allows Juvenal to instruct "*the rising Generations against such fatal and scandalous Abuses.*"[45]

These several examples make plain that by the later 1730s Juvenal was practically as well as theoretically a member of the literary opposition. Whitehead and Gilbert make just as plain, as Hodgson would in 1807, that Pope's opposition satire was regarded by both friend and enemy as in the Juvenalian camp, however much it was ironically "*Something like Horace.*" The "image" of Juvenal, then, is that of the virtuous outsider, the largely isolated enemy of absolutism, the brave little man rendered dangerous to the tyrant because he would not be silent and could not be bought, the defender of law and scourge of the lawless, the "tragic" declaimer who sometimes violated the standards of genteel decency in order to tell the truth about the ugliness he saw in corrupted and corrupting power. Juvenal and strident opposition are virtually synonymous, especially so in a particular cause circa 1737-1739, and in a more general cause ("freedom") from approximately 1763 (Greene) to 1807 (Hodgson). It need hardly be said that such a description well fits the final satires of Alexander Pope, who by 1737 could no sooner positively imitate the received Horace than he could have been poet laureate. That is, I hope, now clear in the *Epilogue to the Satires*; it was perhaps less clear in the *Epistle to Augustus* of 1737, which, as a result, was brilliantly obfuscating.

---

[45] *The Satires of Juvenal* (n. 38, above), pp. xii, vi. Juvenal lashed Walpole as late as 1763, in Edward Burnaby Greene's imitation (n. 39, above) of Juvenal's tenth satire.

CHAPTER 6

~~~~~~

Pope's *Epistle to Augustus*: The Ironic and the Literal

BY 1737 MANY REGARDED HORACE AND JUVENAL AS BEING on warring sides—one representing the proper, restrained, supportive satire the administration sought, the other the forthright, outraged, hostile satire the opposition offered. Conviction of the blemished reputation of Augustus, we recall, was something large segments of each group could share, for each was, in theory, committed to the limited monarchy and balanced constitution obnoxious to the Augustan settlement. Seventeen thirty-seven was also a year of rejuvenation for the sputtering opposition cause. Walpole was nearly defeated on the question of the Prince of Wales' income; the Duke of Argyle pressured him into reducing the penalties on the city of Edinburgh for its Porteous riots; Queen Caroline, Walpole's most significant ally, died in November; and the Spanish "depredations" upon English shipping were undermining Walpole's peace policy.[1] The time must have seemed auspicious for the further reinforcement of political with literary forces. What better way for Pope to infiltrate the enemy's lines than by (apparently) putting on the ample habit of the loyal muse; on the one hand by attacking the common enemy, and on the other by seeming to flatter him, thus (again apparently) mollifying those who still thought well of the princeps and his Georgian namesake? To those understanding and approving his intention, a smile of approbation would follow; to those understanding and disapproving, silence

---

[1] For these see John Butt, Introduction, in The Twickenham Edition of the Poems of Alexander Pope, vol. 4, *Alexander Pope: Imitations of Horace*, 2nd ed. (New Haven: Yale Univ. Press, 1961), pp. xxxv-xxxvi.

was preferable to a response that would publicize so subtle yet strong an attack; to those not understanding, there was at last the welcome vision of Pope's reform that would soon pass into disillusion requiring temporary silence.[2] Though the administration makes several direct and indirect responses to *Augustus*, it throws its heaviest artillery against the blunter assault of the *Epilogue to the Satires* (1738).

In the process of writing such a poem Pope would have done violence to Horace's intention, but that would have been new neither for Pope nor other adapters of the classics. From the beginning of his career as an imitator Pope had felt free to change and transcend his parent-poem. In 1712 he says that the "Messiah" was "written with this particular view, that the reader by comparing the several thoughts might see how far the images and descriptions of the Prophet are superior to those of the Poet."[3] Similarly, Pope's *First Satire of the Second Book of Horace Imitated* (1733) is harsher than anything Horace intended, sets its speaker against rather than for the government, adopts a Juvenalian not Horatian pose of attacking highly placed government appointees (lines 105-110), and contrasts Horace's serious with his own mocking view that the heads of state can in fact make proper legal and moral distinctions between kinds of satire. Pope's compartmentalized response allows him to admire and learn from Horace and Virgil as poets while—especially during the heat of opposition rhetoric—rejecting them as below the best standards in ethics and politics. An imitation of an author need not imply acceptance of his values.

Such freedom toward the original was long an option for the imitator. As William King put it in the Preface to his

[2] For further discussion of the response to Pope's poem, see Appendix I, below.

[3] The Twickenham Edition of the Poems of Alexander Pope, vol. 1, *Alexander Pope: Pastoral Poetry and an Essay on Criticism*, ed. E. Audra and Aubrey Williams (New Haven: Yale Univ. Press, 1961), p. 111.

version of Ovid's *Art of Love* (1709), "An Imitator and his Author stand much upon the same terms as *Ben* does with his Father in the Comedy [*Love for Love*]: '*What th'of he be my Father, I an't bound Prentice to 'en!'* " And as William Clubbe noted regarding Swift's and Pope's imitations, "in general they . . . have imitated (and that loosely) such parts of him [Horace] only as suited the purpose of their own immediate Satire."[4]

Perhaps more than any other of Horace's works, the epistle to Augustus was appropriate for Pope's "own immediate Satire." It was commonly read as being full of genuine praise for the wisdom and achievements of Augustus. As far as I can tell, only Shaftesbury even conjectured that Horace might be ironic; others agreed that "the Epistle of *Horace* to *Augustus*" embodied what the poet thought "just Commendations and due Encomiums."[5] The "major" discussion and translation of the poem chronologically closest and prior to Pope's was Charles Carthy's Dublin performance of 1731; these dubious blank-verse splendors were subscribed by Ambrose Philips, the Earl of Roscommon, Swift, and several of his friends. If Pope did not know this effort then, he might have a few years later when it helped to spawn several epigrams against Carthy by William Dunkin and others, published in part and in whole in 1734.[6] In any case, Carthy is properly

<hr/>

[4] King (London), p. xxxix; Clubbe, *Six Satires of Horace In a Style Between Free Imitation and Literal Version* (Ipswich, 1795), p. v.

[5] Shaftesbury, Anthony Ashley Cooper, *Advice to an Author*, in *Characteristics of Men, Manners, Opinions, Times* (1711), ed. John M. Robertson, 2 vols. in 1 (rpt. Indianapolis: Bobbs-Merrill, 1964), 1:175-76, n. 1; Nathaniel Lee, *The Tragedy of Nero, Emperor of Rome* (1675; London, 1735), sig. A2^r.

[6] Carthy's work is titled, *A Translation of the Second Book of Horace's Epistles, Together with Some of the most select in the First, with Notes*. Page references are cited in the text. Harold Williams provides the background in *The Poems of Jonathan Swift*, 3 vols., 2nd ed. (Oxford: Clarendon Press, 1958) 2:665-72. Pope may also have known [Francis Manning] *An Essay on the Vicious Bent and Taste of the Times. In an Epistle to . . . Sir Robert Walpole* (London, 1737). This

high serious, sings Augustan and Georgian praises (sigs. A2ʳ-B1ʳ), and offers the standard interpretation and history of Horace's poem, one available to Pope in several sources.

> This Epistle is justly looked upon, as one of the finest Pieces of Antiquity, both for Panegyric and Criticism. Nothing can be imagin'd more noble and solemn than the Introduction, nor more delicate than the Compliments therein paid to *Caesar*; whom although he raises far above all the Heroes that went before him, yet, in all he says, we meet with nothing extravagant, but the whole supported by a suitable Decency, as well as Grandeur of Thought and Diction. It was written on Account of a kind Rebuke our Author received from *Augustus*, who, as *Suetonius* informs us, finding no mention of himself in several of *Horace*'s Satyrs and Epistles, which he had seen, and with the Reading whereof he was charmed, gave him to understand, that he was not a little displeased with him, for not conversing chiefly with himself in that kind of Writing; concluding with this generous Expostulation, *whether he was afraid it would be a Disgrace to him, that Posterity should know he was his familiar Friend.* (P. 36, note a)

Surely here was enough to move a stoic, much less an opposition poet eager to find ways to goad the administration. Pope had of course already mentioned his Augustus, would do so again shortly, and was not likely to have charmed his royal, or other, court readers.[7] More important, Pope's answer to the question recorded by Suetonius would have been—yes, it is disgraceful to be known as the friend of such a king, and he would have added that the disgrace was Horace's as well, since making Augustus smile was

---

adapts much of the more fulsome praise of Augustus and applies it to Walpole (e.g., pp. 5-7).

[7] See *Fortescue* (imitation of *Satires*, ii. 1), line 21; *Arbuthnot*, line 222; *Bolingbroke* (imitation of *Epistles*, i. 1), line 106.

giving aid and comfort to the enemy, to the man who agreed to proscribe Cicero, and who banished Ovid and induced Virgil's dishonest, indeed slavish, *Aeneid*. Moreover, as Harold Williams observes, "Carthy, printing Latin on one side and English on the other, brought upon himself the nickname of Mezentius, in allusion to that King of Caere in Etruria, famous for his cruelties, one of whose tortures was the tying of the living to the dead." If Pope did know Carthy and the tumult his poem caused, his own standard practice of printing the original facing his imitation would have taken on a new function: not the punishment Carthy-Mezentius inflicted on Horace by tying him to his own dead lines, but the punishment Pope inflicts on Horace by bringing his shame to light.

Furthermore, 1734 also offered the anonymous *A Satire*, an attack upon Walpole's enemies—the *Craftsman*, *Fog's*, Pope, Bolingbroke, Lyttelton, and others—that turns the opening of Horace's epistle to Augustus into celebration of Walpole, who is "engag'd in *Britain*'s Cause, / To aid her Senates, or enforce her Laws." We soon hear commendation of George Augustus borrowed from Virgil that translates as, "Freedom's Monarch! Prince of Liberty!" Similarly, on 3 October 1735 the *Gazetteer* published an imitation of Horace, *Odes*, iv. 5, in order to "oblige a true Friend to his Majesty's Person and Government." The poet of "*To* Augustus" is pleased because George's "Laws, thy Manners have subdu'd / The Vices of a Multitude." Moreover,

> Who dreads the Pride of France or Spain?
> Or who the Feuds which Poets maintain?
> Too trivial they to give us Pain,
>   If mighty George be safe.[8]

[8] For Williams, see *Poems of . . . Swift*, 2:665; *A Satire* (London), p. 3, with a note directing us to "*Hor. Epist.* I. Lib. 2," p. 14. The latter page also includes this line from "*Virg.* 6. aen.": "Lo! *Britain* smiles; for lo! *Augustus* reigns." Moreover, Mighty George was very safe indeed, in

It seems reasonable to assume that for Pope the association of George II and Walpole with Augustus was all too accurate. *Epistles,* ii. 1 and its Augustan ambiance were so polluted that they could serve as a norm only in the negative way of Pope's own invention.

Indeed, Pope had already been invited to praise his Augustus. On 13 January 1731 the *Grub-street Journal,* no. 100, makes clear that such encomia of George II as Augustus were all too common. It also may have contributed to the genesis of Pope's poem, since Pope read and contributed to the *Journal.* In that number Philarchaeus tells of reading Horace, "*Epist.* Liv. I., esp. XVI, ver. 25, & c.," and finds from "an old Scholiast" that Horace has borrowed his compliment from Varius' panegyric upon Augustus.

HORACE makes a great compliment both to AUGUSTUS and *Varius,* by producing these verses, and 'tis pity we have not more remains of that excellent Poet. For, in my opinion, these are the finest lines, and contain the finest compliment that ever was made by any mortal. The more you consider, the more you admire. There's the judgment and solidity of VIRGIL, the ease and unaffectedness of OVID. 'Tis as lofty and strong as HOMER; and as to expression, short and natural as HORACE himself. I wish I could translate them into† two English ones as good; I would give 50 pounds. Let Pope himself do it, if he can, and apply them to our AUGUSTUS.

† It is, no doubt, impossible to do this. . . . However, the very thought of applying them to our AUGUSTUS, incited Mr. Maevius [Richard Russel] to attempt them. . . . The Society highly approved them . . . as a short specimen of unpensioned Panegyric; intirely different from some *New-years Odes,* which

part because he was protected by the *Gazetteer's* pens. Hence, on 28 October 1737, and again on 6 April 1738, that journal parodies the opening of Pope's and Horace's poems through applying to Lyttelton what had been applied to Augustus. See Appendix, I, below.

if the Author was not well known, might justly be looked upon
as grave burlesques upon the Court.[9]

The interpretation I am suggesting is quite different from
the conventional one that applauds Pope's genius in contrasting Horace's honest praise with his own ironic praise of
the monarch. According to this view, Pope draws his own
British king and poet as enemies in a declining society, and
contrasts them with the Roman princeps and poet as allies
in a flourishing society. One distinguished critic says that
the Roman "universal Augustan metaphor or 'myth' " serves
as "a paradigm of the great and good now lost in the corruptions of the present, as in the comparison of George II
with Augustus Caesar." A more recent commentator insists,
"There could be no more vivid contrast to Caesar Augustus
than in King George Augustus."[10] To paraphrase one of
the putative Augustans, there can be only one objection to
this reading—namely, that it is not true; or, with more
academic refinements, that it needs radical revision and
probable abandonment in light of the counter tradition to
which Pope and his friends contributed.

Pope was not considerate enough to write a poem that
fits a perfect anti-Augustan paradigm; like some other attacks upon Horace and his ruler, *To Augustus* includes restrained admiration for each man. We recall Blackwell's
belief that Horace and Virgil made the best of a bad job
in their efforts to moderate the barbarity of their master

[9] For Pope and the *Grub-street Journal*, see James T. Hillhouse, *The
Grub-street Journal* (Durham, N.C.: Duke Univ. Press, 1928), pp. 4-5,
25-39. See also Bertrand A. Goldgar, *Walpole and the Wits: The Rela-
tion of Politics to Literature, 1722-1742* (Lincoln: Univ. of Nebraska
Press, 1976), pp. 123, 160, and Goldgar's "Pope and the *Grub-street
Journal*," *MP*, 74 (1977): 366-80.

[10] Maynard Mack, " 'Wit and Poetry and Pope': Some Observations
on his Imagery," in *Eighteenth-Century English Literature: Modern
Essays in Criticism*, ed. James L. Clifford (New York: Oxford Univ.
Press, 1959), p. 34; John Paul Russo, *Alexander Pope: Tradition and
Identity* (Cambridge, Mass.: Harvard Univ. Press, 1972), p. 217.

through song and false compliment. Pope's own Advertisement to his poem states "that *Horace* made his Court to this Great Prince, by writing with a decent Freedom toward him, with a just Contempt of his low Flatterers, and with a manly Regard to his own Character." If it were not for Pope's letter to Arbuthnot of 26 July 1734, which praises Augustus for encouraging Horace's moral satire, one would suppose that these lines were also ironic, and they may in fact be so.[11] Nevertheless, there are clear signposts that indicate Pope's assault upon Caesar Augustus, his poet Horace, and the world they have made and inhabit. Along the way, Pope gains authority by dissociating himself from Augustan—Horatian and Georgian—courtly values, and by associating himself with the opposition in general and Swift in particular. Horace and Pope do have different ends in view, but Pope's are unlike those commonly ascribed to him. The better to see their divergence, I will offer a brief overview of Horace's poem, drawn from what I take to be basic insights regarding its theme and structure, Pope's own remarks, and those of contemporary editors, commentators, and interpreters.

I: HORACE, AUGUSTUS, AND "SCRIBERE COGAS"

Horace's poem is essentially social, one of inclusion of the poet with Augustus, the court, the aims of the state in general, the Roman present and past, and of Rome with the provinces she governs and civilizes. It also relates the poet to social and literary concerns—Roman simplicity and

11 Pope's remark is from *Imitations of Horace*, p. 192. Subsequent citations will be given in the text. Roman and italic type are inverted in quotations from the Advertisement. For Pope's letter, see *Correspondence of Alexander Pope*, ed. George Sherburn, 5 vols. (Oxford: Clarendon Press, 1956), 3:420. For a recent and healthy sign of the new trend, see Malcolm Kelsall, "Augustus and Pope," *HLQ*, 39 (1976): 117-31. See also Professor Kelsall's inaugural lecture, *Imperious Caesar, Dead and Turned to Clay* (Cardiff: University College Press, 1977).

Greek sophistication, Roman and Greek literary traditions, drama with its imagination and spectacle, and written verse with its cerebration. The poet is a necessary, cooperating part of the good he describes and a friendly critic of the less good. At the poem's outset, Horace praises Augustus' moral and military concerns for all of Italy, and likens him to the greatest of heroes and gods; unlike these, however, he gains his fame while living, and is venerated by his people. Considering their wisdom in so honoring him, they are curiously incompetent in literary matters and are so partial to the ancients, especially the old dramatists, that they have denied the value of contemporary literature—precisely that literature Augustus himself should nurture as valuable to the state and his own interests. Through several paragraphs of amiably acerbic literary criticism, Horace praises the ancients while indicating their roughness and lack of polish; he also discusses Greek literary sophistication and personal frivolity, Roman stoic manliness and unpolished letters, and the current madness that makes everyone scribble. At nearly the exact center of the poem, however, Horace stops his attacks upon poets and poetry and signals their moral and practical values to the state in a section that, as Richard Hurd said in 1751, "will be found to comprize every thing, that any, or all, of [poetry's] most zealous advocates have ever pretended in its behalf."[12] The poet is personally harmless and upright. Though not much of a soldier, he serves the state by teaching children to speak well, adults to be better human beings, the nation to emulate the best examples, and the disconsolate to take comfort. He inculcates religion and, through the inspired muse, teaches youths to

[12] *Q. Horatii Flacci Epistola ad Augustum. With an English Commentary and Notes* (London, 1751), p. 72. For more-recent commentary on this poem, see Edward Fraenkel, *Horace* (Oxford: Clarendon Press, 1957; rpt. 1966), pp. 383-99, and several remarks in Gordon Williams, *Tradition and Originality in Roman Poetry* (Oxford: Clarendon Press, 1968), pp. 443-59.

gain favor from heaven, avoid calamities, and seek peace and fertility.

The development of such inspired poetry was long in coming. Rough Roman satyr drama had to be checked by law and then polished by Greek arts, and even now the older Roman comedy on the stage is more concerned with low entertainments, the pockets of the writer, and the gross ocular pleasures of plebeians as well as knights and lords. The best sort of dramatist appeals to the imagination, not the eye; he controls the heart and his audience. Admittedly, poets—self-centered, proud, wishing to be attached to the princeps himself—can be nuisances. But they are vital to Augustus. Alexander had the good sense to let only the best painters and sculptors preserve his image, but the bad taste to allow one Choerilus to commend him in verse. Augustus, on the other hand, has used good judgment, chosen Virgil and Varius to sing him, honored them with gifts, and received the honor of their praise. The manners and soul of Augustus are set forth truly in their poetry. Horace feels inadequate to the task of recording Augustus' military and other achievements, and he fears that his talents cannot do justice to the ruler he loves, especially since the people more easily remember what has been blamed than praised. The poet would not wish to see himself badly carved and sold in wax or receive a panegyric in a bad poem; then the sheet of verse would wrap the statue and, to his humiliation, he would be hawked about in the streets—an indignity, by implication, even worse for a monarch who protects and reforms the state. The greatest service that Horace can render Augustus at this moment is to urge that he encourage distinguished poets whose art will immortalize his greatness.

That is, I believe, a reasonable gloss of *Epistles*, ii. 1 as Pope and his contemporaries might have seen it; and it provides a backdrop for Pope's own intention and achievement. He substitutes hostility for affection, national disgrace for national honor, opposition politics for courtly reconciliation, and, normally, exclusion for Horace's inclusion. Along the way, with indirection worthy of the master he rejects, Pope belabors the notions of state-supported poetry, absolute monarchy, and the virtues of the Augustan settlement. What Pope wishes us to see is not that George Augustus is unlike but shockingly like his Roman namesake; and it is not in Pope's similarity to but difference from Horace that he finds his greatest moral force. *"An Answer from* Horace" may have been an argument on authority in 1733;[13] by 1737 Pope thinks rather less of that court-poet, and by 1738 it will be worse yet. In the Advertisement of *To Augustus*, for example, he remarks that Horace

> paints [his prince] with all the great and good Qualities of a Monarch, upon whom the *Romans* depended for the Encrease of an *Absolute Empire.* But to make the Poem entirely English, I was willing to add one or two of those Virtues which contribute to the Happiness of *a Free People*, and are more consistent with the Welfare of our Neighbours. (P. 191)

The word *paints* is important for two reasons: it suggests the end of Horace's poem, where one function of the artist —painter, sculptor or poet—is to make a noble artistic object of the monarch. Pope thus shows that Horace is living up to his own standards for the role of the poet in the state. He is also implying subterfuge. The ambiguous term *paint* means, among other definitions in Johnson's *Dictionary* (1755), "To deck with artificial colours." As the next sentence indicates, for Pope, Horace is praising—painting—an absolute ruler who increases his nation's power at the expense of the freedom of others. Pope has already divorced himself from both painter and subject, proclaimed his English virtue and freedom and, thereby, the need for opposition to Walpole and his king.

[13] Advertisement to *The First Satire of the Second Book of Horace Imitated*, in *Imitations of Horace*, p. 3.

Other aspects of the Advertisement further these hints of the anti-Augustan and anti-Horatian. Few causes more exercised Walpole's literate enemies than the stage Licensing Act of 1737 and the administration's apparent and frequent attacks upon the freedom of the press. Though the *Gazetteer*, 8 June 1737, insisted that it was "the greatest Stupidity or Impudence . . . to put the licentiousness of the *Press* and the *Stage* upon the same foot," many critics nevertheless equated the two. Lord Chesterfield insisted that restraint upon the stage would lead to "a Restraint on the Liberty of the *Press*" and "even of *Liberty* itself." Samuel Johnson's *Compleat Vindication of the Licensers of the Stage* (1739) feared that the act would be extended to the press and would bring sloth and ignorance.[14] On the other hand, in *Fortescue* Pope proclaimed himself "Un-plac'd, un-pension'd, No Man's Heir, or Slave" (line 116) and, of course, would have resisted licensing. Whether Pope was in opposition in 1737, or still trying to appear friendly with Walpole in 1733, the independence of the artist was paramount—or at least independence from the ruling Hanoverians, however more attractive the Stuarts may have been in *Windsor Forest*. Yet Horace was enrolled in the government's campaign to control opposition literature, and this Horatian poem encourages greater friendship between poet and absolute monarch, and the latter's manipulation of both artistic process and product. Pope makes this clear in the second paragraph of the Advertisement. Augustus was not a patron of poets in general: "he not only prohibited all but the Best Writers to name him, but recommended that Care even to the Civil Magistrate" (p. 191).[15] Moreover, like the satirist in

14 *Gentleman's Magazine*, 7 (1737): 409. Johnson's words are from the conclusion of the *Compleat Vindication*. See chap. 7, sec. II, at n. 22 in text, below, for Chesterfield's relevant attack on Augustus.

15 Pope is referring to Suetonius, Augustus 89. He may also be alluding to British stage licensing and the Roman *lex laesae majestatis*; if so, he is characterizing Augustus not as a monarch of discretion, but as a tyrant and censor of harmless books. The remarks regarding patronage,

the *Gazetteer*, Horace invites the tyranny that Pope and his friends feared. The Roman pleads the case of his contemporary poets "against the Emperor himself, who had conceived them of little use to the Government"; but he shows that "the Writers of his Time" [had] great advantages over their Predecessors, that their *Morals* were much improved, and the License of those ancient Poets restrained: that *Satire* and *Comedy* were become more just and useful; that whatever extravagancies were left on the Stage, were owing to the Ill Taste of the Nobility, that Poets under due Regulations, were in many respects useful to the *State*." Horace concludes, Pope says, that it is upon such regulated poets that Augustus "must depend, for his Fame with Posterity" (pp. 191-92). In the *Epilogue to the Satires* Pope's adversarius unconsciously portrays Horace as a fawning court-toady to the king. He is more subtle here, but Horace already is a tool of Walpole, the advocate of Augustan—Georgian and Caesarean—licensing, restraints upon stage and satire, and the "due Regulations" that make poets "in many respects useful to the State." Such utility, Pope may well have remembered, included silence regarding Cicero, Brutus, and Ovid, and vocal support for the principate and its great men.

The validity of this interpretation is supported on the basis of evidence within the poem, external historical evidence of the evils of Augustus, opposition concerns already cited, and later contemporary comments. Joseph Warton was important as a classicist and as a reader of Pope. In his

---

and Pope's consistent refusal to seek or accept a patron, cast doubt on the familiar assumption that Pope was unhappy because Britain lacked the patronage of a true Augustus. For these views, see Ian Watt, ed., *The Augustan Age: Approaches to Its Literature, Life, and Thought* (Greenwich, Conn.: Fawcett, 1968), p. 15, and Maynard Mack, *The Garden and the City: Retirement and Politics in the Later Poetry of Pope 1731-1743* (Toronto: Univ. of Toronto Press, 1969), p. 168. One point of Pope's imitation, I believe, is that to her cost Britain already had a proper Augustus on the throne.

edition of the *Works* (1797) he criticizes Warburton and
Hurd for missing much of the point of *To Augustus*, especially in the final 16 lines. Neither takes "the least notice of
any irony being intended in this imitation," he says. "To
what motive shall we ascribe this cautious silence?" Warton
has no such timidity, and in his explication of the respective
beginnings of Pope's and Horace's poems he amplifies the
spirit of the anti-Augustanism he had expressed as early as
1753 and 1756. Warton's gloss of Pope's opening lines even
scolds him for an apparent oversight in his hostility to the
parent-poem.

> All those nauseous and outrageous compliments, which
> Horace, in a strain of abject adulation, degraded himself
> by paying to Augustus, Pope has converted into bitter
> and pointed sarcasms, conveyed under the form of the
> most artful irony.
> "Horace," says Pope in the advertisement to this piece,
> "made his court to this great prince, (or rather this cool
> and subtle tyrant [Warton adds],) by writing with a
> decent freedom towards him, with a just contempt of his
> low flatterers, and with a manly regard to his own char-
> acter." Surely he forgot the 15th and 16th lines:
>
>> Jurandasque tibi per numen ponimus aras, [sic]
>> Nil oriturum alias, nil ortum tale fatentas, &c.

He goes on to say that we speak incorrectly of the so-called
Augustan writers, since many of them predated Augustus
and many others did not owe their excellence to patronage.
Moreover, he regards the celebration of Augustus' clemency
as overwhelmingly "unaccountable," agrees with Seneca that
such clemency was merely fatigue, and reminds us of Augustus' "cruel proscriptions, . . . unjust banishment of Ovid," and
"the infamous obscenity of his verses." He concludes this long
note with a quotation from Voltaire's article on Augustus
in the *Questions sur l'encyclopédie*, in which the princeps is
"Un fourbe, un assasin, . . . parvenu à l'Empire par des

crimes qui meritaient le dernier supplice," that is, capital punishment.[16]

As Warton's reaction suggests, Pope's anti-Augustanism is not limited to the poem's Advertisement. The opening 30 lines have been meticulously explicated by Jay Arnold Levine, who urges Pope's ultimate association of Augustus not with "Apollo, but Apollyon; not the true God, but the Adversary, or anti-Christ."[17] However convincing this might be, I suspect that Pope has also used the familiar historical knowledge of Augustus' sexual excesses, cowardice, absolutism, political usurpation, and other violations of law. If so, it is likely that Pope is not ironic in the received sense. Instead of improperly applying to George II what was properly applied to Augustus, the opening paragraph is equally improper for each man. Pope's targets include Horace for flattering his monarch, Augustus for not doing what Horace attributes to him yet coercing the moral equivalent of a Cibberian birthday ode, and George II for being all too "Augustan."

> While You, great Patron of Mankind, sustain
> The balanc'd World, and open all the Main;
> Your Country, chief, in Arms abroad defend,
> At home, with Morals, Arts, and Laws amend;
> How shall the Muse, from such a Monarch, steal
> An hour, and not defraud the Publick Weal?
>
> (Lines 1-6)

Indeed, it is probable that the real poem being positively imitated in this section is Lyttelton's then unpublished "To Mr. Glover on his Poem of Leonidas. Written in the Year 1734"; and the real norm is not the absolute tyrant but the

16 Warton, *The Works of Alexander Pope, Esq.*, 9 vols. (London), 4:208; Voltaire, *Questions*, 9 vols. (Geneva [?], 1770-1772), 4:146-47. At about the same time, Henri Ophellot de la Pause [J. B. C. Isoard Delisle] also complained about the inaccuracy of the opening of Horace's poem. See the *Histoire des douze Césars de Suétone*, 4 vols. (Paris, 1771), 1:338.

17 "Pope's *Epistle to Augustus*, Lines 1-30," *SEL*, 7 (1967): 448.

English patriot Godolphin. There the opposition's Lyttelton wrote lines that both illuminate Pope's first paragraph and, in the final couplet, provide an immediate source.

> Say, what is now th' ambition of the great?
> Is it to raise their country's sinking state;
> Her load of debt to ease by frugal care,
> Her trade to guard, her harass'd poor to spare?
> Is it, like honest Somers, to inspire
> The love of laws, and freedom's sacred fire?
> Is it, like wise Godolphin, to sustain
> The balanc'd world and boundless power restrain?[18]

Instead of Lyttelton's patriot limiting power, George II and Augustus extend it by violation of law and debasement of freedom. Instead of Lyttelton's positive image of balance and praise—an image that appears in an antiadministration poem celebrating another antiadministration poem—Pope presents an image of moral and political imbalance in a tottering world. Instead of Lyttelton's deserved praise for Glover's attack on the court, we hear the assumed voice of the court sycophant, inappropriately praising George II just as Horace, Pope would have felt, inappropriately praised Augustus Caesar.

Pope's opposition bias is also made clear in his poem's second paragraph, which replaces Horace's Romulus, Castor, and Pollux with the patriot kings, Edward, Henry, and Alfred, each of whom protected English liberty, honor, or letters as George II did not, and each of whom, Pope claims, died without proper recognition in his lifetime.[19] Today's king, in contrast, is widely accepted—"To Thee, the World

---

[18] *The Works of George Lord Lyttelton*, ed. George Edward Ayscough, 3 vols., 3rd ed. (London, 1776), 3:194-95. For further discussion of this poem, see Howard D. Weinbrot, "Lyttelton and Pope's 'Balanc'd World': The 'Epistle to Augustus,' Lines One and Two," *N&Q*, 216 (1971): 332-33.

[19] As a few examples of praise for these monarchs "who were most indulgent to the Liberties of the People," see the *Craftsman*, no. 377 (22 September 1733, quoted), stanza four of Thomson's *Ode to the Prince of Wales* (1737), and Johnson's *London* (1738), lines 23-30, 120, 248.

its present homage pays" (line 23); George II is thus once more likened to Augustus, who also gained fame within his own age. In stating the apparent fact, however, Pope uses Roman and religious background to "flatter" his monarch in ways different from anything Horace attempted.

> Great Friend of LIBERTY! in *Kings* a Name
> Above all Greek, above all Roman Fame:
> Whose Word is Truth, as sacred and rever'd,
> As Heav'n's own Oracles from Altars heard.
>
> (Lines 25-28)

Of course George and Walpole were less than friends of opposition liberty. The real attack, though, comes not in the obvious misstatement but in the more subtle lines on George as a greater tyrant than any of the Roman kings. It had long been one of the canons of classical historiography that Rome began its ascent to greatness only after the expulsion of Tarquin the Proud, the last of her absolute kings. Hence Nathan Hooke, in the volume of his *Roman History* dedicated to Pope in 1738, says that "the freedom which the *Romans* recovered by the expulsion of *Tarquin the Proud* was now secured to them by his death; a freedom that was indisputably the source of all their future grandeur."[20] One reason for the murder of Julius Caesar was the fear that he might be king. Augustus, well aware of the power of names and associations, scrupulously avoided that deadly title and styled himself *princeps senatus*, a chief among senatorial equals. Horace therefore avoids *rex* and instead describes his ruler as *dux*, a leader. Pope sets off

---

20 *The Roman History, From the Building of Rome to the Ruin of the Commonwealth*, 4 vols. (London, 1738-1771), 1:168. History was, of course, relevant for literary glosses. Père Catrou observes of Virgil's *Eclogues*, v. 5: "A la vérité, c'eut été une indiscretion au Poëte, de se servir du mot odieux de *Regnat*, s'il eut fait tomber directement & sans metaphor sur César" (*Les Poësies de Virgile*, 4 vols. [Paris, 1729], 1:109). For a later, but useful and relevant, compilation of classical remarks on kings, see Alexander Adam, *Classical Biography* (Edinburgh, 1800), pp. 74-76.

most of the line in roman rather than the usual italic type on the facing page and thus draws this difference to our attention.[21] He probably wished us to contrast the two words: "Te nostris Ducibus, Te Graiis *anteferendo*" (line 19). For all Horace's delicacy, it should be pointed out, Joseph Warton nevertheless found this section "the most unpardonable strain of flattery in one who had served under Brutus."[22]

Pope also adds to Horace's poem in the reference to "Heav'n's own Oracles from Altars heard." The persona is outdoing the Augustan poet in praise; but behind the mask Pope is calling George II the tool of either the devil or his first minister. Whether or not the oracles were ever genuine, they commonly were thought to have been destroyed upon the birth of Christ. The controversy was discussed at length in Thomas Broughton's *Bibliotheca historico-sacra* (1737) and summed up briefly in Ephraim Chambers' popular *Cyclopaedia* (1728). "It is," he says, "a pretty general opinion among the more learned, that *oracles* were all mere cheats, and impostures; either calculated to serve the avaricious ends of the heathen priests, or the political views of the princes. . . . There are two points in dispute on the subject of *oracles; viz.* whether they were human, or diabolical machines? and whether or no they ceased upon publication or preaching of the gospel?"[23] In either case, the oracular and "Heav'n" are more likely to be antonyms than synonyms. Indeed, the word *oracle* normally modified by *false* was frequently smacked across the political net during the

[21] The importance of such a device has been well shown by Aubrey L. Williams, "*Pope and Horace*: The Second Epistle of the Second Book," in *Restoration and Eighteenth-Century Literature: Essays in Honor of Alan Dugald McKillop*, ed. Carroll Camden (Chicago: Published for Rice Univ. by Univ. of Chicago Press, 1963), pp. 309-21.

[22] Pope's *Works*, 4:150n.

[23] Broughton, 2 vols. (London), 2:193-202, especially, 201-2; Chambers, 2 vols., 6th ed. (London, 1750). By 1765 the rejection of oracles was part of the philosophes' attack upon superstition. See chap. 31 of Voltaire's *Philosophy of History* (London, 1766), pp. 174-75.

height of the paper war between the *Craftsman* and the *Gazetteer*, each side agreeing that the other was miserably wrong in its predictions. As Maynard Mack has shown, the oracle was also the voice of Walpole emerging from the Golden Rump, before which a multitude of courtiers prostrated themselves.[24]

The Advertisement and opening 30 lines of Pope's imitation, then, proceed not by the irony of appropriate vs. inappropriate praise, but the irony of applying inappropriately to George II what Horace had applied inappropriately to Augustus Caesar, and by implicitly criticizing Horace for flattering and Augustus for prompting such stuff. The title-page motto of the 1737 folio edition is from line 267 of Horace's poem: *"Ne Rubeam, pingui donatus Munere!"*—lest I should blush at being presented with the foolish gift. Horace has been hoist with his own petard. Pope's apparently sycophantic poet thus is the "Horace" of Augustus' stable; Pope actually differentiates himself from Horace as an exemplar, but likens the subjects of each dramatic speaker's praise. In the process, he announces his own opposition bias, holds up norms of other English kings, and makes clear that George II is not Roman *dux* but *rex* and negatively oracular.

Anti-Augustanism and anti-Horatianism are in fact thematically important throughout the poem, as lines and sections remind us of British hatred of absolutism and those who support it. Let us look first at the passage in which

[24] At times, *oracle* was also used with positive denotations, but in general, and in this political context, to be oracular was to be mistaken. See the *London Journal*, 4 April 1730; the *Craftsman*, no. 219 (12 September 1730); the *Gazetteer*, 23 September, 15 October, 17 October, 25 November, 9 December, 16 December, 1735; 6 January, 10 February, 24 February 1736. The list can easily be expanded and includes theological and historical as well as political texts. As a final example, however, here is a remark from the *Gazetteer* for 2 March 1736. Fog is "the chief Oracle of his Party (but with less subtlety than the D——l at *Delphos*)." *Attainted, imposture, ambiguous, juggling,* and *corrupted* commonly appear as modifiers. See also Mack's *The Garden and the City*, pp. 145-46.

Pope comments upon Horace's portrait of the poet's national function.

Horace had hoped to show the poet's utility to Augustus and thus to encourage his patronage; Pope ridicules parts of this passage that Dacier before and Hurd after him so admired.[25] He does so because he rejects the basis of Horace's argument, namely, that "a Poet's of some weight, / And (tho' no Soldier) useful to the State" (lines 203-4). At the battle of Philippi Horace, then an officer in Brutus' republican army, threw down his sword, ran from his colors, and was later pardoned by Octavian, whose virtues and achievements he celebrated. Pope draws our attention to these deficiencies by printing the facing Latin in roman letters: "Militiæ *quanquam piger & malus,* utilis urbi" (line 125). To remind us of our Roman history, however, he adds a note to his own line 204:

> Horace had not acquitted himself much to his credit in this capacity . . . in the battle of Philippi. It is manifest he alludes to himself in this whole account of a Poet's character; but with an intermixture of Irony. . . . The nobler office of a Poet follows, . . . which the Imitator has apply'd where he thinks it more due than to himself. He hopes to be pardoned, if, as he is sincerely inclined to praise what deserves to be praised, he arraigns what deserves to be arraigned, in the 210, 211, and 212th Verses. (P. 211n)

Pope makes three important points: Horace abandoned the cause of freedom; he portrayed his own courtly and other virtues in the character of the poet; Pope himself does neither, but contrasts himself and other friends with Horace and "arraigns" those who praise the court. He thus insists that the poet is valuable not for his service but his opposition to the court, and that the equation of poetic and govern-

---

[25] See André Dacier, *Oeuvres d'Horace . . . avec des remarques critiques et historiques* (1681-1689), 10 vols., 3rd ed. (Paris, 1709), 9:378: "Nous n'avons pas aujourd'hui de ces delicatesses."

mental interests is pernicious. The poet has practical value, and

> I scarce can think him such a worthless thing,
> Unless he praise some monster of a King,
> Or Virtue, or Religion turn to sport,
> To please a lewd, or un-believing Court.
>
> (Lines 209-12)

The immediate target becomes "Unhappy Dryden" (line 213); the ultimate target is all poets who praise monstrous kings. There is, of course, no parallel passage in Horace for this attack upon state-poetry. Pope literally and metaphorically abandons his original; when he rejoins it he again gives it a strikingly anti-Horatian and anti-Augustan turn.

That is, he diminishes the praise of Addison by insisting upon his "Courtly stains" (line 215), while urging that the genuine norm is the opposition Swift, who actually does for Ireland what George II was supposed to have done for all of Britain (lines 3-4). Swift serves his nation not by subjecting himself to the court's "due Regulations," but by opposing its tyranny. Horace surrenders freedom under stress; Swift nurtures it and, along the way, turns a personified nation into a memorializing poet.

> Let Ireland tell, how Wit upheld her cause,
> Her Trade supported, and supply'd her Laws;
> And leave on SWIFT this grateful verse ingrav'd,
> The Rights a Court attack'd, a Poet sav'd.
> Behold the hand that wrought a Nation's cure,
> Stretch'd to relieve the Idiot and the Poor,
> Proud Vice to brand, or injur'd Worth adorn,
> And stretch the Ray to Ages yet unborn.
>
> (Lines 221-28)

Though Swift resisted regulation, the same cannot be said for all British poets. Horace's history of Roman dramatic satire is intended as a brief sketch of the progress of letters,

from the savagely rude to the discreetly civilized. When satire became too harsh, laws against abuse were passed, and
dread of the cudgel led to good and delightful modes of
speech. Again Pope wishes us to pay particular attention to
a corresponding line and sets it off in dominant type: "*Ad
benedicendum, delectandumque redacti*" (line 155). John
Butt has complained that "Pope is not well served by the
need to imitate Horace at this point. Latin satire was of
native growth; the satire of Hall and the later Elizabethans
was inspired by literary models" (p. 215n). Pope knew this
and needed merely to omit or alter the passage if it seemed
inappropriate; however, he is not imitating the development
of satire, but the development of regulation in each state.
Horace and the administration see such regulation as
healthy; Pope and the opposition see it as dangerous, since
most poets are all too willing to follow the state's decrees,
and only the unusual writer, satirist or otherwise, preserves
his independence. The earlier passage about poetry in the
days of Charles II remarks that "The willing Muses were
debauch'd at Court" (line 152): that is relevant to the court
of George II as well, and even more in terms of politics than
love or mockery of religion, though Pope surely disapproved
of the latter debaucheries.[26]

[26] Pope's suggestion of a similarity between licensing under Charles
II and George II would have been recognized by like-minded readers.
That is made clear in Chesterfield's speech to the House of Lords, as
recorded in the *Gentleman's Magazine* for July, 1737.

> The C—rt is always for favouring its *own Schemes*, and is fond of
> making every Thing in its Power *subservient* to them; *our Stage* has
> been formerly made very *useful* in this Particular; in King *Charles
> II*d's Time there was a Licenser at Court, what was the *Practice*
> then? Why, when we were out of *Humour* with *Holland, Dryden* the
> Laureat wrote his Play of the Cruelty of the *Dutch* at *Amboyna.*
> When the Affair of the *Exclusion Bill* was depending, he wrote his
> *Duke of Guise.* When the Court took offence at the Citizens, . . . the
> Stage was employ'd to expose them as Fools, Cheats, Usurers, and to
> compleat their Characters, Cuckolds. The *Cavaliers* . . . were to be
> *flattered*, tho' the worst of Characters, . . . and the *Dissenters*, who
> were to be *abused*, were always *Scoundrels* and *quaint mischievous*

Pope's discussion of the development of satire also has a double referent—the primary but unimportant one of the excesses of and reaction to Hall and Marston, and the secondary but essential one of the effect of stage licensing and attempts to intimidate poets and publishers. We should recall that the printer of *Fog's*, 16 July 1737, was taken into custody, that Henry Haines was criminally prosecuted after he printed the *Craftsman* of 2 July and 10 December 1737, and that Pope himself feared prosecution as a result of line 224, in praise of Swift.[27] Pope's final note to the *Epilogue to the Satires* (a response in part, perhaps, to the *Gazetteer*, 27 October 1738) claims that he must stop writing satire because "bad men were grown so shameless and so powerful, that Ridicule was become as unsafe as it was ineffectual" (p. 327n). For Horace the lines regarding regulation are positive: "*Vetere modum, formidine fustis | Ad* benedicendum, delectandumque *redacti*" (lines 154-55). For Pope they are signs of the court's Augustan extension of power and the need for the resistance of even the few:

> Who felt the wrong, or fear'd it, took th' alarm,
> Appeal'd to Law, and Justice lent her arm.
> At length, by wholesom dread of statutes bound,
> The Poets learn'd to please, and not to wound:
> Most warp'd to Flatt'ry's side; but some, more nice,
> Preserv'd the freedom, and forebore the vice.
> Hence Satire rose, that just the medium hit,
> And heals with Morals what it hurts with Wit.
>
> (Lines 255-62)

Fellows. . . . In this Manner was the Stage managed under a *Licenser.*

Chesterfield is lamentably confident that a licenser "will generally regulate his Judgment according to the Humour of the Court, whatever the Humour of the Court may be" (7:410).

[27] For further discussion of such threats, see Laurence Hanson, *Government and the Press, 1695-1763* (London: Oxford Univ. Press, 1936), pp. 51, 66-70. Warton's gloss to line 224 also repeats that "For this passage our Author was threatened with a prosecution" (4:183n). As

Horace's *formidine fustis* is a civilizing step that leads to Virgil and Varius and their glorification of Augustus. Pope's ironic "wholesom dread of statutes" leads to the decline of the arts and civilization.

This is made clear through an image of the stage as an emblem of politics. Edward appeared earlier as one of the opposition's kings of a pre-Georgian golden age; he now re-appears on the stage soon to be licensed by the court's first minister, and is acted, or parodied, by the man soon to be the king's own poet. The scene Pope is referring to took place in 1727 as part of the coronation festivities of George II, ten years before the Licensing Act and three years before Cibber's elevation to the laureateship. But it is not chronology so much as metaphor that is important here—the reduction of a great old English king to the level of actor-courtier in service to a destructive new king, and the results of regulatory state interference in the arts. Pope strengthens his point by once more emphasizing a key word in Horace's facing Latin.

> *Mox trahitur manibus* Regum *fortuna retortis;*
> *Esseda festinant, pilenta, pertorrita, naves,*
> *Captivum portatur ebur, captiva Corinthus.*
>
> (Lines 191-93)

In the performed drama that Horace describes the author drags in bound *kings*, once fortune's favorites, and places them in the Roman triumph and its hurried procession of chariots, carriages, wagons, ships, and captured ivory and Corinthian bronze. With a startling inversion, Pope turns Horace's Roman triumph into an English disgrace, and metamorphoses the foreign, defeated kings into the apparently victorious but really debased Edward. The English monarchy has become low enough to be acted by Colley Cibber, and thus is the captive king, while the nobility is

---

we have seen, Johnson's political works of 1738-1739 *may* have placed him in jeopardy as well. See above, chap. 5, sec. III, n. 42.

part of an unannounced "triumph" of its own defeat. In the elaborate English spectacles, during which, Pope tells us, "the Playhouses vied with each other to represent all the pomp of a Coronation" (p. 222n), there is neither plot nor discourse. Instead,

> Back fly the scenes, and enter foot and horse;
> Pageants on pageants, in long order drawn,
> Peers, Heralds, Bishops, Ermin, Gold, and Lawn;
> The Champion too! and, to complete the jest,
> Old Edward's Armour beams on Cibber's breast!
>
> (Lines 315-19)

Moreover, in Pope's poem—unlike Horace's—the court steps directly in and contributes to the degradation of the theater. Intelligence gives way to mere visual stimulation. The audience is debased and howls like wolves when it sees "Quin's high plume, or Oldfield's petticoat" (line 331),

> Or when from Court a birth-day suit bestow'd
> Sinks the lost Actor in the tawdry load.
>
> (Lines 332-33)

In order to appear something other than a grumbling malcontent, Pope follows Horace in offering a norm for the good dramatic artist. On the surface, their views are similar, but their respective contexts lend each a different meaning. They celebrate the playwright who can use imagination to induce imagination, evoke passion, responses of the heart as well as pity and terror, and thus control the viewer and deliver him "To Thebes, to Athens, when he will, and where" (line 347). But Pope's artist is significantly free of due regulations and anything except the poet's own genius; he is an example of a nonsatiric poet able to flourish without the court's intrusion. Pope therefore stresses Horace's word *inaniter* (line 211) to indicate, I believe, freedom from government meddling as well as the paradox of poetry's "empty" words moving one so deeply. Horace, on the other hand, uses his norm to gain further support for his own poetry and its utility for Augustan interests.

Pope's continuing difference of intention and negative evaluation of his presumed models appear again in the adaptation of the poet's desire to serve the crown. Horace grants that poets are often excessively sensitive to criticism, vain about their work, and seekers of preferment from the throne. Pope distinguishes the words he wishes us to see adapted—verses (*Carmina*), send for us (*arcessas*), and force us to write (*scribere cogas*).

> *Cum speramus eo rem venturam, ut simul atque*
> Carmina *rescieris nos fingere, commodus ultro*
> Arcessas, & *egere vetes,* & scribere cogas.
>
> (Lines 226-28)

Dacier notes that Horace criticized the vanity of poets for wishing to be so close to their prince who would supply topics for them (9:435). Hurd seconds this view, and adds that poets too easily thought "that *preferment is the constant pay of merit*, and that, from the moment their talents became known to the public, distinction and advancement are sure to follow," since they must "deserve the favour and countenance of their prince" (p. 23n). Horace nowhere suggests that this is wrong—merely that it is presumptuous in all but the best poets, and that Augustus himself is wise to seek fame through Virgil and Varius rather than through lesser talents. He is showing how Augustus can best use the poets for his own ends. Such state employment is a positive good; Pope sees it as a positive evil because it is an invitation to untruth. Poets are troublesome

> But most, when straining with too weak a wing,
> We needs will write Epistles to the King;
> And from the moment we oblige the town,
> Expect a Place, or Pension from the Crown;
> Or dubb'd Historians by express command,
> T' enroll your triumphs o'er the seas and land;
> Be call'd to Court, to plan some work divine,
> As once for Louis, Boileau and Racine.
>
> (Lines 368-75)

Pope deplores the job of official liar, whether Roman, French, or English "historiographer royal." Only by an earthly "express command"—*scribere cogas*—may one's "divine" work celebrate George's pre-Dettingen military virtues, Louis' achievements, and Augustus' deeds.[28]

In order to buttress his case, Pope takes a combination of steps unprecedented in his imitations of Horace: (1) he places three consecutive lines in roman rather than italic letters; (2) he places brackets around them; and (3) after those eye-catching devices, he leaves blank the opposite, English section of the page in which the Latin would have been imitated.

[At neque dedocorant tua de se judicia, atque
Munera quae, multa dantis cum laude, tulerunt
Dilecti tibi Virgilius Variusque poetæ:] (Lines 245-47)

Horace, Virgil, and Varius, those poets whom Augustus loves and who love Augustus, do not discredit his judgment in receiving the gifts Augustus has given them, to his glory. At the appropriate place, Pope says nothing. Since these lines were not part of a textual crux, and were commented

---

[28] Prior had also comically deplored Boileau's lies regarding Louis XIV's brave accomplishments. See Prior's *English Ballad, on the Taking of Namur* (1695), a parody of Boileau's *Ode sur la prise de Namur* (1692). Pope almost certainly knew both poems. In any case, as it was put by the anonymous author of *A Short Review of Mr. Hooke's Observations . . . concerning the Roman Senate and the Character of Dionysius of Halicarnassus* (London, 1758), "it is well known that Lewis XIV had a band of writers as regularly retained in his service as his guards; for which reason, every thing that was written during his reign concerning his person and government, was rather a panegyric than a history" (p. 31). See also John Duncombe, trans. and ed., *The Works of Horace in English Verse. By Several Hands*, 2 vols. (London, 1757), regarding Horace's lines 28-33 of his epistle to Augustus. Since the Romans were not as good at wrestling as the Greeks, "might not *Horace* be willing to flatter the Vanity of the Emperor in this Instance, as, we know, he actually did in many others? And thus of late Years, the *French* Writers have prostituted their Pens in Honour of *Lewis* XIVth's *Golden Age?*" (2:514).

upon and translated in the normal run of events, Pope is not being pedantic but emphatic. He probably wishes us to see that there is neither a Virgil nor a Varius to sing George II and that, in a grotesque adaptation of those poets, the new Augustus has only "such forgotten things / As Eusden, Philips, Settle, writ of Kings" (lines 416-17).[29] Though Varius' works were almost wholly lost, he was sufficiently well known to appear in the *Grub-street Journal* and in Moréri's *Grand dictionnaire historique*, where he is described as "Poëte Latin, ami de Virgile & d'Horace, eut aussi beaucoup de part aux bonnes graces de l'Empereur Auguste."[30] Moréri cites Horace's line 247, above, as his source. Horace, Virgil, and Varius thus unite in praise of their princeps, and oppose the forgotten Eusden, Philips, and Settle.

This is an attractive reading. But there is another hypothesis that suggests itself—namely, that Pope is dissociating himself from Virgil and Varius, especially the former, by refusing to imitate the lines positively, since they would be as much flattery of George II as they are of Augustus. We know that Virgil's moral force had been weakened by his support for the usurping Augustan settlement, and that Pope himself was offended by the dishonesty of the *Aeneid*. Virgil and Varius are court-poets, as unlike Pope as they are like Horace. Hence, "Well may he blush, who gives . . . or receives" flattery (line 414) includes all three Roman as well as

[29] Considering the nature of this poem's satire, one must suspect that "writ of Kings" means both what Eusden et al. wrote about kings, and what the king himself "writ." Johnson (*Dictionary*, 1755) defines *writ* in three relevant senses: "1. Any thing written; scripture . . . now chiefly used in speaking of the Bible. . . . 2. A judicial process. . . . 3. A legal instrument." Pope uses *writ* in the Biblical sense three times, and in the sense of *old* and *learned* once. See *A Concordance to the Poems of Alexander Pope*, comp. Emmett G. Bedford and Robert J. Dilligan, 2 vols. (Detroit: Gale Research Co., 1974). Either the king's sacred words, or his judicial processes, or his legal instruments, or all three will be forgotten because they are worthless.

[30] Four vols., 8th ed. (Amsterdam, 1698). This is the edition from which Jeremy Collier's translation was made.

British fawners. Creech's translation of the bracketed lines
supports both interpretations: the lines are inapplicable to
George II and his poets; but they are also further examples
of courtly lies and thus inapplicable for Pope.

> But *Virgil*, *Varius*, and the learned few,
> That are applauded, and belov'd by You;
> Declare your Skill is great, your Judgment true.
> The Honors you bestow do raise your Fame,
> They gratefully reflect upon your Name,
> And kindly praise the Author whence they came.[31]

I suggested that the opening of the poem, which sings Augustus' moral achievements, was not applied ironically in the
received sense, for Pope knew Augustus to be at least as corrupt as George II. The final praise of each man's military
achievements is comparably misstated. Augustus negotiated
with the Parthians, he did not defeat them; he normally did
not visit the battlefields, and neither traversed seas (to conquer England, for instance) nor, barring two campaigns, en-
gaged in battle except through lieutenants, one of whom
(Varus) was catastrophically defeated; his policies were
largely those of peace, protection of borders, encouragement of trade, and solidification of his own power, partly
through the creation of new families in his debt.[32] All of
this would have been painfully familiar to the opposition.
Horace's encomia, delivered in exalted Virgilian tones, are
as erroneous as Pope's; but Horace's are willful if friendly

[31] *The Odes, Satyrs, and Epistles of Horace* (London, 1684), p. 537.
[32] For the Parthians, see Ezekiel Spanheim, *Les Césars de l'empereur Julien* (Amsterdam, 1728), p. 204, n. 695, which notes Horace's "license de Poëte" in speaking of the "Perses & des Parthes subjuguez par Au-guste." Gibbon calls the consequences of the Parthian venture "an honourable treaty," but notes that the vain "marble of Ancyra, on which Augustus recorded his own exploits, asserts that *he compelled* the Parthians to restore the ensigns of Crassus" (*The History of the Decline and Fall of the Roman Empire*, ed. J. B. Bury, 7 vols. [London, 1900], 1:2, and 2, n. 1). The opening of Tacitus' *Annals* shows Augustus rewarding those willing to serve him.

misrepresentations and a sign of the value of a docile poet
usefully serving his master. Pope's encomia break the limits
of the court-persona's credibility—"Your Arms, your Actions, your Repose to sing" (line 395)—and reveal the hostile
poet who is proudly un-Horatian, unkept, unsullied by the
mailed gentility of *scribere cogas*, and sane enough to stay
away from the worlds of the mad and of old curiosities, as
the praisers of king and minister are not:

> A vile Encomium doubly ridicules;
> There's nothing blackens like the ink of fools;
> If true, a woful likeness, and if lyes,
> "Praise undeserv'd is scandal in disguise:"
> Well may he blush, who gives it, or receives;
> And when I flatter, let my dirty leaves
> (Like Journals, Odes, and such forgotten things
> As Eusden, Philips, Settle, writ of Kings)
> Cloath spice, line trunks, or flutt'ring in a row,
> Befringe the rails of Bedlam and Sohoe.
>
> (Lines 410-19)

The *blush* and *flatter* above are used differently in Horace.
There only the receiver and not the giver of flattery blushes;
but they are used similarly in the epitaph Pope wrote for
himself, probably about this time, in which he insists that
he "never flatter'd" heroes and kings, and demands: "Let
Horace blush, and Virgil too."[33]

Horace concludes with a gesture of solidarity and humil-
ity: poet and princeps have a distaste for clumsy praise in
verse or wax statue and would not wish to be hawked about
in the street as wrapping paper or wrapped object. Horace's
own low *sermones*—so different from the sublime strains of
a Virgil or Varius—cannot equal his longing to praise well.
For Pope, however, "Well may he blush" is another sign of
the break from Horace, Augustus, George II, and the court.
The awkward flatterer's sheets in Horace will be used as

[33] See opening of chap. 4, above, for the full context.

wrapping paper; Pope wishes that fate on his own verse if he should be so guilty. Earlier, Horace cited the foolish lines of Choerilus in praise of Alexander; Pope triples the number of native fools who "writ of Kings," includes Eusden, Philips, and Settle, and suggests that they are a brief selection of zealous Georgian flatterers. Horace thus supports his own character by union with his monarch; Pope supports his by dissociation from both monarch and Horace. Pope's extant norm is Swift, whom he praises as holding views contrary to the apparently accommodating values of the Advertisement and *Epistles*, ii. 1, itself. "The Rights a Court attack'd, a Poet sav'd" contrasts with Horace's "a Poet's of some weight, / And (tho' no Soldier) useful to the State" in praising its leader.

From the poem's Advertisement to its conclusion, then, Pope characterizes his monarch and court as being lamentably Augustan. He also characterizes Horace as the literary and Augustus as the political paradigms of what should not be the relationship between the coercive power of the state and the freer needs of the artist. Pope wishes to shift *scribere cogas* to *nolo serviam*, and the ideal of the poet from Horace and Virgil to Swift—that is, in this instance, the Juvenalian Swift who opposes tyranny whatever the cost. The anti-Augustanism of his imitation, however, is intended as more than a protest and contrasting affirmation. It also shows how the currently dominant Augustan world has induced what may be irreversible decay. Lines 398-402 portray George II not as the feeble contrast to a successful leader of an absolute empire bullying its neighbors, but as spiritual father to the Queen of Dullness. Pope expects to sing "How, when you nodded, o'er the land and deep, / Peace stole her wing, and wrapt the world in sleep" (lines 400-1). The poem depicts a world running down, one still distant from *The Dunciad* of 1743, but already on that road. *To Augustus* proceeds in part through the likening of George II and his court to the domineering princeps and his, and in part through the inversion of Horace's methods and their replacement with rhetoric of isolation and an important syllogism whose "proof" undercuts the values of government intrusion in the arts.

II. Augustan Darkness

We remember that the poem begins with the praise of the opposition's favorite kings—Edward III, Henry V, and Alfred the Great—and a lamentation that they did not receive adequate recognition during their lifetimes. George II is a happy exception to the rule:

> All human Virtue to its latest breath
> Finds Envy *never* conquer'd, but by Death.
> . . . .
> *Sure* fate of all, beneath whose rising ray
> Each Star of meaner merit fades away;
> Oppress'd we feel the Beam directly beat,
> Those Suns of Glory please not till they set.
> To Thee, the World its present homage pays,
> The Harvest early, but mature the Praise.
>
> (Lines 15-16; 19-24)

The words I have italicized suggest that Pope is establishing a syllogism with the following terms: only the great and virtuous are denied fame and are envied in this world; George is not envied and gets fame in this world; therefore George is neither great nor virtuous. George lacks human virtue and is not a sun of glory—merely the son of George I, hardly an auspicious parent as far as the patriots could see.

Pope departs radically from Horace, for whom the public follows the wrong poets and the right leader. Horace thus contrasts Rome's wise political with its unwise aesthetic judgments, and urges the monarch himself to bring the two into balance by his example, so that the citizens will honor today's good poets as they do today's good emperor. For Pope, however, political judgment is a function of poetic judgment (and vice versa); the people who revere bad poets also revere the bad king. Pope must therefore show that the society praising George II is as mistaken here as in its poetic judgment. For purposes of self-protection, among others, he attacks George II by attacking the audience that simultaneously overpraises him and the flawed or incompetent artists.

We see that the people who are "Foes to all living worth except your own," are also "Advocates for Folly dead and gone" (lines 33-34); that "the People's Voice is odd, / It is, and it is not, the voice of God" (lines 89-90); that "the Publick is a fool" (line 94); that in the face of older poets' violation of "all Reason's laws, / These fools demand not Pardon, but Applause" (lines 117-18); that "all shame is lost in George's Age!" (line 126); that some "Examples yet remain" of "Fools" who "disgrac'd the former Reign" (lines 127-28); that in the present times a "Poetick Itch" (line 169) has inappropriately seized everyone and serious standards have been lost (lines 169-88); that Cibber, the Poet Laureate, "breaks the laws" of the theater "with vast applause" (lines 292-93); that one had best say "Farewel the stage!" (line 302) if getting money is the essential criterion of success; that lords and mobs alike prefer farce and pantomime to serious drama (line 311); that the "monster of a King" (line 210) is transformed into "The many-headed Monster of the Pit: / A sense-less, worth-less, and unhonour'd crowd" (lines 305-6) wolflike in its howling at the stage (lines 328-29); that poets are all too eager to lie—favorably—about their king in order to gain preferment (lines 368-75); and that the journals, odes, and other "forgotten things" that have been written about kings (lines 416-17) should evoke blushes from both giver and receiver and be subject to disgraceful sale and use.

The cumulative effect of such debasing of mob, lords, poets, and public at large is to render them utterly unreliable as guides of any sort, whether aesthetic or political. Socially high or low, dramatic, satiric, political, or religious poet, priest or layman, the literary judgment is atrocious—"I say

the Publick is a fool," and "all shame is lost in George's Age!"
The reflection upon the public's opening praise of the monarch is inevitable: the advocates for literary folly are also advocates for regal folly. They are so to some degree because the
king himself is a fool and the people imitate him as much
as they did Charles II, on the principle of *ad exemplum
regis*—"All, by the King's Example, liv'd and lov'd" (line
142).[34] They are also such foolish advocates because the king
himself encourages poets like Cibber, Eusden, and Settle.
The words applied to Charles II are again intended for
George II: "The willing Muses were debauch'd at Court"
(line 152).

The results of these major errors in judgment are clear in
the social and artistic disruptions that, unlike those in the
Horatian model, have little chance for improvement. The
perhaps incorrigible quality of Pope's world is indicated in
the contrast between his and Horace's view of the function
and value of the poet. Horace seriously insists that the poet
teaches the worth of prayer, makes the supplicant feel the
god within him, and allows him to win the gods' favor
through the prayers taught by the muses; for Pope, Christian
prayer is turned into unchristian uses and impressive shout-
ing to a misguided minister.

> How could Devotion touch the country pews,
> Unless the Gods bestow'd a proper Muse?
> Verse chears their leisure, Verse assists their work,
> Verse prays for Peace, or sings down Pope and Turk.

[34] The notion is mentioned in Swift's "On Reading Dr. Young's
Satires, Called the Universal Passion" (1726; pub. 1734), line 24. Thomas
Blackwell, in his fashion, is more expansive—but also illuminating: "It
is universally acknowledged, that the Happiness of Nations depends, in
a great measure, upon their Governors, whose *Manners* the People are
rather more ready to imitate than to obey their Commands. This
should render Men in power equally circumspect in private life, as at-
tentive to the Duties of their public Stations" (*Memoirs of the Court
of Augustus*, 3 vols. [Edinburgh and London, 1753-1763], 3:1).

The silenc'd Preacher yields to potent strain,
And feels that grace his pray'r besought in vain,
The blessing thrills thro' all the lab'ring throng,
And Heav'n is won by violence of Song.

(Lines 233-40)[35]

Horace's defense of the poet's value is at the quantitative and qualitative center of his poem; and well it might be, since without it much of the rationale of the importance and value of contemporary poetry would disappear. Pope's debasing of that poetic norm thus reverses Horace's intention: Pope wishes to show that on the whole modern poetry cannot be defended. Both audience and artist have accepted the Horatian premise of due regulations and artistic service to the state—defined as serving the monarch's and court's self-interest and public image. The one unsullied poetic norm is Swift in opposition. Pope must retreat to the *Drapier's Letters* of 1724 to offer praise in 1737 and the inverted modern equivalent of Virgil.

There are times when Horace does supply a positive model for Pope, but largely in those sections of the epistle addressed to literary criticism. In his corresponding sections Pope lowers the mask of sycophantic courtier and becomes the wise "Horatian" speaker able to see through excesses of praise and blame, arrive at earned not received literary opinions, and accurately evaluate the literary milieu. This authority also carries positively into the political milieu, just as the bad literary evaluations by the foolish people carry

[35] This passage won less than universal approbation. Warburton admired it (*Works of Alexander Pope*, 9 vols. [London, 1751], 4:138n), but others were extremely critical. Duncombe, *Works of Horace*, 2:519-20, regarded Horace as more Christian than Pope in his "burlesque Imitation" that mocks established worship. Warton argued that "Pope has indulged a vein of ill-placed humour and pleasantry" (Pope's *Works*, 4:183n). But Sternhold and Hopkins had long been in doubtful odor, and were even subject to attack by a friend of the administration. See [Thomas Newcomb] *A Miscellaneous Collection of Original Poems* (London, 1740), pp. 244-45, where those two worthies are labeled defaming vandals.

negatively into their political evaluations. But aside from literary standards and talents, and perhaps some aspects of his willingness to talk freely to his prince, Horace is the enemy—and even in those aspects of the imitation Pope's vision and context are ethically and politically superior to the amiable friend of C. Julius Caesar Octavianus, who took the name Augustus in 27 B.C. in order to obviate the hated names of triumvir and proscriber.

In his own *Epistle to Augustus* Pope shows the implications of eagerness to serve an absolute monarch who destroys liberty; he quarrels with Horace's lies and collaboration, Augustus' tyranny and control of art and his own king's and court's adaptations of Augustanism and Horatianism. A world moving toward the sleep of dullness results: the mythic king is played by Cibber, who can only wear the shell of English greatness; modern poetry, all too generously supported by the throne and administration, is created in their image, and only the honor of opposition remains.

One is hardly overstating to say that the later Pope rejects most of the nonliterary, especially political, standards that Augustus and Horace had come to represent. Pope's essential pose becomes that of the indignant satirist whose moral virtue, outrage, and preservation of old, free values distinguish him from establishment corruption. That is, of course, the mask not of the polite *enfant gâté* of the court, but of the Juvenalian lasher of vice, the blessedly rejected true Roman who describes his world and says, "*difficile est saturam non scribere*" (i. 30), just as Pope would say he shall defend Virtue's cause or die fighting the rich, powerful, and corrupt who dominate his world (*Fortescue*, lines 91-122). So noble an ironist as Pope would no doubt have been pleased with Juvenal's revolution within Horace's own walls.

CHAPTER 7

~~~~~~

Conclusion: Mutatis Mutandis

I. The Response in France

A T SEVERAL PLACES IN THIS STUDY I HAVE USED CONTINENTAL, largely French, sources to buttress particular points. One could, I believe, write a comparable book on the acceptance and rejection of Augustus in France, the changing attitudes toward the empire and republic, and the consequences for political, historical, and literary works. Some emphases would differ from those in Britain but, with one major exception, the general shape of such response would be similar—Augustanism rises and falls with royalism and absolutism. For example, the power and *gloire* of Louis XIV made him a splendid reincarnation of Augustus. In 1664 Puget de la Serre dedicated *L'Histoire d'Auguste* to his king and told him that *"cette Histoire . . . est un Miroir qui represente parfaitement vostre Majesté."* The mirror was polished by a short poem indicating the greatness of each man *"Pour faire graver sous les Portraites du Roy & d'Auguste, peints ensemble."* Boileau took a similar tack in 1668. In his first epistle, written at Colbert's request, he hopes to reconcile Louis to the Treaty of Aix-la-Chapelle that temporarily ended the War of the Spanish Succession. Even the greatest of heroes and kings are immortalized by poets singing their deeds rather than by the deeds themselves (as Horace in his epistle to Augustus and *Odes*, iv. 9 also urged). Hence, he tells Louis,

> En poëtes fameux rends nos climats fertiles:
> Un Auguste aisément peut faire des Virgiles.
> Que d'illustres témoins de ta vaste bonté
> Vont pour toi déposer à la postérité.[1]

---

[1] De la Serre (Roüen), sig. aii^r and ai^v; *Oeuvres de Boileau: Texte de l'édition Gidel*, ed. Georges Mongrédien (Paris: Garnier Frères, 1952),

In 1674 Louis Moréri's *Grand dictionnaire historique* praises every aspect of Augustus' reign. Some time later, St. Evremond, not blind to Augustus' faults, still believes that his government was excellent, and that "The Good of the State was his first Thought." René le Bossu, a believer in strong monarchy, states that "*Augustus* destroyed nothing, he only re-established a tottering State." Bossu thus praises Virgil for aiding Augustus and his wise design. In the *Aeneid*, Virgil "was oblig'd to make ["the *Subjects* of *Augustus*"] lay aside the old Antipathy they had to *Monarchy*, to convince them of the Justice, and the legal Prerogative of *Augustus*, to divert them from so much as desiring to oppose his Designs, and to raise in them a Love and Veneration for this Prince." Père Catrou's edition of Virgil is filled with comparable glosses and praise for the close relationship between Augustus and Virgil, though even he thinks that Virgil's flattery sometimes went too far.[2] Catrou knows that Virgil copied the character of Aeneas from Augustus: "Quel art en cela! quelle sagesse! C'étoit particuliérement à son Prince, que le Poëte prétendoit plaire. Auroit-il atteint son but, s'il avoit donné à son Héros des traits, qu' Auguste n'eut pû trouver en soi? Mais quelle satisfaction secrete pour un Empereur, de se reconnoitre dans le portrait d'un demi-Dieu, & de voir son caractère, en quelque sorte, divinisé dans le fils de Venus?" (3:585). The people themselves were equally ecstatic, though, no doubt wisely, less secret in their pleasure (3:587). J. B. L. Crevier's 1749 *Histoire des empereurs romains* rationalizes Octavian's youthful excesses under the guise of necessary policy in an exquisitely prudent

---

p. 112. Of course, the controversy regarding Charles Perrault's *Parallèlle des anciens et des modernes* (1688) would also have enhanced the comparison between the two rulers.

[2] St. Evremond, *Miscellaneous Essays*, 2 vols. (London, 1692), 1:96; Bossu, *Monsieur Bossu's Treatise of the Epick Poem*, trans. W. J., 2 vols., 2nd ed. (London, 1719), 1:59; 1:54-55; François Catrou, *Les Poësies de Virgile*, 4 vols. (Paris, 1729), 2:20-21 for Virgil's excessive flattery. Subsequent citations from Catrou are given in the text.

rise to benevolent "monarchical authority."[3] In the process, Augustus had to control "defamatory libels" and make them "high treason, and punishable accordingly" (1:329)—much to the betterment of the state, though later emperors were unjust in applying the law.

But there were many misgivings, many puzzles, and much outright hostility to Augustus, even before the philosophes hit their stride. Bossuet and Tillemont, for example, were certainly aware of Augustus' depravities and the results for the state. "*Caesar* and *Anthony* defeated *Brutus* and *Cassius*: Liberty expired with them," Bossuet says. Yet he sees contradictions reconciled by God's wisdom, especially in the stability and peace that Augustus created throughout the empire, so that "then came Jesus Christ into the World." Tillemont, clearly a reader of Tacitus, is even more conscious of Augustus' blemishes and his absolute power, but also stresses stability and "la douceur de la paix," so that "on sçait toujours assez de choses pour admirer l'ordre & la sagesse de Dieu dans la conduite du monde."[4]

[3] *Histoire des empereurs romains depuis Auguste jusqu'à Constantin*, 11 vols. (Paris, 1749-1755). I quote from John Mills' translation (1755), 10 vols. (London, 1814), 1:13. Subsequent references are cited in the text. Crevier's conclusion that "the real and solid benefits that flowed from monarchy" were ample recompense for Augustus' depravity along the way, was attacked by Sir Tanfield Leman in the *Monthly Review*, 12 (1755): 410. Such heresy may be fit for a Frenchman, but "no *Briton*, sensible of the sweets of liberty, would easily be prevailed on to think in the same manner." See also the review of a subsequent volume of Crevier by "N" in the *Monthly*, 23 (1760): 497-98. The attributions are from Benjamin Christie Nangle, *The Monthly Review First Series 1749-1789. Indexes of Contributors and Articles* (Oxford: Clarendon Press, 1934), p. 84 (cited hereafter as Nangle).

[4] Jacques Bénigne Bossuet, *A Discourse on the History of the whole World*, trans. [R. Spencer] (London, 1686), pp. 552, 88; Louis Sebastian le Nain de Tillemont, *Histoire des empereurs . . . durant les six premiers siècles de l'église*, 3 vols., 2nd ed. (Brussels, 1732), 1:2, 1:7. Crevier, 1:44, acknowledges his debt to Tillemont, who was also, in a very different manner, a tutor to Gibbon. See David P. Jordan, *Gibbon and His Roman Empire* (Urbana: Univ. of Illinois Press, 1971), especially pp. 140, 142-44.

Such spiritual histories and faith in divine order were not convincing to all, and as the century progressed perhaps not to many. Catrou blandly states that Virgil could not praise Cato of Utica because he was an enemy of the Caesars (3:571n), and that he pleased Augustus by parodying Cicero's style through Drances' bombast in Book Eleven of the *Aeneid* (4:460). François Macé, however, in the *Histoire des quatre Cicérons* (1715), is angry at contemporary Roman historians' silence regarding Cicero and at Augustus' change of government. He deplores Octavian's manipulation and proscription of Cicero,[5] the deadly horrors of the proscription in general (pp. 189, 193), and the fate of the nation and its posterity:

> La République n'avoit alors qu'une ombre de liberté, & il ne restoit plus d'esperance aux grands, plus de liberté pour les suffrages, plus de crédit au peuple; ainsi plus d' emulation à la vertu, plus d'amour pour l'étude, plus de gloire à acquerir. De-là, les grands hommes désoccupez tomberent dans la langueur, & ensuite dans le vice. (P. 236)

Readers interested in feminine concerns in Rome would have had even more expansive lessons to read. Jacques Roergas de Serviez' popular *Les Femmes des douze Césars* (1718) describes and bemoans the scenes of the triumvirate's proscription. The patriotic and elegant flattery Catrou so admired is now viewed quite differently: "ce que les Poëtes ne manquerent pas de lui attribuer dans leurs vers, qui sont autant de honteux monumens de leur flatterie & de leur impieté."[6] Roergas de Serviez grants Augustus' good rule after Actium, but this harsh description in a section, after all, about Livia must have been noticed, especially since the book went into a fourth edition by 1722, was translated into English in 1723, again in 1752, and into Italian in 1734.

Discussions of Cicero were one source of French, as of

---

[5] (The Hague, 1715), p. 164. Subsequent quotations are cited in the text.

[6] Two vols., 4th ed. (Amsterdam, 1722), 1:69 (proscription); 1:97.

British, hostility to Augustus. Another source was those writers focussing largely (Roergas de Serviez) or almost exclusively on Octavian's rise to power—as does the Abbé de Vertot in *Histoire des révolutions arrivées dans le gouvernement de la république romaine* (1721). Here we find the familiar portrait of a grasping, malicious, cruel, cowardly, tyrannical, contradictory ruler who used art, games, and shows gradually to soften "the too great Fierceness of the *Roman* Temper," and thus artfully and "insensibly accustom men freeborn to bear with Slavery."[7] By 1734 Montesquieu's *Considérations sur les causes de la grandeur des romains et de leur décadence* places Augustus' activities within a reasoned framework of the rise and fall of nations, and thus adds philosophic reflections not in Vertot. In the process, he is harder on Cicero than Macé had been earlier. That injudicious orator introduced "an Enemy into the Republick" far more dangerous than Antony had been.[8] He also characterizes Augustus' reign in words that would later appear in the Chevalier de Jaucourt's remarks on Rome in the *Encyclopédie* and in Goldsmith's *Roman History* (1769): "*Augustus* (for that was the Name offered by Flattery to *Octavius*) was careful to establish Order, or rather a durable Servitude; for when once the Sovereignty has been usurped in a free State, every Transaction, on which an unlimited Authority can be founded, is called a Regulation, and all Instances of Disorder, Commotion, and bad Government, are represented as the only Expedients to preserve the just Liberty of the Subject" (p. 128). Moreover, Montesquieu does not adhere to the convenient theory of Augustus' controlled schizophrenia, his nice move from hor-

[7] *The History of the Revolutions That happened in the Government of the Roman Republic*, trans. John Ozell, 2 vols., 3rd ed. (London, 1723-1724), 2:409.

[8] *Reflections on the Causes of the Grandeur and Declension of the Romans* (London, 1734), p. 121. Subsequent references are cited in the text. The Chevalier de Jaucourt's remarks are in vol. 14 (1765), "Romain Empire," and Goldsmith's in his *Roman History*, 2 vols. (London, 1769), 2:98-99, and chap. 3, sec. 1, at n. 11, above.

rid Octavian to happy Augustus. "A compleat key to the whole Life of *Augustus*," he says, is that "He wore a Coat of Mail, under his Robe, in the Senate House" (p. 130). That is, presumably, he recognized that the senate was the symbolic home of liberty in which he, as heir to the assassinated dictator, was neither welcome nor safe. As a result, he had to change the Roman republic into a monarchy. The "smooth and subtle Tyrant led [the Romans] gently into Slavery" (p. 132).

Montesquieu's even more influential *De l'Esprit des lois* (1748) enlarges on the essential bias of his *Considérations*: namely, the balance necessary in a free state, whether republic or monarchy, in order to insure liberty (see bk. xi, chap. 6, for instance). One important aspect of this balance and freedom is the people's right to publish works that "are no way preparative to high treason." Crevier thinks Augustus' suppression of satire good, though wrongly used by others thereafter; Dryden and then the British opposition to Walpole had long ago argued against such suppression, and Montesquieu now adds that "nothing was more fatal to Roman liberty" (p. 285).

Bonnot de Mably also tells readers of his *Observations sur les romains* (1751) that Cicero foolishly helped to ruin the commonwealth by helping Octavian (pp. 78, 82), that Augustus killed satire because it disturbed his vices, and that "Tiberius, emboldened by his example, extended the sense of this law [*laesae majestatis*], to everything that offended him" and was a bad ruler in part because he thought himself, as Augustus' heir, "an usurper." It can be no surprise that in the *philosophe Encyclopédie* Augustus emerges as the destroyer of the republic, the enchainer of his people, and the murderer of accurate historical writing.[9] By then

[9] Montesquieu, *The Spirit of the Laws*, trans. Thomas Nugent, 2 vols., 5th ed. (London, 1773), 1:285; Mably, *Observations on the Romans* (London, 1751), pp. 78, 82 (Cicero ruins the commonwealth), p. 94 (Tiberius follows Augustus' precedent), p. 91 (usurper); *Encyclopédie*, vol. 14, "Romain Empire."

Virgil's once-admired flattery is less than warmly received in several quarters. Similarly, Dubois-Fontanelle finds that Ovid's praises must be pleasing to few readers, and at another place frankly says: "Ce seroit lui avoir fait sa cour d'une façon bien ridicule; mais le Poëte vouloit flatter, & le Prince aimoit sans doute à l'être." We remember that François-Jean, Marquis de Chastellux, and Jean Dusaulx each used political criteria to cast doubt upon the moral and literary distinction of the court-poets. Juvenal, Dusaulx insisted, always railed "against usurped power" and preserved the republic's love of freedom.[10]

Much of the ugliness of Octavian's and Augustus' depravity reached the stage in France, as it did in England: Crébillon the elder's *Le Triumvirat ou la mort de Cicéron* (1754: pub. 1755) and, more forcefully, Voltaire's *Le Triumvirat* (1764: pub. 1766) illustrate this reaction, especially so since those two men were political and philosophical enemies, yet agreed on Octavian's wretched conduct. In the latter play, Augustus' few decent or magnanimous words in the text are disowned in the notes as necessary theatrical fictions: "le poëte lui fait ici un honneur qu'il [Augustus] ne meritait pas."[11] Those notes scold Cicero's folly (p. 182), almost all aspects of Augustus' private life and public ca-

[10] Jean Gaspard Dubois-Fontanelle, *Nouvelle traduction des métamorphoses d'Ovide*, 2 vols. (Lille, 1772), 2:321, 1:92; Chastellux and Dusaulx, pp. 133, 167-68, above.

[11] *Le Triumvirat*, in *Oeuvres complètes de Voltaire*, 70 vols. (Paris, 1785-1789), 5:186. Subsequent references are cited in the text. Voltaire's play—his only complete dramatic failure—was not among the many of his efforts adapted in England. For a study of those, including *Brutus* and *La Mort de César*, each inspired in part by Voltaire's English experiences, see Harold Lawton Bruce, *Voltaire on the English Stage*, University of California Publications in Modern Philology, vol. 8 (Berkeley: Univ. of California Press, 1918). For discussion of the relationship between these two plays by Voltaire and Crébillon, see Paul O. Le Clerc, *Voltaire and Crébillon père: History of an Enmity*, in *Studies on Voltaire and the Eighteenth Century*, ed. Theodore Besterman, 115 (Banberry, Oxfordshire: The Voltaire Foundation, 1973): 57-58, 118-119, 130-34.

reer, the error of thinking him good rather than lucky (p. 174) and, among other things, the poets' offensive flattery of the princeps. The historians are bad enough, but "il faut avouer que *Virgile* et *Horace* ont montré plus de bassesse dans les éloges prodigués à Auguste, qu'ils n'ont deployé de goût et de génie dans ces tristes monumens de la plus lâche servitude." Many of these notes were transplanted for Voltaire's article on "Auguste Octave" in the *Questions sur l'encyclopédie* (1770-1772), where they were more easily accessible to British readers. There one would see that "il est donc permis aujourd'hui de regarder Auguste comme un monstre adroit & heureux," and later see that Virgil and Horace, in praising the wicked Augustus, show "des âmes serviles."[12]

One more example of the French hostility to Augustus should be instructive. In 1771 Henri Ophellot de la Pause (J. B. C. Isoard Delisle) published his four-volume translation of the *Histoire des douze Césars de Suétone*; in the same year, Gilbert Stuart issued his favorable review for the *Monthly*. Since the translator's own comments "under the title of Mélanges Philosophiques" are "the favourite part of his work," Stuart is glad to reproduce some of the major ones, Augustus of course among them. Though the successive emperors took his name, "we cannot possibly imagine that by doing so they proposed to do homage to the memory of that detestable prince." Could Marcus Aurelius imitate him? "What relation is there between the sublime

---

12 *Questions*, 9 vols. (Geneva [?] 1770-1772) 2:351-52. British knowledge of Voltaire's attack on Augustus is plain in the *Monthly*'s quotations from it (see chap. 2, sec. II, at n. 29, above), and in William Kenrick's characteristically cranky review of the *Dictionnaire philosophique*, also in the *Monthly*. Voltaire is not sufficiently harsh and clear on the "odious practice" of pederasty; but Kenrick does quote and approve of Voltaire's blast at the princeps: "Octavius Augustus, that sensualist, that cowardly murderer, dared to banish Ovid, at the same time that he was well pleased with Virgil's singing the beauty and flights of Alexis, and Horace's making little odes for Ligurinus" (*Monthly Review*, 33 [1765]: 283; attribution in Nangle, p. 173).

soul of a sovereign, the disciple of Zeno, and the atrocious mind of a tyrant, whose destructive policy had made despicable slaves of those Romans whose fathers he butchered?" Ophellot makes clear the sort of nation in which such a ruler could or could not thrive:

> if a Caesar should arise in any of our modern republics, I would advise its magistrates to lead him to the gibbet. If such a man should appear in a monarchy like France, it would be prudent to confine him in the Bastile. He should receive no protection but under an absolute government; and there he might rise to be an excellent despot.[13]

This brief review has suggested similarities between British and French reactions to Augustus. Such similarities are significant but need to be tested further: if Augustanism is in part a function of absolutism, we should expect an Augustan retread to emerge at some time during the French Revolution.[14] That movement was, of course, republican

[13] As quoted in the *Monthly Review*, 45 (1771): 577; attribution in Nangle, p. 105. For the French, see Ophellot de la Pause, *Histoire des douze Césars de Suétone*, 4 vols. (Paris, 1771), 1:253-55. The section is headed, "Portrait de César fait par un philosophe." Part of Ophellot's *Mélanges Philosophiques* is indebted to Voltaire's notes to *Le Triumvirat*. See 1:253-54.

[14] The use of the classics in colonial and revolutionary America supports this point as well, though there the main target is Julius Caesar rather than Augustus. Cato of Utica, Brutus, Cassius, and Cicero are among the most often evoked heroes—all republicans, of course. Charles F. Mullett observes that the bulk of the colonial pamphleteers derived their knowledge of Roman history "from Plutarch and Tacitus, with some help from Livy and Polybius, and in consequence conceived of themselves as the analogues of the farmer-republicans who sought to prevent the establishment of Caesarism." They also disliked Rome's deification of emperors and "ultimate transition to an empire built on military power; for both, it was felt, characterized arbitrary government" ("Classical Influences on the American Revolution," *Classical Journal*, 35 [1939-40]: 96-97). For further relevant discussion, see Richard M. Gummere, *The American Colonial Mind and the Classical Tradition: Essays in Comparative Culture* (Cambridge, Mass.: Harvard

in spirit, if not in outcome, and at the beginning was anti-imperial and anti-Caesarean by definition. But the Terror and Napoleon changed much of the original impetus and revived some political values that sat poorly beneath the cap of liberty. Tacitus would have been guillotined by the Gallic emperor, if it were possible—but at least one compliant modern historian would not have been. That was Pierre-Charles Levesque, whose three-volume *Histoire critique de la république romaine* appeared in 1807, seemed to have Bonaparte's own moral support, and looked at Rome's history in a new, or at least inverted, light.[15]

Levesque argues that Rome was most glorious not, as vulgar thought had it, following the expulsion of the last king (Tarquin) until the end of the republic, but during the days of those early kings themselves. The subsequent historians, who were all Pompeians and republicans at heart, slandered the kings, Julius, Augustus, and the empire in general, and falsely glorified the miserably unheroic, barbaric republic. As Stephen Jones put it in his review of

---

Univ. Press, 1963); Robert Middlekauf, *Ancients and Axioms: Secondary Education in Eighteenth-Century New England*, Yale Historical Publications, Miscellany 77 (New Haven: Yale Univ. Press, 1963); H. Trevor Colbourn, *The Lamp of Experience: Whig History and the Intellectual Origins of the American Revolution*, Institute of Early American History and Culture (Chapel Hill: Univ. of North Carolina Press, 1965); Bernard Bailyn, *The Ideological Origins of the American Revolution* (Cambridge, Mass.: Belknap Press of Harvard Univ. Press, 1969).

[15] Levesque had already initiated his process of discrediting the historians of Rome. On 27 May and 2 September 1803 he read his "Doutes, conjectures et discussions sur différens points de l'histoire romaine" to the Institut Impérial de France. Those were published in the *Histoire et mémoires de l'Institut Impérial . . . class d'histoire et de littérature ancienne*, 2 (Paris, 1815): 307-93. He says that "les historiens peuvent se tromper ou mentir" (p. 353) regarding the origin of Rome and her growth under the kings. He concludes that the republic enfeebled the Romans and cost them their earlier "acquisitions" which they had to reacquire by force of arms (p. 392). This view, he admits, is an attempt largely to reverse the received history of Rome's first centuries (p. 393).

Levesque for the *Monthly*, Rome's republican "history is represented as pregnant with lessons of a dangerous tendency; since it inculcates hatred of kings, extols tyrannicide, and . . . excites a spirit at variance with civil obedience and subordination, and a disposition unfriendly to a dutiful submission to governors."[16] As Jones further says, one of Levesque's miraculous achievements has been to "unsay and undo all that [the French] had so ostentatiously said and done from the beginning of the revolution . . . and to force them to act and labour in a course absolutely opposite to that in which he found them" (p. 521). The political aim of "his patron" (p. 525) was to banish the Revolution's love of Greek and Roman republics, to discredit antiroyal and anti-imperial historians and to insist that the noblest models were not Cato, Brutus, or Cicero, but Julius and Augustus. Pompey is inferior to Julius; Octavian, though bloody, is far less the evil triumvir than prejudiced historians have painted him. He has, in fact, been excessively blamed for his proscription of Cicero. Christopher Lake Moody, who was inspired to write a second long review of Levesque for the *Monthly*, insists that such insensitivity "disgraces the

16 *Monthly Review*, second series, 54 (1807): 517-18. Subsequent quotations are cited in the text. The attributions to Jones and to Moody, below, are in Nangle, *The Monthly Review Second Series 1790-1815. Index of Contributors and Articles* (Oxford: Clarendon Press, 1955), p. 236. Levesque was reviewed in the *Critical Review*, third series, 14 (1808): 449-62 which, like the *Monthly*, admired Levesque's independent cast of mind but deplored his distortion of history and hostility to Britain and freedom. Here is one example of the *Critical*'s reaction: "*Mark Antony*, while the creature of Julius, is held up to our admiration and esteem; no sooner does he become the rival of Augustus, than he is represented in the most degrading light. The triumviral proscriptions are palliated with excessive charity" (p. 460). Levesque's view marked a change in French reaction to Augustus. The British reaction, however, was stable, as Moody and others make clear. For a good example of early nineteenth-century evaluation of Augustus, an evaluation "Designed Chiefly for the Junior Students in the Universities, and the Higher Classes in Schools," see Henry Kett, *Elements of General Knowledge* (1802), 2 vols., 4th ed. (1803), 1:392-97.

author before us." Indeed, he seems unaware of the "deep stain which this base concession has inflicted on [Augustus'] memory, the odium of which his subsequent high fortunes have been ineffectual to wipe away." "Disgust" has become Moody's reaction to Levesque, who here is worse than the worst Romans he describes: they "never sunk to that pitch of degeneracy . . . in abstractedly extolling despotism and depreciating liberty." Augustus is part of the odious "incessant tyranny" established by Julius Caesar; yet both men comprise Levesque's imperial model.[17]

We have, as it were, come full circle: The royalists of seventeenth-century France are reincarnated in the supporter of the Emperor Napoleon; the republican Roman and the British and philosophe legacies are discarded.[18] The

[17] *Monthly Review*, second series, 55 (1806): 485. Levesque writes in the *Histoire critique*:

> On est touché de la fin tragique du plus grand des orateurs romains. . . . Mais il faut considérer aussi qu'il aurait été frappé de la proscription, quand elle n'aurait atteint qu'un fort petit nombre de têtes. Il avait affecté de se montrer, en intention, l'un des meurtriers de César, puisqu'il avait témoigné hautement le regret de n'avoir pas été mis du complot par les conjurés. Il avait été, en intention, l'un des meurtriers d'Antoine, puisqu'il avait reproché à Brutus de l'avoir épargné. Il avait proscrit, autant qu'il était en lui, Caïus Antonius, frère du triumvir, lorsqu'il avait blâmé Brutus, qui l'avait fait prisonnier, de lui avoir laissé la vie. Enfin il avait été proscripteur lui-même en intention, quand Brutus lui ayant écrit qu'il fallait mettre plus de zèle à empêcher la guerre civile qu'à punir les vaincus, il avait répondu qu'il était d'un avis fort différent; qu'une salutaire sévérite l'emportait sur une vaine clémence, et que si l'on voulait être clément, les guerres civiles ne manqueraient jamais. Il fallait donc, suivant son principe, que l'un des deux partis fût proscripteur: sa faction devint la plus faible, et il fut proscrit. (3:360-61)

[18] The association of Caesar(s) and Napoleon was frequently made by hostile British and friendly French commentators. In 1802 Coleridge says that Napoleonic France resembles that period "when Rome ceased to be a Republic, and the government was reorganized into a masked and military despotism . . . and all the powers of consul, tribune, and generalissimo centered in one person." Napoleon combines the qualities of the first two Caesars. See "Comparison of the Present State of France

British remain anti-Julian and anti-Augustan (while normally recognizing each man's genius), because by 1807 their own history of a balanced constitution, now actually tilted in the commons' direction, made Roman absolutism impossible. If there was any doubt, Napoleon's machinations would have galvanized British resistance as the *Histoire critique* galvanized Moody's, who is as conservative in his review as Levesque is reactionary in his volumes. In words that had over a century's precedent in Britain, Moody makes plain that Levesque's readers will see Rome's "inroads on those constitutional forms which were the guards of the freedom of the state." The offensive events at the end of the republic helped to subvert "those forms under which Rome had risen to be the mistress of the world, and the human mind had attained" its greatest "intellectual height." The geniuses of the Augustan age were the offspring of that earlier and "different order," though despotism "bribed them to offer incense to it, and to gild the slavery which it introduced" (p. 482).

Earlier, I suggested that the true Augustans for the eighteenth century would have been Oliver Cromwell and Louis XIV, each unacceptable to contemporary British literary, historical, and political thought. The true Augustus, or Julius, for the early nineteenth century would have been Napoleon—the completion of a triumvirate surely as hateful and un-British as Octavian, Antony, and Lepidus. The example of Levesque supports the hypothesis that Augustanism can flourish only under absolutism, a form of government that became progressively more odious in England after 1688. His example also serves as an effective contrast to the characteristic attitudes of the earlier British and French philosophe commentators upon Augustus, commentators

---

with that of Rome under Julius and Augustus Caesar," from *The Morning Post* (21 September 1802), in *Essays on his own Times* (1850), ed. Sara Coleridge, rpt., 3 vols. (New York: AMS Press, 1971), 2:480.

who even more effectively help us to evaluate the utility of the label *Augustan* in understanding Restoration and eighteenth-century literature.

II. Quo Vademus?

Let us assume for the moment that all or some of these major figures are Augustans: Dryden, Swift, Pope, Fielding, Goldsmith, Johnson, and Gibbon. Let us also collect some of their representative remarks regarding that ruler and his values. For Dryden, Augustus was guilty of "usurpation" of Roman freedom, slaughtered "many noble Romans" in the process, and forced the softening of satire "to provide for his own reputation"; for Swift, Octavian induced bloody faction, destroyed Rome's freedom and "entailed the vilest Tyranny that Heaven in its Anger ever inflicted"; for Pope, Augustus as proscriber was a "severe & barbarous" tyrant and as emperor was a corrupting manipulator of art; for Fielding, Echard's pro-Augustan history was offensive to the republican Livy who, in Fielding's view, prefers Hooke's "patriot," antityrannic "judicious collection"; for Goldsmith, the apparently benign Augustus created "permanent servitude" and insured a debilitated empire through his precedent of imperial succession and an unbalanced constitution; for Johnson, who regarded the Romans in general as first poor and then rich thieves, "no modern flattery . . . is so gross as that of the Augustan age," as in Horace, *Odes*, iii. 5. 2; for Gibbon, Augustus violated the division of powers that made Rome great, assumed all authority, demolished Roman genius, and created subsequent Roman degeneracy: "Tyran sanguinaire, . . . il parvient au trône, et fait oublier aux républicains qu'ils eussent jamais été libre."[19] We could, of course, enlarge this cento to include

[19] These references may be found above: Dryden, pp. 75-76; Pope, p. 63 and chap. 6 *passim*; Fielding, p. 58; Goldsmith, p. 92; Gibbon, p. 66. Johnson's remark is in Boswell's *Life of Johnson, together with Boswell's Journal of a Tour to the Hebrides*, ed G. B. Hill, rev. L. F. Powell, 6

the words of Cowley, Shaftesbury, Thomson, Akenside, Gordon, Bolingbroke, Lyttelton, Hooke, Blackwell, King, Warton, Spence, Pitt, and many others presumed to live and write somewhere in a British Augustan age. The point, however, should be clear: Augustus may have been admired for certain traits and actions, but his career and its implications were foreign to many ideals basic to eighteenth-century Britain. His personal behavior as ruler and private citizen, his destruction of the balanced constitution, solidification of slavery, establishment of absolutist precedent that drained Rome's energy and talent, management or destruction of art, artists, and letters for personal aggrandizement at the cost of truth and liberty—all of these several charges helped, in Voltaire's words, to characterize Augustus as "Un fourbe, un assasin" whose crimes merited capital punishment. All this is unlikely evidence in support of "the enormous prestige enjoyed by the Roman Augustan age all over Europe in the seventeenth and eighteenth centuries." Nor is Pope's portrait of a screening Horace who pleases at court, or the anonymous insistence that Horace serves to *"ornament a Tyrant's Nest,"* support for the view that the British Augustans saw in "Horace's poetry a concentrated image of a life and a civilization to which they more or less consciously aspired." Students of eighteenth-century satire may also wish to reconsider the notion of Horace as dominant and Juvenal as dormant until the second half of the century. Praise of Juvenal as a great poet of the "resistance" is shared for 200 years. From Rigault, to Dryden, to Crusius, to Dusaulx, numerous readers would have agreed with Hodgson's later belief that "while blaze the fires of Liberty. . . . / So long th' Aquinian shall transcend [Horace] in praise." With these revisionist points in mind, it may be time to reex-

---

vols. (Oxford: Clarendon Press, 1934-1950), 2:234. He calls the Romans thieves in his 1756 *Literary Magazine* review of Blackwell's *Memoirs of the Court of Augustus*, vol. 2. See also Richard Peterson, "Johnson at War with the Classics," *ECS*, 9 (1975): 69-86.

amine the accepted wisdom regarding Pope's *Epistle to Augustus* as a simple inversion of wise Horace's wise praise of his wise monarch. The "universal Augustan metaphor or 'myth' " on which such a reading has long been based is, in a different sense of the word, just that—a myth. The Juvenalian Pope would consider himself disgraced *"that Posterity should know he was* [Augustus Caesar's or George Augustus'] *familiar Friend."*[20]

As the first chapter made clear, hostility to Augustus by the major classical historians, especially Suetonius and Tacitus, was transmitted to Renaissance Florence and then much of Western Europe; it temporarily submerged during the triumph of sixteenth- and seventeenth-century royalism, reemerged in England late in the seventeenth century, and by the earlier eighteenth century had become entrenched in libertarian commonplaces, historical discussions, and practical politics. The years of verbal and printed combat during the opposition to Walpole were especially rich in anti-Augustanism, as Whig and Tory, administration and opposition smeared each other with the same brush. Given the consistent British opposition to tyranny, it is altogether fitting that those authors and genres most clearly associated with the Augustan dispensation should be most clearly suspect. Horatian satire and Virgilian epic dramatically lose force and credibility as the century progresses, and offer a splendid example of the influence of political judgments on the mutations of literary history.

[20] See Voltaire, *Questions sur l'encyclopédie*, 9 vols. (Geneva [?], 1770-1772), 4:146-47; V. de Sola Pinto on the prestige of the Augustan age, "Augustan or Augustinian?" *ECS*, 2 (1969): 292; Pope, the first *Dialogue* of the *Epilogue to the Satires* (1738), lines 11-22; the anonymous *Plain Truth* (1740), pp. 15-16; Reuben Brower, *Alexander Pope: The Poetry of Allusion* (Oxford: Clarendon Press, 1959), p. 176; Francis Hodgson, *The Satires of Juvenal* (London, 1807), pp. xxxviii-xxxix; Maynard Mack, " 'Wit and Poetry and Pope,' " in *Eighteenth-Century English Literature*, ed. James L. Clifford (New York: Oxford Univ. Press, 1959), p. 34; Charles Carthy, *A Translation of the Second Book of Horace's Epistles* (Dublin, 1731), p. 36, note a.

The modern concept of eighteenth-century benevolent Augustanism, then, is an idea whose time has passed. During its course it left a variety of distorted illuminations, one of which is the belief in a persistently Horatian satiric mode, preeminently so in Alexander Pope. The *Epistle to Augustus* and *Epilogue to the Satires*, however, demonstrate that Horatian means may be used for Juvenalian ends and thus be essentially un-Horatian. The administration recognized this difference between technique and intention in Pope's reworking of *Epistles*, i. 1, to Maecenas. Walpole's *Gazetteer* is outraged that Pope should celebrate a patron so hostile to the government and, therefore, the nation (6 April, 12 April, 24 August, 19 October, 10 November 1738). On 27 March 1738 the *Gazetteer* complains about the "very great Writer [who] has lately published an Epistle of *Horace*, which is not only inscribed, but also is full of very fine Compliments" to Bolingbroke. That enemy does not deserve such praise, for he "was endeavouring to subvert the Laws and Constitution of his Country, and to introduce in the stead of it, Tyranny and absolute Power." On 13 December the *Gazetteer*'s true Maecenas appears—not as an absolutist, but as a faithful member of the court of Augustus, as one whose good qualities are preserved and whose bad are lessened "by the *Learned,* whom he so kindly and generously protected." Pope's *Bolingbroke* is as inappropriately "Horatian" as his *Augustus.* The apparently genteel tones both mask and reveal a hostility lacking in Horace's epistle. In each of Pope's poems, he is most true to his own art and character when politically Juvenalian in an imitation of Horace.

My emphasis upon anti-Augustanism does not ignore the substantial body of positive remarks regarding Augustus during the Restoration and eighteenth century. Probably the bulk of these come from outright royalists, those more sympathetic to the power of the king than the commons in the balanced state, and those admiring particular aspects of the Augustan order without necessarily endorsing it in whole or in part. Such remarks are spread throughout our 140 years, but predominate between roughly 1660 and 1700, and especially before 1688. Most praise of Augustus falls into three classes: he restored political stability through his sole governance and control of a factious senate; in the process, he encouraged and nurtured great art and artists; he also increased the prestige and wealth of Rome and its empire. Though these are not, in general, offensive achievements, they do have several "but" clauses that soon made them uncongenial to many experiencing eighteenth-century Britain's historical processes of relative "democratization" and pride in its unique national identity.

The notion of sole governance, for example, was an aspect not only of Roman Caesarism, but also of a rejected French autocracy and, closer to home, equally offensive Stuart divine right and Cromwellian military dictatorship. However appealing the Augustan norm might—briefly— have been in 1660, it came trailing clouds of corruption. Furthermore, the political squabbling by commons and others was recognized as a troublesome but necessary alternative to absolutism and its concomitant intellectual sloth. The sense of Halifax's remark, in the *Character of a Trimmer* (written 1684), that "Parliaments, notwithstanding all their faults, and excesses, . . . yet . . . add the greatest strength to . . . a wise Administration," was incorporated into British political thought.[21] Party, with its fierceness of debate, Walpole's *London Journal* said on 20 July 1734, is "so far from being a reproach [to Britain], that 'tis an honor to us; and shews, that we have a sense of liberty and public virtue." In 1737 Chesterfield, opposing the first minister's Licensing Act, said, "The Restraint of Licentiousness is always a very popular and plausible Pretence; and arbitrary Power at first exerts itself in the Prosecution of it. Thus *Augustus* valued himself upon restoring Order and Decency to *Rome*; but

[21] The text is from the *Miscellanies* (1700), as in *The Complete Works of George Savile First Marquess of Halifax*, ed. Walter Raleigh, 2 vols. (Oxford: Clarendon Press, 1912), 1:64.

God forbid that we should ever pay as dear for the Restraint of Licentiousness, as the *Romans* did to that Emperor."[22]

Consequently, the Augustan model would have been regarded as one possible way to provide stability—but a stability apparent rather than real, temporary rather than permanent. For the dominant Whigs, the Tiberian succession and ultimate decline of Rome were in clear contrast to the commons' invitation of William of Orange, the orderly succession by Anne and then the naturalized Hanoverians, under whom England defeated Jacobite disruptions and enhanced her own imperial expansion. Augustus' marble buildings rose only to fall because of the political bogs on which they were built. Even granting opposition jeremiads, the British seemed to have great glory before them while building, as the tireless propagandists had it, on the granite of the Magna Charta and the Glorious Revolution. These cliotherapeutic strains were not seriously diminished by the harsher realities of the political situation. As J. H. Plumb has shown, the three major causes of England's political stability after 1715 were "single-party government; the legislature firmly under executive control; and a sense of common identity in those who wielded economic, social and political power."[23] That is no doubt true; it is equally true that the single-party frequently was challenged from within and without its ranks, that the legislature could on occasion chastize, defeat, and check the executive, and that the common identity included a shared belief

---

[22] As in the *Gentleman's Magazine*, 7 (1737): 411. The *London Journal* is quoted from Isaac Kramnick, *Bolingbroke and His Circle: The Politics of Nostalgia in the Age of Walpole* (Cambridge, Mass.: Harvard Univ. Press, 1968), p. 120. Both the administration and opposition may have been aware of Machiavelli's view, in the *Discourses*, that "Rome came to perfection through discord." See Harvey C. Mansfield, Jr., "Burke and Machiavelli on Principles in Politics," in *Edmund Burke: The Enlightenment and the Modern World*, ed. Peter J. Stanlis (Detroit: Univ. of Detroit Press, 1967), pp. 56-57.

[23] *The Growth of Political Stability in England 1675-1725* (London: Peregrine Books, 1969), p. 14.

in limitation of power—all impossibilities under archaic Augustanism. "God forbid that we should ever pay as dear . . . as the *Romans* did to that Emperor."

One of the shared beliefs was the necessity of domestic and foreign trade for Britain's financial success. That is immediately relevant to each of the other points in celebration of Augustus. He and Maecenas received much praise for their presumed nurturing of the arts; but, as we know, that was amply balanced by awareness of the base and costly reasons for such patronage. Furthermore, the careers of Pope and Johnson demonstrated that the court's or aristocracy's patronage was no longer necessary for financial well-being and was a detriment to moral well-being. The "celebrated letter" to Chesterfield is a result not a cause of the decline in patronage. On Thursday 19 August 1773 Johnson observed to Boswell and Dr. Watson:

> now learning itself is a trade. A man goes to a bookseller, and gets what he can. We have done with patronage. In the infancy of learning, we find some great man praised for it. This diffused it among others. When it becomes general, an author leaves the great, and applies to the multitude. . . . With patronage, what flattery! what falsehood! While a man is in equilibrio, he throws truth among the multitude, and lets them take it as they please: in patronage, he must say what pleases his patron, and it is an equal chance whether that be truth or falsehood.[24]

In contrast, the court of Augustus emerges as an elegant but sinister classical fossil.

That contrast between different national genius and history is clear in British and Augustan imperial expansion as well. The nationalism of eighteenth-century Britain had its ugly side and was not ignored; but numerous commentators believed that her hegemony was based on mutually profit-

---

[24] *Journal of a Tour to the Hebrides*, in *Boswell's Life of Johnson*, 5:59. For other relevant information see Paul J. Korshin, "Types of Eighteenth-Century Literary Patronage," *ECS*, 7 (1974): 453-73.

able trade, Rome's on destructive arms. This view was part of the government's defense of its peace policy in the 1730s. On 15 March 1738 one of the *Gazetteer*'s poets urged that the Spanish depredations need not bring fear, since George was guarding the state and its people's rights. George II "Shall *Honour* with fair Peace impart, / And *Trade* with *Freedom* shall unite." On 30 September a comparable poet made overt the difference between the administration's peace and liberty and the Romans' and others' war and slavery. The world was a pleasant place until Nimrod and fellow "Tyrants fed their Lusts with Spoils":

> Till *Caesar*, with as wild and wasteful Aims,
> Gave Tyranny and Rapine softer Names.
> Conquest and Glory they were then miscall'd;
> And Nations, said to be reduc'd, enthrall'd.
> A *Cato* then, and then a *Brutus* rose,
> To War for Freedom, and Mankind's Repose;
> Nor will the World, oppressing Kings to awe,
> A *Brunswick* ever want, or a *Nassau*.
>
> . . . .
>
> Oh Liberty! how truly art thou great,
> When thus with Empire thou'rt allow'd a Seat!
> Oh Empire! how refulgent is thy Throne,
> When Liberty, among thy Stars, is one!

Some years later, on 30 October 1742, the same journal extended the contrast to France, a familiar reincarnation of Roman attempts at universal monarchy. Britain is "the Protectress of Publick Liberty, and the sole Refuge of Affrighted Nations." Unlike France, "we promote our own Welfare by attending to that of others; we do not grow Rich by impoverishing, or powerful by distressing our Neighbours." Accordingly, foreigners "love us, in the very same proportion" they hate France. "By supporting the Rights of our Neighbours we extend our Interest, heighten our Authority" and thereby "procure . . . Advantages in favour of our Commerce." These unexceptionable remarks would have been supported by the opposition or administration: each wished the Thames a wider path in the commercial seas, so that it could better export empire through trade and freedom. The Tiber exported empire through conquest and subjection. Hence, even in this third area in which Augustus and his goals were praised, the British model left the Roman, and its French surrogate, far behind. In politics, in patronage and cultural attitudes, in aims and achievement, Augustus' Roman values were often inimical or irrelevant for those of contemporary Britain. When they were relevant, they may have been so as negative examples.

We could, I believe, expand this discussion along other broadly cultural lines. Britain's parity with or superiority to France, for instance, was emerging in several fields. Whether one compared Shakespeare and Corneille, Marlborough and Tallard, Pope and Boileau, or Johnson and the forty Frenchmen, the most immediate Augustan model was hardly as impressive as it had been; as Voltaire, Diderot, Montesquieu, and de Lolme amply demonstrate, the French themselves were beginning to cross the Channel to find their guides. The British character could no more than the British climate stay enthralled by a single model, much less a 1700-year-old pagan model foreign to many native standards. Other readers will no doubt add their own examples of Britain's growing national pride—in Newton, Milton, and Bentley; in the exuberant language that prospered without courtly refinements; in James II's un-Caesarean "abdication" and the peaceful change in government; in new research into native and northern-European mythology and literature; in a Christian religion that seemed to offer a world of peace and order beyond Augustus' comprehension. Whether the political developments I have outlined are father to these— as I think—or whether they are among these several children cannot be decided on the basis of brief speculation, if at all. What is clear, however, is that from several vantage points, Augustanism in eighteenth-century Britain commonly appears as a temporary and antiquated royalist intrusion, or a series of individual achievements which, many Britons felt, their own country could equal or improve upon. It is the republic, the creator of an early form of constitutional monarchy and the noblest achievements of Roman history, that Britain is proudest to emulate, and even then only in what Bolingbroke called her "spirit and force: . . . only the particular graces."[25] The rest is gilded decline and fall, enhanced by hundreds of years of associations, the grandeur of the fall, the greatness and influence of the language and literature, and the beautiful dying-songs of the republic's final poets finally reduced to the role of salesmen for a forced purchase.

The issues raised in this study far transcend disagreement with the inadequacy of a particular label and its ancillary tags; but the label itself has contributed to ignorance regarding the issues. "Augustanism" brings with it a panoply of inferences, hypotheses, and critical and scholarly methods (or lack of them) that dictate conclusions and evaluation of recalcitrant evidence. If we must have something to come

[25] *Letters on the Study . . . of History*, 2 vols. (London, 1752), 1:67. The British, especially when confronted with Cromwell and then the French Revolution, drew a sharp distinction between Rome's constitutional, conservative republic, and the chaos of a destructive democracy. As T. J. Mathias put it in 1798, "We all regret the loss of that Republick which the genius of Cicero had constructed." A few fragments remain, "though the plan . . . of that consummate practical Statesman, and experienced Philosopher" cannot be wholly reclaimed. Modern republics, especially the French, however, offer only "insolent domination; sanguinary and unrelenting ordinances; and the tyrannical suppression and overthrow of every existing Institution." There is nothing in the French model that "the good can approve, and the wise ratify" (*The Shade of Alexander Pope on the Banks of the Thames. A Satirical Poem* [London], pp. 57, 65, note q). As early as 1716 Joseph Addison warned his countrymen of the dangers of imitating Roman history—especially the conduct of the later Brutus: "Instructions . . . to be learned from histories . . . are only such as arise from particulars agreeable to all communities, or from such as are common to our own constitution." See *The Freeholder*, no. 51, in *The Works of . . . Addison*, ed. Richard Hurd, 6 vols. (London, 1811), 6:233.

between the "Renaissance" and the "Romantics," what shall we call the several ages between 1660 and 1800? Is there a name that does not imply value judgments and pre-selection of the "right" literature? "Neoclassical," always a misrepresentation, never very fruitful, and subject to some of the dangers of "Augustan," has all but been dismissed in any case. "Preromanticism" was a candidate for the dustbin from the moment of its inception. An "Age of . . ." with the blank to be filled in by Dryden, Pope, Johnson, or some other worthy, has obvious chronological, generic, and authorial limitations. Perhaps a radical step is in order: let us call the years from 1660 to 1700 the later seventeenth century or, if we prefer and are aware of difficulties after 1688 and with an author like Congreve, the Restoration period. We then may call the years from 1700 to 1799 the eighteenth century, with further refinements like early, middle, and later eighteenth century as required. If yet more nomenclature is necessary, we may refer to, say, the 1730s, the period between 1726 and 1742, the reign of Anne or other monarchs, and so on. Whether such descriptions will be adequate only time and practice can tell; but they may avoid some of the unfortunate implicit and explicit assumptions, the distortions and misreadings that stem from the Augustanism now prominent in literary studies of the Restoration and eighteenth century. And they will at least avoid the curious practice of saddling those 140 years, or significant parts of them, with the name of a man who would have been as welcome there as hemlock to a philosopher.

Appendix: Two Notes on Pope's *Epistle to Augustus*

I: POPE'S "TO AUGUSTUS" AND THE "DAILY GAZETTEER"

The special success of Pope's *Epistle to Augustus* (1737) has long been an accepted truth. Pope, it is thought, so cleverly applied to George II what Horace said of Augustus Caesar that the court was pleased to see his reform and welcome him to the fold. The administration *Gazetteer* for 3 January 1740 quotes approvingly some lines from 89-127 and says that "Mr. *Pope* has beautifully paraphrased them" from Horace. Even the opposition *Common Sense* seems to have been taken in. On 8 October 1737 Chesterfield says: "Excepting a late Imitation of *Horace,* by Mr *Pope,* who but seldom meddles with publick Matters, I challenge the Ministerial Advocates to produce one line of *Sense,* or *English,* written on their Side of the Question for these last Seven Years."[1] As late as 1797 Joseph Warton retrospectively notes that Pope's satire was so well concealed "that many persons, and some of the highest rank in the court, as I have been well informed, read it as a panegyric on the king and ministry, and congratulated themselves that Pope had left the opposition."[2]

This hypothesis has much to be said for it, but may need

---

[1] As quoted by John Butt, in The Twickenham Edition of the Poems of Alexander Pope, vol. 4, *Alexander Pope: Imitations of Horace,* 2nd ed. (New Haven: Yale Univ. Press, 1961), p. xxxviii. Butt, however, thought this was to be taken as a nonironic, if quaint, statement. Quotations from Pope's *Epistle to Augustus* are taken from this edition. This number of *Common Sense* is in *Miscellaneous Works of . . . Chesterfield,* ed. Matthew Maty, 2 vols. (London, 1777), 1:72-76, p. 75 quoted. For further comment on this passage, see Bertrand A. Goldgar, *Walpole and the Wits: The Relation of Politics to Literature, 1722-1742* (Lincoln: Univ. of Nebraska Press, 1976), p. 161, and p. 240, n. 68.

[2] *Works of Alexander Pope, Esq.,* 9 vols. (London, 1797), 4:148n.

modification. For one thing, most students of the period assume that "many persons" implies the court's virtually general hoodwinking. For another, a satire without a reasonably clear object of attack probably will not be successful and is, in any case, an unlikely citizen of the opposition's republic of hostile letters. More important, there is ample evidence to suggest that the administration was not made up wholly of the dull and uncomprehending, was far from being unanimously taken in, if at all, that unlike the apparent point of *Common Sense* (surely ironic taunting from Chesterfield and his friends), several of its writers knew very well what Pope was saying and so informed him by his own method of indirection. A few years later, and after the blunt *Epilogue to the Satires* (1738), they reminded him of their annoyance in a more overt way, and thus suggested that further such performances would be neither welcome nor prudent.

We recall that Pope begins his imitation by praising George II: ". . . You, great Patron of Mankind, sustain / The balanc'd World and open all the Main" (lines 1-2). The facing Latin reads: *"Cum tot sustineas & tanta negotia, solus."* Since "balanc'd World" is not a common translation for "tot," I have suggested that Pope borrowed this phrase from Lyttelton's "To Mr. Glover on his Poem of Leonidas. Written in . . . 1734." That work was either read to the "patriots" at Stowe, circulated in manuscript, or both. There Pope would have read a question asking whether "th' ambition of the great" is to be "like wise Godolphin, . . . sustain / The balanc'd world, and boundless power restrain?"[3]

If Pope attacks George II by alluding to Lyttelton, is it not possible for the administration to alter the process, to

[3] Howard D. Weinbrot, "Lyttelton and Pope's 'Balanc'd World': The 'Epistle to Augustus,' Lines One and Two," *N&Q*, 216 (1971): 332-33. For Lyttleton's poem, see *The Works of George Lord Lyttelton*, ed. George Edward Ayscough, 3 vols., 3rd ed. (London, 1776), 3:194-95. See also chap. 6, sec. I, at n. 18, above.

attack Pope by alluding to Lyttelton? On 28 October 1737 the *Gazetteer* replies to *Common Sense* and, in the process, hints that it is aware of the true nature of Pope's poem. The justice of that writer's "claiming *all* the *Wit* to *his Party*, and fixing all the Dullness on the contrary," will not be examined but, he says, left to the public "to judge from the following *Epistle* to the reputed chief Author of that Paper." The enclosed "Familiar *Epistle*" is designed for "*those other* Patriot Wits, *the* ingenious Dissertators, Epigrammatists, Essayists, Balladmongers, &c. &c. &c. *in the* Opposition." The first two paragraphs are in sublimely bad couplets in the putative style of the opposition. The latter two are in the administration's competent verse. The opening lines of the epistle, however, are most relevant, since they parody Pope's comparable opening of his *Epistle to Augustus*. The *Gazetteer* may have read or heard Lyttelton's poem to Glover or, as is more likely, had its author's imagination fertilized by the allusion to Pope's *Augustus* in the issue of *Common Sense* to which it was replying. I suspect that the *Gazetteer* understood Pope's meaning and the difficulty of a direct reply, and tried to communicate its knowledge to the opposition in the following lines in "praise" of Lyttelton.

> While You, Sir, sustain all the wonderful Cares
> Of Foreign Transactions, Domestick Affairs,
> When with Patriot Schemes, *Britain*'s State to amend,
> With *Ballads* adorn, and with *Journals* defend;
> 'Gainst the Good of Nation a Crime 'twou'd appear,
> To desire you'd attend to a long *Gazetteer*;
> Yet to read this Epistle familiarly deign
> —Then return to your *Journals* and *Ballads* again.

Moreover, on 6 April 1738 the *Gazetteer* imitated the "First Part" of Horace's *Satires*, i. 6, attacked Lyttelton, Bolingbroke, Pope and the patriots in general, and characterized Lyttelton with a familiar phrase presumed to be spoken by that "boy patriot" himself: "Were I, Sir, to sustain *Great*

Britain's Weight, / Her *King* should happy be, her *People* great."

The jabs at Lyttelton as mock Augustus are only one sign of the administration's response to Pope's imitation. If there really were general belief in the *Epistle to Augustus* "as a panegyric on the king and ministry," the court writers either would ignore otherwise offensive parts or be gentle in their criticism. Such is not the case. Indeed, they even sought to quarrel with Pope regarding Sternhold and Hopkins' version of the Psalms, an effort that the administration's ally Thomas Newcomb was to call the defaming effort of Vandals.[4] On 26 August 1738 one Rusticus berated Pope's *Essay on Man*, his politics, and cast of mind and body. The second line below applies to *Augustus'* controversial dispute with those Renaissance translators (lines 229-40). Rusticus argues that Pope,

> . . . as impell'd by diff'rent Fits and Qualms,
> [Can] Applaud loose Sonnets, and lampoon the Psalms:
> Can cry down others for their lewd Amours,
> Yet keep at home a Brace, or so, of Wh—res.
> His Country's Foes caress, and Friends revile,
> Frown on the Loyal, on the Factious smile.
> Against his Prince, his Keenest Malice arm,
> Then wipe his Mouth, and cry, pray where's the Harm?

Some of this anger was evoked by Pope's imitation of Horace's *Epistles*, i. 1, in which Maecenas becomes Bolingbroke; some was evoked by the bitter *Epilogue to the Satires*; but some, the first lines make clear, was evoked by *To Augustus* which, by late summer of 1738, was seen in part as a typically outrageous opposition tirade by a typically self-seeking opposition poet.

4 [Thomas Newcomb], *A Miscellaneous Collection of Original Poems* (London, 1740), pp. 244-45. This effort, "*On* Sternhold *and* Hopkins's translation *of the Psalms*," could easily have been written before 1737, as were other poems in this volume.

The latter point is amplified by a writer in the *Gazetteer* for 9 January 1739, who dismisses Warburton's ineffectual defense against Crousaz's attacks on the *Essay on Man*. For "W. W.," Pope does not believe that all human actions can be justified, since if that were so there could be no point in writing satire which hopes to reform the corrigible part of humanity. The *Gazetteer* has a better explanation for Pope's satiric zeal—not the correction of erroneous action, but the venting of excessive "Gall, which might otherwise have endanger'd his *precious* Life." In addition, his satire allows him to destroy the reputations of "all the greatest Poets of our Nation: such as *Chaucer*, and *Spenser*, and *Milton*, and *Shakespeare*, and *Johnson*, and *Beaumont*, and *Fletcher*, and even his pretendedly admired *Dryden* and his dear Friend *Congreve*; upon the Ruins of all whose *Fame*, has he, in his Imitation of *Horace*'s celebrated Epistle *to Augustus*, endeavoured to erect his own *Poetical Throne*, that he may reign the *sole Tyrant of Parnassus*."

Walpole's writers provided jaundiced readings of the beginning and middle of Pope's poem; they provided comparable reading of the conclusion as well, in which Pope drops the already crumbling mask of sycophantic court-poet and insists:

> A vile Encomium doubly ridicules;
> There's nothing blackens like the ink of fools;
> If true, a woful likeness, and if lyes,
> "Praise undeserv'd is scandal in disguise."
>   (Lines 410-13)

The administration was stung by this section well after its appearance in May of 1737. On 3 September 1740 the *Gazetteer* berated those parasites who attacked their benefactors.

> For tho' their Invectives are not sharp enough to wound; yet their Panegyricks are blunt enough to knock a Man

down. It is Mr. *Pope*'s Observation, That Praise undeserved is Satire [sic] in Disguise. But to say the Truth,
this lies rather in the Construction than in the Intention;
for if a Man praises excessively it is thro' Simplicity, and
a Redundancy of Good Nature, which is the direct Reverse of the People I·speak of, whose Gall overflows to
such a Degree, that it mixes even with their Compliments,
and poisons all their Commendations.

The significantly misquoted, or misremembered, allusion to
Pope's "scandal in disguise,"[5] and the *Gazetteer*'s recollec-
tion of its own earlier portrait of Pope's overflowing gall,
both again suggest that the administration quickly saw *To
Augustus* as a poisoned well from which it was dangerous
to drink. Pope's frequently subtle rhetoric in that poem
would have made extended political and historical refutation painful; besides, there were soon to be the easier targets
of *Bolingbroke* and the *Epilogue*. But any armor has its exposed gaps and the administration saw those in Pope's link
with Lyttelton's "balanc'd world," with Pope's own attacks
on English rulers, writers, and religious psalms, and with
the traditional, often nonpartisan suspicion of satire's motives and ends. Some of these connections, with Lyttelton for
instance, admittedly are speculative, though at the very
least possible and perhaps probable. When combined, however, they give us a view different from the usual one that
assumes the court and administration blind to a hostile
poem. Many readers no doubt were taken in upon first
reading; many soon realized *To Augustus'* real aims; and
others must have known at once that they were being so
cleverly bombarded that they had little room for return of
fire. But return they did, and at least told Pope, other enemies, and their own advocates that they knew just what he
was doing.

[5] The same "error"—or accurate reading—was made in the anonymous *One Thousand Seven Hundred Thirty Nine. A Rhapsody*, 2nd
ed. (London, 1740), p. 5.

II: POPE'S "TO AUGUSTUS" (LINES 221-24) AND THE RESPONSE TO SWIFT'S DRAPIER

> Let Ireland tell, how Wit upheld her cause,
> Her Trade supported, and supply'd her Laws;
> And leave on SWIFT this grateful verse ingrav'd,
> The Rights a Court attack'd, a Poet sav'd.

So Pope says, without classical warrant, in the *Epistle to Augustus*. His praise of Swift includes lines that contrast sharply with the diminished norm of Addison and the impossibility of any norm in the Augustan world of 1737. "Ireland" has become both personified poet and, presumably, engraver of the base of a statue built to honor the victory over Wood and his court-backed coinage. The passage clearly has its function at this point in the poem. Among other things, it shatters any lingering façade of Pope as apostate from the opposition; it galls the administration by reminding it of an embarrassing defeat; it shows how, in the world of George II, the only moral art and poetry can come under opposition impetus; and it hits the administration where it thought itself strongest, the propagation of trade.

The passage also evokes a specific body of literature, much of it Dublin broadside, that supports the notion of Ireland's becoming vocal and graphic in response to Swift's triumphant Drapier. On 12 October 1725 Bishop Nicolson wrote to the Archbishop of Canterbury telling him that Swift "is, at present, in great Repute; the Darling of the populace; His Image and Superscription on a great many Sign Posts in this city [Dublin] and other great Towns." On 4 October 1727, the Society of Weavers presented him with an adulatory broadside, reminding him that he secured his "Country's Rights, and preserv'd it from being Ruined by designing and avaritious Men."[6] Pope may have

---

[6] *The Drapier's Letters*, ed. Herbert Davis (Oxford, 1935), p. lxvi for Bishop Nicolson; see pp. 323-24 for the Society of Weavers. Swift

known this broadside, and he almost certainly knew some of the many others that flew from the presses in 1725. Pope's lines above make three points: (1) grateful Ireland becomes a rhetorician, poet, or engraver on Swift's behalf; (2) Swift encouraged Ireland's trade by rectifying and supporting her laws; (3) he was a poet who preserved rights the court attacked. These appear in the broadsides as virtual topoi.

For example, the author of *A Second Poem to Dr. Jo—n Sw—t*[7] insists that "Our Gratitude, with Ease, may be express'd, / We'll strive to be, what you wou'd make us,— bless'd." That gratitude is again recorded in *A New Song. Sung at the Club at Mr. Taplin's The Sign of the Drapier's Head in Truck-Street* (1724). We hear that

> ... Juries shall join,
> And Sheriffs Combine
> To thank him in well written Paper.

The *Song* also predicts that "In Ages to come, / ... They'll Monuments raise to the DRAPIER." Robert Ashton was inspired to raise his own poetic monument in the present age. Though others may glorify Albion's ancient fame,

> I raise my Thoughts, to touch a nobler Theme,
> And sound the Merits of a Reverend Dean.

The gratitude was commonly expressed in terms of the essential legality of Swift's cause. *The Drapier Anatomized; A Song* (1724; printed with the *New Song*) loves and reveres its subject because

---

alluded to that broadside in a letter to Pope, 12 October 1727. See *The Correspondence of Alexander Pope*, ed. George Sherburn, 5 vols. (Oxford: Clarendon Press, 1956), 2:452.

[7] Unless otherwise specified, the date of publication is 1725, the place Dublin. All of the broadsides quoted, together with several others of relevance, are preserved in a British Library volume: "Poems 1703-55," shelf mark C 121. g. 8. Shelf mark C 121. g. 9 includes the apposite *Ireland's Warning, Being an Excellent New Song, upon Wood's Base Half-pence. To the tune of Packington's Pound* (Dublin, n.d.).

> Like a Patriot Good,
> He gallantly Stood,
> And will stand by Justice and Reason.

The *New Song* was delighted because "He sav'd us our Goods, / And Dumbfounder'd *Woods*," and Ashton praised the Dean who "can guide our Laws when Judges are misled."

Woods and *brass* and *copper* were often code-words for the tyranny of the court. *Satyr Satirised* (1725?) praises the Drapier who is "always for his Country's good / And values neither *Brass nor Wood*." *The Drapier's Ballad* (1724-1725) describes the warrior in "Copper *Armour* Clad, / A *Wooden Tool* of Might," with "*Brazen* Pride" who had to be conquered by the courageous, patriotic Drapier. At least one writer, securely cloaked with anonymity, broke that code. *The Drapier Anatomized* knows that Swift

> Will lash and Chastise,
> All such Villanies,
> As tend to Oppression or Treason.

And it makes clear who those oppressors are:

> Some Court Alligators,
> To God and King Traytors,
> And Devoted to Lust and Ambition.

All three of Pope's points were included in *A Poem to D—— S——* of 1724-1725. Though there may be some distant verbal echoing in Pope's lines, it seems to me more likely that Pope is drawing on the conventions and general language of these many-faceted poems rather than recalling one in particular. It is, however, a convenient, competent, and touching tribute, the sort of work, I believe, that Pope had in mind when writing his own praise of Swift in *Augustus*.

> As Joyful Sailors when the Tempest's o'er,
> When the Wind's hust, and Surges cease to roar,
> To that great Power direct their ardent Prayer,

That laid at once the Tempest and their Fear:
So we deliver'd from the curs'd Design,
Of Faithless WOODS, and his more Faithless Coin;
First to high Heaven our pious Prayers direct,
That kindly sent a Patriot to protect
His bleeding Country, to restore its Laws,
Maintain its Rights, and vindicate its Cause:
Next to that great Protector we bestow,
Immortal Praise who broke the dreadful Blow;
Accept Great Sir the poor Return we make,
'Tis all we have to give, and all that you can take;
Kindly accept (nor think my Judgment wrong)
The grateful Tribute of a Muse's Song;
Which as my Duty owes my Zeal inspires,
And paints with Pleasure what the World admires.

It is hardly any wonder that, on 9 February 1737, Swift wrote to Pope thanking him for the lines in *Augustus* "which are to do me the greatest honour I shall ever receive from posterity, and will outweigh the malignity of ten thousand enemies."[8] They are not only noble in their own right, but also recall Swift's and Ireland's great triumph, and Ireland's grateful response.

8 Pope's *Correspondence*, 4:56.

Index

Académie des Inscriptions et Belles-Lettres, 166, 166n
Addison, Joseph: on art and liberty, 71; on Augustus, 80; on Boccalini, 39; criticized, 84; in Pope's *Augustus*, 202, 249; Pope's Prologue to his *Cato*, 176n
Advice. A Satire, 148n
Aeneas, 124-25, 127, 219
A. F., *The Bucolicks of Virgilius*, 121
Agrippa, Marcus Vipsanius, 10, 21, 25, 26, 99
Aix-la-Chapelle, Treaty of, 218
Akenside, Mark, 132, 232
Alexander the Great, 176, 197, 213
Alley, Rev. Jerom, 57
Amelot de la Houssaye, Abraham-Nicolas: translation of Tacitus, 29n, 32, 33, 48n, 67, 68
Andrews, Robert, 75, 124
Anne, Queen of England, 49, 51, 52, 236, 241
Antonines, the (emperors of Rome), 102, 104, 106
Antoninus, Marcus Aurelius (Emperor), 44, 61, 102, 225-26
Antony, Mark (Caius Marcus Antonius): attacked, 10, 11, 15, 220, 222, 228n, 229n; battle at Philippi, 25, 220; berates Octavian, 23, 26; defeated by Octavian, 10, 12, 31, 34n, 65, 92; proscribes Cicero, 74, 81; Shakespeare's play about, 46; as triumvir, 20, 21, 26, 30, 60, 156, 157, 228n
Apollo, 36, 40, 42, 196

Appian of Alexandria, 9, 21n; on Octavian, 20, 25, 27
A. R., *An Oration of Agrippa to Augustus*, 21, 21n
Ariosto, Ludovico: on Augustus, 66-68
Aristophanes, 143
Aristotle, 90n
art and liberty: Augustus destroys, 69-79 *passim*; British on, 70, 71-72, 73-74, 73n-74n, 76-79; French on, 71, 76-77, 78; Romans on, 69-71
Art of Poetry, The, 130
Ashton, Robert, 250, 251
Atticus, Titus Pomponius, 15, 40n
Augustan age (and relevant "Augustan"), 123, 151, 213: analogues of, 52, 88-89, 108, 118-19, 218, 229n-30n, 230; British attack, 64, 68-79 *passim*, 82-83, 88-89, 102, 231; British praise, 49-51, 91, 114-16; classical writers and commentators attack, 14-48 *passim*, 69-71; classical writers praise, 9-13; its genius formed prior to Augustus, 71, 72, 76-79, 195-96, 230; modern views of, 4-9, 4n-5n, 50, 128n, 137, 182, 232; as seen by eighteenth-century in Horace, 189-91
Augustus Anglicus, 49, 50
Augustus, Caius Julius Caesar Octavianus:
    analogues of: Cromwell, 70n, 89-90, 89n, 108, 230; Charles I, 116; Charles II, 5, 49, 78n; Demetrius Phalareus, 14; George II, 51, 113, 114,

INDEX

Augustus (*cont.*)

117-18, 142, 186, 186n; Hitler, 118-19; James II, 53, 61n, 62, 88; Louis XIV, 88-89, 160, 218, 230; Napoleon, 52, 230; Pitt (the younger), 77; Walpole, 110
art and statuary of, 60-62, 61n-62n, 80

British ambivalent toward: Blackwell, 78-79, 97-98, 135-36, 189; *Craftsman*, 109-10; Goldsmith, 9, 91n, 94, 100n; *London Journal*, 109, 114-16; *Old England*, 112

British attack: Akenside, 132; Andrews, 75; A. R., 21; *Biographia Classica*, 163; Blackwell, 18, 97-99, 100, 125, 135-36; Bolingbroke, 7, 38, 63, 76, 232; Chesterfield, 235-36, 237; commentators on Cicero, 15-17, 16n-17n; Clarke, 27-28; Cleland, 65, 66; Crusius, 64-65, 162-63; Denman, 170-72; Dryden, 52, 62-63, 64, 75-76, 122, 124, 161-62, 163, 231; Gibbon, 44, 66, 100n, 101-8, 107n-8n, 231; Gifford, 167, 171, 174; Goldsmith, 51, 91-94, 100, 231; Gordon, 60, 69n-70n, 74, 76, 87, 100n, 107n, 129-30; Grainger, 132; Greene, 89, 127-28; Griffiths, 132; Hill, 87-88; Hodgson, 171-72, 232; Hooke, 75; Hurd, 134; Jephson, 72n, 75; Johnson, 153, 176-78, 231; King, 84; Lee, 72-73; 73n; Lyttelton, 14, 17, 84n; Meadley, 88; Middleton, 74; *Mirth in Ridicule*, 162; Montagu, 88; Moody, 169-70, 229; Pitt, 65, 122; *Plain Truth*, 131, 131n-32n, 142, 232; Pope in *Augustus*, 137, 182-217 *passim*, 243, 249, 252; Pope in

Epilogue, 137-41, 147-48; Pope in epitaph, 120, 129; Rose, 167; Shaftesbury, 64, 123, 160; Sheffield, 80-82; Spence, 65, 125; Swift, 82-83, 86-87, 231; Thomson, 71, 72n, 232; Trapp, 162; Warton, 65, 195-96, 232

British praise: Biddle, 49, 59; Blackwall, 49-50; Blount, 49; Bohun, 11; Dryden, 49; Eusden, 51; Echard, 54-57, 100n; *Gazetteer*, 117-18, 234; Hearne and others, 56, 57, 100n; *London Journal*, 113-16; Manning, 13; Otway (translates de Bröe), 54, 55, 57, 100n

classical writers attack: Appian, 20, 25, 27; Asinius Pollio (in Macrobius), 70; Brutus, 15; Dio Cassius, 20-22, 25-27, 45, 86, 102; Florus, 27; Juvenal, 156-58, 159, 160, 162, 165, 172-74, 176-78, 179-80; Livy, 19; Plutarch, 15, 20; Seneca, 34, 69, 71; Suetonius, 9, 22-24, 22n, 24n, 26, 102, 233; Tacitus, 28-32, 48, 57-58, 69, 70, 86, 113, 210n, 232

classical writers praise, 9-10; Appian, 9; Cicero, 11-12, 15-17, 16n-17n, 38, 40n, 128, 221, 222, 223; Dio Cassius, 9, 13, 20, 176-77; Florus, 19; Horace, ix, 68, 74, 75, 120, 120n, 123, 129-36, 137, 137n, 160, 165-69, 182-217 *passim*, 232; Suetonius, 9, 14, 21, 176-77; Tacitus, 30; Velleius, 12-13, 26; Virgil, 83, 121n, 127n, 129, 130, 131, 133, 134, 137, 219

French writers attack: Bossuet, 220; Chastellux, 133, 224; Crébillon, 60, 61, 61n, 224, 224n; Dubois-Fontanelle, 224; Du-

INDEX

saulx, 8, 133, 167-68, 224, 232; *Encyclopédie*, 223; Malby, 223; Macé, 221; Montesquieu (and Jaucourt), 222-23; Ophellot, 168-69, 225-26; Racine, 133, 133n-34n; Roergas de Serviez, 221; Tillemont, 220; Vertot, 222; Voltaire, 24n, 60-61, 61n, 67, 133, 195-96, 224-25, 232

French writers praise: Blondell, 49; Boileau, 218; le Bossu, 219; Bossuet, 220; de Bröe, 54, 55, 57, 100n; Catrou, 121n, 210; Crevier, 219-20, 223; Levesque, 227-28; St. Evremond, 71; de la Serre, 218; Tillemont, 220

Italian Renaissance writers attack: Ariosto, 66-68, 66n-67n; Boccalini, 39-42; Bruni and Florentines, 33-34, 44; Machiavelli, 37-38; Malvezzi, 44-45

modern views of: positive, ix, 3-7, 28, 80, 188, 232, 233, 243-44; revised or negative, 6-9, 32, 196, 243-48

traits or actions attacked: banishes Ovid, 23, 24, 24n-25n, 73, 73n, 84, 85n, 186, 194, 195, 225; censors and destroys art, 29, 34, 59, 64, 69-79, 73n, 110, 113-15, 193-94, 223; cowardice in battle, 31, 66, 84, 103, 196, 210; creates tyrannic precedent, 28-29, 33-34, 37-39, 44-45, 64-65, 66, 87, 92-94, 99, 101-2, 104-6, 118, 153, 197, 222-23, 226; cruel, 62-63, 66, 84, 195-96, 221, 226; destroys balanced constitution, 8, 27, 29-30, 55, 57, 58, 77, 86, 88, 92-94, 94-95, 100-8, 112, 114, 117, 182, 233, 230; deviant sexuality, 19, 23-24, 24n, 31, 56, 63, 67, 76, 81, 82, 84,

111, 196; governed by Livia, 31, 45, 82; hostile to other states, 73n, 192, 238-39; hypocrite, 30, 84, 87, 102-3; irreligious, 31, 61; proscribes Cicero, 14, 57, 74, 74n, 81-82, 186, 220, 221-22, 224, 228-29; taxes the people for personal benefits, 176-78; Tiberius chosen to highlight his own virtues, 21-22, 31, 32n, 45, 47, 86, 87

traits or actions praised: balances constitution, 10, 13, 98; creates empire, 13, 57, 235; martial hero, 10, 11, 12, 43; patron of art, ix, 10, 11, 49-50, 50-51, 68, 77, 84, 117-18, 196, 201, 207, 235, 237; stabilizes Rome and brings happiness, 10, 11, 12, 13, 30, 43, 49, 55-57, 235. *See also* Octavian.

Baker, George, 19, 19n
Baker, Sir Richard, 42, 43n
Baron, Hans, 33, 34
Bayle, Pierre, 39, 60
Beaumont, Francis, 247
Bentley, Richard, 239
Beroaldus, Philippus (the younger), 33
Biddle, Edward, 49-50
Binniman, Henry, 21n
Biographia Classica: Augustus in, 65; Dryden, Horace, and Juvenal in, 163, 163n-64n; Rapin in, 169n; Suetonius in, 22n; Tacitus and Gordon in, 46n; Velleius in, 18n
Blackwall, Anthony, 50-51
Blackwell, Thomas (the elder), 72n
Blackwell, Thomas (the younger): on Appian and Dio, 18, 20n; on Augustus, 78-79, 97-99, 100, 125, 135-36, 232; on balanced

Octavian (C. Julius Caesar Octavianus): Cicero's help for, 11-12, 15-17, 16n-17n, 38, 40n, 128, 221, 222, 223; coward or incompetent in battle, 21, 22-23, 25-26, 31, 222; cruel, 22-23, 92, 99, 115-16, 172-74, 222; private and sexual life, 21, 23-24, 24n; triumvir and proscriber, 10, 20, 21, 22, 30-31, 59-61, 63, 91, 156-57, 221; tyrannical usurper, 20, 22, 87, 91, 95, 115-16, 165, 171, 222. *See also* Augustus, Cicero, Horace, Virgil

Octavius, Caius (father of Augustus), 27

Old Comedy, 139n, 143-44

Old England, 112

Oldham, John, 151

One Thousand Seven Hundred Thirty Nine. A Rhapsody, 248n

Ophellot de la Pause, Henri [J. B. C. Isoard Delisle]: on Augustus, 84n-85n, 169, 196n, 225-26; on Horace and Virgil, 84n-85n, 169n, 196n; on Juvenal and Horace, 168-69; praised, 225-26

oracle: in politics and religion, 124, 199-200, 199n-200n

Osborne, Francis, 114-16

Otway, Thomas, 54

Ovid (Publius Ovidius Naso), 94, 165, 187: Augustus banishes, 24, 24n-25n, 73n, 84, 85n, 186, 194, 195, 225; Augustus flattered by, 73, 73n, 84, 85n, 224; Augustus' incest discovered by, 24, 24n-25n, 76

Owen, Edward, 170n, 174, 174n

Ozell, John, 288n

Pansa, Caius Vibius, 10, 12, 22, 30, 47

Paschalius, Carolus, 35

patronage: Augustus gives, 10, 11, 49-51, 68, 84, 196, 201, 207; Augustus uses to destroy art, 69-79 *passim*; Augustus uses for political purposes, 68-69, 118-19, 126-27, 207-11; Napoleon gives, 228; Pope refuses to seek, 189, 193-94, 193n-94n, 207-12. *See also*, art and liberty, Augustus, Horace, Johnson, Juvenal, Maecenas, Pope, Virgil, Voltaire

Patterson, James, 18

Pax Romana, 40

Pemberton, Henry, 123

Perrault, Charles, 219n

Persius (Aulus Persius Flaccus): Dryden on, 139, 160, 161; follows Lucilius, 139n-40n; Horace and Juvenal superior to, 150, 161, 163, 172; Horace's politics inferior to, 169; Pope adapts, 139; seldom smiles, 152; Whitehead adapts, 178-79

Philips, Ambrose: in Pope's *Augustus*, 184, 209, 211, 212

Pinkerton, John [Robert Heron], 77-78, 78n, 128

Pinto, V. de Sola, 4, 232

Pitt, Christopher: on Augustus, Horace, and Virgil, 65, 122, 123, 124, 232

Pitt, William (the younger), 77

Plain Truth, or Downright Dunstable, 131, 131n-32n, 142, 232

Pliny (the younger), 22n, 107

Plumb, J. H., 236

Plutarch, 15, 20, 226n

A Poem to D—— S——, 251-52

Poggio, Bracciolini, 34, 34n-35n

Pollio, C. Asinius, 34n, 70, 79

Polybius, 90n, 226n

Pompey (Sextus Pompeius Mag-

INDEX

Rochester, John Wilmot, Earl of,
6n
Rogers, Pat, 3n
Romulus, 196
Roscommon, Wentworth Dillon,
Earl of, 184
Rose, William, 89n, 96n-97n, 167
Rosinus, Joannes, 11
Rothstein, Eric, 32n
Rowe, John, 16
Ruffhead, Owen, 89n, 94n
Rufus, Corellius, 154
Russel, Richard [Mr. Maevius],
187
Russo, John Paul, 188

Sackville, Charles, Earl of Dorset,
152, 159
Saint-André, François de, 59
Salutati, Coluccio, 34
satire, 6, 74n, 203, 204, 232, 243,
244: and contest between Horace, Persius, Juvenal, 142, 150-
53, 150n-51n, 161-63, 169-72;
and Emperor Julian's *Caesars*
and Verrio's mural of, 61-62,
61n-62n, 80; "Horatian," 109,
119, 142-45, 147, 149, 182, 194;
"Juvenalian," 109, 113, 137-41,
139-40n, 148-49, 154-74 *passim*,
154n, 157n, 158n, 170n, 174n,
182, 183, 232, 234; used by opposition to Walpole, 76n, 82-
83, 131, 148-49, 153, 175-81, 183-
217, 249-52; used by Walpole
administration, 113n, 130-31,
145-47, 183, 186, 245-46, 247-48.
See also, Boileau-Despréaux,
Horace, Juvenal, Persius, Pope
Satire, A, 186
"Satire in Answer to a Friend, A,"
158
Satyr Satirised, 251
Savile, Sir Henry, 29n, 42

Scaliger, Julius Caesar, 73, 73n,
167
Schrevelius, Cornelius, 156-57
*Second Poem to Dr. Jo———n
Sw—t, A*, 250
Sejanus, Lucius Aelius, 18
Seneca, Lucius Annaeus (the
elder): attacks Augustus, 34, 69,
71; attacks known, 34n-35n, 70,
110, 195
Serre, Puget de la, 218
Serviez, Jacques Roergas de, 221,
222
Settle, Elkanah: in Pope's *Au-
gustus*, 209, 211, 212, 215
Severus, Alexander, Marcus Au-
relius (Emperor), 102
Shadwell, Thomas, 158-59
Shaftesbury, Anthony Ashley
Cooper, 3rd Earl of: on art and
liberty, 64; on Augustus, Hor-
ace, Virgil, 123, 160, 184, 231;
on Juvenal, 159-60
Shakespeare, William, 239, 247
Sheffield, John, Duke of Bucking-
ham and Normanby, 50: on
Augustus, 80-82, 80n-81n; on
Cicero, 16-17
Shelley, Percy Bysshe, 97
Sherburn, Sir Edward, 51
Sheridan, Thomas, 172, 180-81
*Short Review of Mr. Hooke's
Observations, A*, 54n, 208n
Sidney, Algernon, 38, 45n
Smart, Christopher, 68
Spanheim, Baron Ezekiel, 61n,
210n
Spanish Succession, War of the,
218
Spectator, nos. 54 (Steele) and 291
(Addison), 39
Spence, Joseph, 65, 232: on the
Aeneid, 65n, 121, 124-25, 125n,

267

INDEX

Warburton, William; criticized,
195, 247; on Pope, 216n; Pope's
letter to, 138n
Warton, Joseph, 122, 132: on
Aeneid, 121, 124, 125, 126, 134;
on Augustus, 7, 51, 65, 77, 94-
96, 232; on Dio, 18, 20; on
Horace and commentators,
134, 195, 199; on Montesquieu,
152; on Pope, 194-95, 204n-5n,
216n, 243
Warwick, Philip, 57
Watson, Dr. Robert, 237
Watson, George, 64n
Watt, Ian, 6, 6n, 194n
Welsted, Leonard, 78n
Wheare, Degory, 21, 21n, 22
Whigs, x, xn: anti-Augustanism
shared with Tories, 7, 18-19, 48,
52, 53-54, 96, 233; battles with
Tories, 45, 52-53, 109, 117;
Juvenal attacks, 158, 175; on
limits of monarchic power, 52-

53, 90, 109, 116-17, 236; Verrio
on, 62. *See also* Tory
Whitehead, Paul, 178-80, 178n,
179n
Whitford, R. C., 150n, 166n
Wicksted (John Churchill?), 126,
126n-27n
Wilcocks, Joseph, 63, 100n
William III, King of England, 53,
62, 83-84, 236
Williams, Harold, 185
Williams, R. D., 128n
Wind, Edgar, 62
W. J., *Ductor Historicus*, 54n
Wolcot, John [Peter Pindar], 169n
Wood, Thomas, 158, 158n, 159n
Wood, William: Irish coinage of,
249, 251, 252
Wren, Matthew, 37

Xiphilinus, Joannes, 13

Zeno, the Stoic, 61n, 62, 226
Zosimus, 9

270

LIBRARY OF CONGRESS CATALOGING IN PUBLICATION DATA

Weinbrot, Howard D.
    Augustus Caesar in "Augustan" England.

    Includes bibliographical references and index.
    1.   English literature—18th century—History
and criticism.   2.   Classicism.   3.   Augustus,
Emperor of Rome, 63 B.C.—A.D. 14, in fiction,
drama, poetry, etc.   4.   Latin literature—History
and criticism.   I.   Title.
PR445.W4   820'.9'1   77-72140
ISBN 0-691-06344-3